FRANCIS GEORGE SCOTT
AND THE SCOTTISH RENAISSANCE

Francis George Scott at the piano (c. 1953)
(Photograph by Lida Moser)

Francis George Scott

and the

Scottish Renaissance

MAURICE LINDSAY

PAUL HARRIS PUBLISHING

EDINBURGH

First published in the United Kingdom 1980
by Paul Harris Publishing
25 London Street
Edinburgh

ISBN 0 904505 43 X

British Library Cataloguing in Publication Data:

Lindsay, Maurice
    Francis George Scott and the Scottish Renaissance
    1. Scott, Francis George
    2. Composers — Scotland — Biography
    I. Title
    780'.9'24   ML410.S/
    ISBN 0-904505-43-X

*The publishers acknowledge the financial assistance of the
Scottish Arts Council in the publication of this volume*

Printed in Scotland by The Shetland Times Ltd., Lerwick, Shetland

CONTENTS

PREFACE

Publication of this book forms part of the celebrations to mark the centenary of the birth of Francis George Scott. I have always believed that, sooner or later, it would be necessary to isolate the qualities of his music, which are considerable, from the propaganda that surrounded it, through no fault of his own, during his lifetime, and militated against its acceptance on its musical merits. Accordingly, in 1977 I invited a number of people to form a committee, the purpose of which would be to organise the writing and publication of a biographical study; to arrange for the re-publication in a new edition of some forty of his best songs; to ensure the issue of a gramophone record on which singers of distinction would perform some of the re-issued songs; and to assist with the promotion of a memorial exhibition around the time of the actual centenary, 25th January, 1980, in the National Library of Scotland.

The Francis George Scott centenary committee consisted of Dr W. R. Aitken, Mr Max Begg, Dr George Bruce, Mr Martin Dalby, Mr A. C. Davis, Mr David Dorwood, Mr Douglas Gray, Mr Neil Mackay, Mrs Diana Milne, Mr George N. Scott, Mr Ronald Stevenson and Professor Michael Tilmouth. Its members elected me as their chairman. All its objectives have been achieved.

Once I had begun to write this book, originally entitled *Francis George Scott: the Man and the Music,* it became apparent that what was evolving, more or less inevitably, was a document which shed some light on the early days of the Scottish Renaissance movement. It therefore seemed advisable to give it its present title, since the scope of its interest has widened, although its main purpose has remained the reassessment of the achievements of Francis George Scott.

I would like to thank Mr George Scott and Mrs Lilias Forbes, two of the composer's three surviving children, for their assistance. Dr George Bruce was also most helpful. I am greatly indebted to the editor of the centenary edition of the *Selected Songs,* Mr Neil Mackay, who kindly allowed me to make use of his unpublished student thesis on Francis George Scott. I have quoted his views on more than one occasion.

Others to whom I am indebted are Mrs Margaret McCance who helped me with material regarding the friendship between her late husband, William McCance, Scott and MacDiarmid and for allowing us reproduce her husband's self-portrait; William Crosbie, for permission to reproduce his portrait of MacDiarmid; Mr K. S. Sorabji, who showed me letters sent to him by Scott; Mr George Barr, the librarian in charge of the Music Department of the Mitchell Library, Glasgow, where the Francis George Scott Archive is housed; Mr Stanley Simpson, Department of Manuscripts, at the National Library of Scotland, who made accessible to me material by William Soutar and others; Dr Benno Schotz, who provided me with a photograph of his fine head of the composer; Mr John Tonge for permission to quote from his essay in the *Festschrift*; Mr Gavin Muir and The Hogarth Press for permission to quote from Willa Muir's *Belonging* and Edwin Muir's *Autobiography;* Dr John Burt of Dunfermline, who made photographs and other material concerning his father available, and Mrs Margaret Turnbull of Hawick, who allowed me to copy early family photographs. The staff of Hawick Area Library gave me information regarding Scott's family tree, as well as other material relating to the composer's early association with the town.

Unaware that Dr C. M. Grieve (Hugh MacDiarmid) was on his deathbed, I wrote asking permission to quote from what he had already written about Scott. Shortly after the poet's death I received permission from his father through his son, Mr Michael Grieve.

I am most grateful to Mr Michael Grieve for his help, and also, of course, to his late father, with whom I enjoyed a variable though often warm friendship lasting more than thirty-five years. I should like to take the opportunity of emphasising here that while Scott's influence on *A drunk Man looks at the Thistle* now seems clear, the greatness of the poem's imaginative power is, of course, entirely MacDiarmid's. It was no part of my fact-searching to seek to diminish his achievement.

A number of F.G.'s students, notably William G. Noble (who later became a well-known exponent of his songs), Mr Ronald Calder, Mrs Margaret Macfarlane and Mrs Catherine Ironside also have my thanks. For permission to quote from a letter by Douglas Young I thank his widow, Mrs Hella Young, and for permission to quote Sir Alexander Gray, his son Mr

John Gray. Mr John Arnott was kind enough to verify the date of the *Men of Mark* broadcast, an illicit tape of which survived. A copy of this is now safely in the National Library of Scotland. The Principal of the College of Piping, Mr Seumas MacNeill, most kindly assisted me with the lecture on 'Pibroch' and Dr W. R. Aitken, bibliographer extraordinary to the Scottish Renaissance, generously provided the Bibliography for this book.

To Trevor Royle and Christie Duncan, the Directors, respectively, of Literature and Music of The Scottish Arts Council, I owe thanks for support in many different ways, and to my publisher, Paul Harris, for his encouraging enthusiasm in finding a solution when the b~ok turned out to be almost twice as long as he had originally intended.

To Miss Helen Logan, who pursued many a factual hare for me, and to Mrs Joan Birkett, who translated Roger-Ducasse's letters from the original French, I extend my gratitude. Last but by no means least, I give both thanks and gratitude to my wife, whose judgment tempered my excesses of enthusiasm and whose sense of style unscrambled my occasional convolutions of construction.

Every effort has been made to trace the holders of the copyright of material I have quoted. If anyone has been overlooked through inability to trace them, I offer my apologies in advance.

While the proofs of this book were being corrected, some fifty letters by Francis George Scott and his family came into the public domain as a result of the purchase of the MacDiarmid archive by Edinburgh University Library. Since they are of considerable significance, they have been considered as an additional Appendix.

MAURICE LINDSAY

Milton Hill
Milton
Dumbarton

November 1979

Chapter 1

HAWICK — BOYHOOD AND ADOLESCENCE

The year 1880 was not without its share of musical interest. During its course Brahms, on holiday at Ischl, completed his *Academic Festival* and *Tragic Overtures* and in November, as a member of the Jury of the competition for the Beethoven Prize, voted to reject Mahler's entry, *Das klagende Lied.* Dvorak wrote his *Violin Concerto,* Tchaikovsky both his *Serenade for Strings* and the *1812 Overture,* while Wagner was at work on the score of *Parsifal.* Medtner, Bloch and Pizzetti came into the world: Wieniawski and Offenbach left it. At this northern knuckle-end of Europe, in the Scottish Border town of Hawick, Roxburghshire, on 25th January — the day celebrated by Scots throughout the world as the birthday of Robert Burns, the National Bard — Francis George Scott was born at his parents' home, 6 Oliver Crescent. When in due course Scott discovered this natal coincidence, he "felt as if a star danced above my head".

He was the fourth child and third son of twice-married George Scott, whose own father had been an estate worker at Thirlestane Castle, Lauder, the home of the Dukes of Lauderdale. It is possible that the family stems from John Scott, fifth son of Sir William Scott, fourth Baron of Harden. The ancestral tree, however, cannot now be traced beyond an older George Scott, a road contractor at Wilton (then a separate burgh from Hawick), who was employed by the Turnpike Trustees, and who married Eleanor Inglis, a lady's-maid at Yair House, Selkirkshire, in 1798. The later George, however, had been trained as an engineer and established himself as a mill-furnisher, or supplier of weaving-loom parts to the Border woollen mills. Since 1771, when four handknitting machines were introduced to Hawick by Baillie John Hardie, using wool from the native Cheviot sheep, the knitting and cloth-making industries had spread and prospered throughout the Borders, and the town of Hawick, by the banks of the Teviot, had become its thriving centre.

On June 18th, 1860, at 9 O'Connell Street, Hawick, George

Scott, then a journeyman, married Elizabeth Pringle, a finisher of woollen hosiery, and the daughter of a warehouseman in a wool hosiery factory. The couple had one son, James. On December 13th 1869, Elizabeth Scott died of consumption. For his second wife, George Scott chose Janet, the daughter of another mill-furnisher, Robert Greenwood, who, in common with many other Lancashire engineers, had arrived in Hawick as a young man at a time when, in spite of opposition, the advantages of machine-operated "power" methods of spinning were becoming obvious. George Scott and Janet Greenwood were married on 17th March, 1871, at the bride's home, "Weemsland", Hawick, "according to the forms of the Congregational Church".

In due course there were born to them Robert, Francis George, the future composer, and a daughter, Margaret Lilias.

James heired his father's business after George Scott's death in 1907. Robert eventually also joined the business. He became a conscientious objector in the First World War (which earned him unpopularity and even threatened eviction in Hawick, as well as visits in Barlinnie Prison, Glasgow, from Francis George). Thereafter, Robert became increasingly obsessed with threats, real or imaginary, to his personal freedom, and was bought out by James. Robert then sailed to America "to see the times", as his sister put it, but soon returned and settled in Liverpool. James continued the business until 1929, but by then his was a dying trade in the face of the depression, changing conditions and methods in the woollen manufacturing industry. Margaret Lilias, who had brought up the three boys after the death of their mother, in due course married and settled in Edinburgh. Her death in 1944 was a serious blow to Francis, with whom she enjoyed a special empathy.

George Scott was imbued with the strong sense of local pride and dour tenaciousness that characterises the temperament of the Borderer, whose ancestors were for long accustomed to the rigours of raid and counter raid, of feuding and violence, in the days when the marches with England were disputed territory. According to his grand-daughter, Lilias, he was "dour, independent and proud to the point of un-reason." She relates that a brother of his, Alexander, the gas-manager at Galashiels, acquired local notoriety by his refusal to answer a summons to carry out repairs at the nearby "Big Hoose". "I'll no rise from my bed for any Duke in hell! ", he declared. A surviving photograph of George Scott shows the bearded severity of a typical successful Victorian business man.

From his father, Francis inherited a down-to-earth practicality in everyday affairs, and a certain wariness in money matters, although according to Lilias, his priorities could be governed by the mood of the moment.

"Purchasing a volume of poetry took priority over a new set of curtains in the sitting-room, and he took his young family on holiday to France and Belgium when household plumbing repairs were more urgently needed. When, on his modest teacher's salary, he spent £200 helping an impecunious friend, he was berated by his sister for not spending the money on his children."

Janet, the composer's mother, though she came of a Rochdale family, seems to have absorbed the balladry of the Borders. Francis was seventeen when she died on 30th August, 1897, but in later life he attributed his sensitive response to poetry largely to her influence.

"When I was five to ten years old, it was no uncommon thing to hear some member of my family singing a stanza or two of say, 'Lord Randal', or of 'Helen o' Kirkconnel Lea', or of 'The Border Widow's Lament' . . . By the time I was in my late teens, I must have been ready to absorb anything I thought was good poetry, so a wide range of the Border Ballads — 'The Dowie Dens of Yarrow', 'Jamie Telfer of the Fair Dodhead', 'Johnnie Armstrong' and many others from various parts of Scotland became known to me; and not only known but, as was the custom of the time, known almost by heart".

Scott's mother had a good, though untrained, singing voice. Although of a religious disposition, she also nourished an almost pantheistic attitude to nature, an attitude she transferred to her son. As a boy, Francis spent much of his leisure time walking the Border hills, cycling the valleys, reaching places as far afield as St. Mary's Loch and Abbotsford, and fishing the rivers, particularly the Teviot, as well as studying local geology and botany and absorbing the rich heritage of Border lore and legend.

His mother's sense of religion perhaps had a less obvious influence upon him, although in later life he acknowledged the part it had played in colouring his spiritual growth. Her granddaughter, then about eight, remembers standing in the Edinburgh home of her aunt, Margaret Lilias, "looking up on a large fading portrait in a brown wooden frame. A woman of grave expression in late Victorian dress looked down on me . . . She seemed to express an intense sadness with a hint of dignity holding her aloof from the din of this world . . . Her gently bowed head revealed an attitude of humility."

Unfortunately, that "fading portrait" of Mrs George Scott has now disappeared altogether. Her son later described her as "a woman of a deeply spiritual nature, a devout church-attending Christian . . . with something of the ardour and zeal of early religious reformers."

Regular church-going was insisted upon by both parents, a practice Francis abandoned in later life — except of necessity when he was a church organist during 1910/11 — and which he did not impose upon his own family.

As in Burns's poem, 'The Cotter's Saturday Night', it was the custom in George Scott's household for the head of the family to read aloud from the Bible. Since the authorised version, with its rich Jacobean word-music, imagery, and re-sounding cadences is great English literature (unlike its styleless successor) this discipline impressed upon Francis the value of the sound of poetry and doubtless helped form his life-long habit of reading aloud to anyone who would listen to a poem or a piece of prose that had particularly caught his fancy.

Although he was not in adult life himself a churchgoer, in the widest sense of the term his attitude to the moral issues of life was broadly that of the traditional Scots Presbyterian. If later there sometimes appeared to be some measure of con-flict in his make-up between the freedom of expression he claimed as an artist and an inborn respect for at least the outward conventions of Scottish Calvinism, it was perhaps some such dichotomy that made him disinclined to take risks.

Scott received his primary education at Hawick Academy. When he was twelve he was transferred by his parents to a private school, Brand's Teviot Grove Academy, later described by its former pupil as "a kind of upper class school, although that was the only thing about it." James Brand, a Fife man, founded the school about 1880. In 1895 it was taken over by a School Board, but Brand remained as rector until two years before his death in 1908. Throughout his career, Brand seems to have been able to produce good academic results. Scott carried off all the prizes, much to the delight of his father, who had the Scots businessman's ambition that his son should somehow 'do better' for himself and graduate at university.

During the primary years, a very old great-uncle who lived in Hawick, blind but a good Scots fiddler, took a great liking for young Francis. He habitually identified him by placing his hands on the boy's head, feeling the frontal bones and declaring that through telepathy he was sure these "musical bones" meant that Francis had a musical gift.

At about the time he transferred to Brand's, Scott also had his first piano lesson from a Yorkshireman, Frank Mather, then organist at Hawick Episcopalian Church. Although Scott had received early encouragement in singing from his mother, Mather (who eventually emigrated to America) laid the foundations of Scott's technique, both as pianist and composer. Until late in life, Scott preserved his first textbook — *The Rudiments of Music* by W. H. Cummings — his name roundly inscribed on the title-page.

Some doubt now exists as to the attitude of Francis's father to his son's future career. Although James and Robert were destined from an early age to succeed George Scott in the family business, the father may not at first have felt that Francis was fit for teaching, or teaching worthy of him. At any rate, according to what, years later, he related to me, the inevitable conflict between music and school work arose as the final school examinations loomed nearer. George Scott would not even entertain the thought of a professional musician in the family. Scott's niece, Mrs Margaret Turnbull, remembers being told by her father, the composer's brother, that at 16 Bourtree Place he had "shared a bedroom with Francis. My father used to tell me about Uncle Francis sitting up half the night studying music. His father would come upstairs, sometimes at 3 a.m. and finding him trying to write music, tell him that he would turn off the gas at the main. That didn't daunt him. He bought candles, and studied by candlelight, pleading with my father not to tell. His father used to tell him that music wasn't a paying job, and that he would be a penniless nothing, but he just said he didn't care, that music was his life." Eventually, George Scott refused to allow the distracting studies with Mather to continue, and to ensure Francis's attention to homework, locked the piano.

One morning George Scott met Mather in the Street. "What are you going to do with Francis?", Mather asked, as they walked along together. "He is going into teaching", George Scott firmly declared. "Hmm", the Yorkshireman snorted, "You might as well make him a bloody butcher."

When the results of the final school examinations were announced, Francis found himself in second place. Totting up his own total of marks and those of his competitors, he discovered that Brand had made an error of addition in favour of a boarding pupil, popular with the masters. Characteristically, Francis did not wait until next day to have the matter put right, but called on the surprised Brand that very night, successfully demonstrating in the empty classroom his right to first place. He was then declared Dux Medalist. Two years earlier, at the age of fifteen, he had composed his first song.

In the days before the Union of the Crowns, when the Borders lived in a state of turmoil, family feuding with family, and almost everyone under the constant threat of English raid or invasion, it was the prudent custom of the town authorities annually to ride round their boundaries or marches to make sure that no one had encroached upon their rightful territory. After 1603, this practice became unnecessary, but Hawick, like most of the Border towns, kept up the custom as a means of expressing and focussing local pride. In modern times, the annual Festival of Riding the Marches has become the occasion for a popular and colourful week of celebration, presided over by an elected Coronet and Coronet's Lass. The festivities involve not only skilled and vigorous horsemanship, but a capacity for hearty and vocal conviviality. To words by a local poetaster, Robert Hunter (1855-1905), the schoolboy composer provided a song for the occasion, 'Oor Bonnie Border Toun', a roistering ballad in the Scottish Victorian music-hall tradition current at that time. 'Oor Bonnie Border Toun' fitted so well the purpose for which it was meant that it was soon in print. It survives today in a published collection of Hawick songs, and gets its quota of performances during each Riding of the Marches. Dutifully memorised, it is enthusiastically roared out every year at the well-washed-down dinner with which the festivities conclude.

Francis was also an enthusiastic versifier during his teenage Hawick years, and some of his literary efforts appeared in the pages of local newspapers and magazines. One of these pieces, 'On Border Hill', goes:

> "Lad in front, and lass in rear;
>   The sun to face, and the hill to climb
> With many a thistle and syke to clear —
>   An' a rare old reel for marking time:
> We'll up the heather and cheerily pass
>   Where whaups are whistling, wild and hollow;
> The bonnie lad will lead — the lass
>   Will follow, follow, follow.
>
> Lass in front, and lad in rear —
>   And the set o' the sun on the Haunted Glen —
> With a rolling song and a parting cheer,
>   We'll dirl the rocks on the windy Pen:
> And hameward — when the blood is mad,
>   And drives us birling down the hollow —
> The bonnie lass will lead — the lad
>   Will follow, follow, follow."

That may not be very good verse. But his deep knowledge of the Scottish poetic tradition, especially as represented by the Border Ballads and the poems of Burns, not only widened into a sustaining force and gave him life-long pleasure, but in due course was to play an important part in helping him fashion his personal musical style.

In the autumn of 1897 Francis George Scott left Hawick for Edinburgh, enrolling simultaneously in the English class of Professor George Saintsbury (1845-1933) at Edinburgh University, and as a pupil-teacher at Moray House College of Education, in his own words settling into "digs . . . practically up against Arthur's Seat."

Chapter 2

THE MAKING OF A COMPOSER

In Edinburgh, liberated from the confining influences of small-town life and a rigidly run household, Francis enjoyed himself to the full. He was much in demand as a pianist for students' 'smoker' concerts, and for accompanying community singing. Having rather more money than many of the students, he was able to indulge the whims of his high spirits.

While in Saintsbury's class, he became both an essay prizeman and *proxime accessit* for verse. He was also Queen's prizeman in science (second place) at the Science and Art Examinations in 1898.

For some reason not exactly clear now,[1] he decided to abandon his university course without taking a degree, probably because he began increasingly to feel that the only degree he would really value must be one in music. Possibly, too, he found the strain of the double training too much for him. In later years he told me that the constraints of university life simply became unacceptable to him. Saintsbury, then about to publish his *Literary History of Criticism, Prosody and Prose Rhythm*, was at the height of his career, although his once-high reputation has somewhat declined in later academic regard. He appeared to Scott, as to so many of his contemporaries, to be "a splendid man who seemed to have read everything."

Scott certainly admired Saintsbury's enormous 'gusto'. Much influenced by Tennyson, Browning and, especially, by Swinburne, Scott submitted his entry for a verse competition, the set theme for which was 'The New Century and the New Age'. Such a theme, Scott reckoned, could not adequately be dealt with in less than "four high-sounding pages". Accordingly, he submitted a piece that seemed to him to be of the appropriate weight and length. "The prize-winning poem", he used to relate, "turned out to be a sonnet". Even though his poem was runner-up for the prize, Scott felt that for once Saintsbury's famous sense of the fitness of subject and form had deserted him.

At Moray House, Scott's combination of high spirits and Border obduracy nearly proved his undoing. Having lent a set square or a rubber to a neighbouring student — the triviality of the object is not without significance — Scott in due course asked for it back. In doing so he attracted the notice, and provoked the wrath, of the lecturer who, in front of the class, thereupon made remarks about Scott's prideful nature that the future composer interpreted as insulting, and said so. The lecturer publicly dressed him down. Scott, furiously angry, picked up a book as if to throw it. Although the book never left his hand, the gesture was enough. The outraged lecturer reported the incident to the Principal, Dr Maurice Patterson. (Scott, in relating the incident to me, mimicked with relish the Principal's censorious tone). "If you do not write an apology to the gentleman concerned, you will have to go down. You have from now until next Friday, when I shall require the written explanation of your conduct."

Instead of writing an apology, Scott and his friends celebrated by holding a party. "I wasn't caring whether he sent me down, up, or in any other direction", Scott commented.

"Though I have difficulty now in remembering even the names of my classmates . . . who came along to drink my beer one Sunday afternoon, I can still remember the zest with which they helped me frame an apology to the redoubtable 'Moses' Patterson."

The beer-inspired communal letter was in due course delivered to Dr Patterson's study. The Principal took a quick look at it and threw it on the floor.

"This isn't an apology," he thundered: "It is an insult."

Unfortunately, the letter has not been preserved, Scott deciding that since Patterson threw it on the floor, "he could damn' well pick it up himself."

A revised version was produced, and proclaimed by Patterson to be "an apology of a kind, but not one which I am willing to accept." Recounting his version of the affair, Scott then stated firmly and finally, that he could go no further in the matter of an apology. In what must have been an interesting contest of wits, Patterson eventually conceded Scott's position, and, gathering together what remained of his pedagogic dignity, said: "Very well, then. I will see if Mr C. will accept this." Scott heard no more of the affair. The spirit of the uncle who had refused to get out of bed to serve a duke, and of his own brother with the nagging sense of the 'aginness' of 'them,' had surfaced, and, for the time being, triumphed. But it was a spirit that in later years was sometimes to make Scott unpopular, and even to stand in the way of the performance and acceptance of his music.

There were other student incidents too, resulting no doubt from Scott's boredom with the formalities of the course. One afternoon "the Doctor spent the last period dealing with 'absenteeism in our class,' and after gravely reading (with appropriate comment) out each culprit on the list, declared me 'facile princeps.' I thought this the most humorous use of the Latin language I had ever heard, but unfortunately none of my classmates seemed willing to share the joke with me . . . If I remember correctly, my last indiscretion (in College at any rate) was in rebutting the Doctor's disapproval that I had never once in two years been present at his voluntary Bible Class meeting on Friday mornings. I was (foolishly) driven to complain to him that as I had no wish to attend his meetings, he had no grounds for reprimanding me. All the same, he docked me of my last quarter or half-year's grant — a sum which (thank goodness) my father (who also was 'a sair saint for the Kirk') immediately forwarded, with something like his compliments."

The sequence of Scott's teaching posts has been preserved in the Scottish Education Department's Record of Service, Superannuation for Teachers, Form M236, dated 11th October, 1928. This shows that on 1st December, 1898, the composer became a teacher at Hawick Drumlanrig School, a post he held until 22nd December, 1899. Previously he had served from 1st November, 1825, as a pupil-teacher at Hawick Trinity School until the last day of October, 1898, at a salary of £20 per year increased by £5 per year "each subsequent year of engagement." He was to be liable for dismissal without notice for "idleness, disobedience, or immoral conduct of a gross kind," according to the information contained in a Memoranda of Agreement between the School Board and George Scott, mill furnisher, 16 Bourtree Place, Hawick, dated 7.12.95.

From Hawick Drumlanrig, Scott moved on 16th August, 1901, to Falkirk Northern Public, and on 7th August, 1903, to Falkirk Carmuirs Public. On 2nd November, 1903, he transferred to Langholm Academy, Dumfriesshire, where he remained until his appointment on 1st August, 1912, to Dunoon Grammar School. From there he transferred to Glasgow Kelvinhaugh (1st May, 1914), Kennedy Street (19th October, 1915) and Townhead (1st February, 1919), where he gave up school teaching on 25th January, 1925, his forty-fifth birthday, to become a lecturer.

No doubt the teaching years in Hawick, when he stayed in the family home with his father's mill furnisher's shop beneath, 16 Bourtree Place, were much taken up with learning the craft that was to earn him his daily bread for so many years. By the time he had reached Falkirk and was at last financially independent, he was determined to extend his musical studies. He therefore took lessons in composition from a Stirling organist, Dr Arthur Merchant. The lessons were supposed to begin at half past two on Saturday afternoons and last for one hour. Week after week Mrs Merchant had to terminate the lessons by reminding her husband that he had a choir practice at 5.30, in twenty minutes. Harmony and counterpoint were the subjects that occupied most of the time spent with Merchant, though study of the piano was not neglected. Although he became a highly capable accompanist, Scott never showed any great interest in a possible career as a pianist.

Towards the end of his stay at Falkirk Northern Public School, Scott found himself unexpectedly transferred over the heads of more senior teachers to the newly completed Falkirk Carmuirs. Characteristically, he attributed the promotion to unexplained rivalries among members of the School Board. When he arrived at the new school, the Headmaster had no class for him, so Scott was given an infant class to keep him quiet. Anxious to get back to the Borders, Scott had applied for a vacant job at Langholm. Having heard nothing, he began to assume that someone else must have been chosen to fill it. One day, without introducing himself, the Langholm Headmaster, John Howie, walked into Scott's classroom and asked if he might watch Scott teach. Nervously, Scott explained that of course his pupils were only infants, and could not absorb a great deal. "Carry on, Mr Scott," Howie interrupted: "I will draw my own conclusions." His conclusions were satisfactory and Scott went to Langholm, a move which was to have a profound effect on his career as a composer.

Clearly, the fact that he had failed to graduate at Edinburgh University was a continuing source of irritation to him. In these days, before the introduction of means-tested grant-aid, university attendance had to be paid for, usually by a pupil's parents. There could therefore be no question of a return to full-time study at Edinburgh in order to take a degree in music. One year after he began taking lessons from Merchant, Scott therefore enrolled at Durham University to read for the degree of Bachelor of Music, a course that could be taken externally. With his constant and necessary commitment to school-teaching, he did not actually graduate until 1909.

His seven years of concentrated musical study involved him in becoming acquainted in detail with the mainstream of the classical repertoire, especially the music of Bach, Handel, Mozart and Beethoven. He spoke with the warmest affection of these great composers to the end of his life. His deepest devotion, however, was reserved for Schubert and Schumann, masters of the German Lied. Towards much of Brahms's achievement his attitude was ambivalent. He admitted Brahms's Lieder to the canon of great songs, but remained decidedly cool towards the four Symphonies, although in later life he made a detailed analysis of the orchestration of the 'St. Anthony Variations.' His complaint against Brahms's large scale works was that, in his view, the joins too often showed. "Brahms will keep on shuffling about as soon as he starts to develop things, as if he was wondering what to do next."

The music of Wagner and of Richard Strauss attracted his enthusiastic attention. The melodic genius and jagged energy of Berlioz, and the broad strokes of rough characterisation deployed by Mussorgsky in their differing ways also appealed greatly to him.

Rather surprisingly, although he was concentrating on taking a degree in music, his creative attentions were still equally divided between music and literature. Indeed, he continued the writing of verses until his twenty-seventh year, before finally coming down on the side of his creative musical urge. His wide knowledge of the technical aspect of poetry, however, equipped him to be a sensitive and constructive critic, and one whose advice many young poets, including the present writer, were eagerly to seek after.

It was during this first decade of the Twentieth Century

that Scott wrote his earliest songs, setting verses culled from popular periodicals of the day like *The Academy,* and from the 'poet's corner' of the *Glasgow Herald.* The poets he favoured included Lady Olive Douglas (Olive Constance, wife of Lord Alfred Douglas, more famous now for the effect of his behaviour on the unfortunate Oscar Wilde than for his once much-admired sonnets); C. K. Scott-Moncrieff (who later became a famous translator, his achievements in this field including the English version of Proust's *A la Recherche du Temps Perdu*); the novelist H. de Vere Stacpoole and the Scottish journalist and playwright, George Reston Malloch (whose play *Soutarness Water* once enjoyed some vogue). Scott also set some verses of his own. These early songs, harmonically unadventurous, reflect the rather facile romantic idiom of the times, though they also reveal Scott's gift as a melodist. He himself regarded them as beginner's work, and never made any attempt to publish them.

Once he had returned to the Borders and become a teacher of English at Langholm, travelling twice weekly the twenty mile journey between Hawick and Langholm, he made two important contacts. One of these, soon after his arrival at Langholm in 1903, was the development of his friendship with his fellow English teacher, William Burt (1883-1949). The other, formed two years later, was with a gifted pupil, Christopher Murray Grieve, the son of the local postman.

Burt was a Highlander from Tarbert, Argyll, who attended the University of St. Andrews and went to teach at Langholm Academy after a year in Loreburn School, Dumfries. He was badly wounded with the Royal Artillery in France in July, 1918. That year he married an Annan girl, Caroline Richardson. One of their children, William, the dedicatee of MacDiarmid's 'Hungry Waters', was killed in 1942 when serving as a Pilot Officer in the Royal Air Force. The other son, now Dr John Burt, remembers "the visits of F.G. to our house and the lively discussions on all manner of things that used to go on into the early hours, with F.G's booming voice carrying upstairs to small people in bed as he sang snatches from his latest composition."

Burt, an enthusiast for the poetry of Meredith, wrote a highly-praised thesis which, in spite of support from high places, unfortunately never achieved publication. He believed passionately in the value of speaking aloud both poetry and prose, and was later to be an enthusiast for sprung rythm related to natural speech, pioneered in the poetry of Gerald Manley Hopkins. As a teacher he was noted for his grasp of a wide range of subjects as well as his own. The friendship between Burt and Scott lasted until Burt's death.

Christopher Murray Grieve, who later became the poet 'Hugh MacDiarmid', has put on record his own account of his first encounter with Francis George Scott.[2]

> I first collided with F.G. Scott — and collided is the correct word — over fifty years ago. He had just joined the staff of Langholm Academy, his first post as a Teacher.[3]
>
> I was a boy of about thirteen in the sixth standard. I am afraid most of we boys had a cynical attitude towards our teachers. We knew, for one thing that behind their respectable facades, they were often pretty wild customers. So were we. The term 'juvenile delinquent' had not come into use in these days.
>
> We were all juvenile delinquents, and consequently up to pranks which today would condemn us to a remand home or Borstal. Our delinquencies were practised inside as well as outside school, and woe betide the teacher who was not an effective disciplinarian.
>
> Mr Scott was. As far as I recall, he thrashed me only once. I have no doubt I well deserved it. If I thought F.G. a brute, I recognise that he was a just brute. As a matter of fact I was his blue-eyed boy, the star pupil. But one did not need to be a star pupil to know — indeed, I think all of us recognised at once — that Mr Scott was out of the ordinary run of teachers, and was, in fact, an eagle among sparrows; or rather, a lion in a den of Daniels, which in regard to the Scottish public he has remained ever since. I think that the basis that was laid then for our later friendship and collaboration was the fact that we were both imbued with the frontier spirit.

During a television interview in the 'Borderline' series[4] put out by Border Television to mark MacDiarmid's seventieth birthday, the poet recollected that in English he did well at Langholm, though getting only two per cent for mathematics, a subject he did not like. He also claimed that it had always been generally assumed he would be a writer, by Scott as well as by others. The composer certainly remembered setting his class the annual essay, 'How I spent my holidays'. All the pens scraped away except Grieve's. "Don't worry, Christopher," Scott said, as the boy sat scratching his head. "There's something in that big head of yours that will come out some day."

In a letter to me dated 20th May, 1945, Scott refers to his days of "school teaching in Langholm, where I seem to have impressed a little boy called Christopher Grieve. It must have been some time in 1923 that a former colleague of mine in Langholm Academy" — William Burt, in fact, who had taught Grieve in the Secondary stage — "sent me a copy of the 'Scottish Chapbook', published in Montrose by a Mr C. M. Grieve, on the staff of the Montrose 'Standard', and who on further enquiry, proved to be the young hopeful we both had taught".

Scott's earliest surviving adult manuscript pieces date from these pre-World War One years. The songs reveal a romantic style of no great individuality and little harmonic adventurousness. The best piece is a lengthy waltz-sequence for piano imitating 'the Viennese style' and entitled 'April Skies'. It is dated 1912.

In the meantime, after receiving his Bachelor of Music degree from Durham in 1909, Scott became concerned about his health. The weekly train journey in all weathers between Hawick and Langholm was made in the company of Netta Jensen, daughter of the station master at Riddings, and with whom Scott shared a travelling rug. The littleness of the social atmosphere of Langholm — a littleness that later manifested itself in the refusal for many years of the civic authorities to honour their most distinguished citizen, Dr C. M. Grieve, by making him a Freeman — also began to seem wearisome. "I fell into a sort of despondency," Scott said, feeling that "Langholm hemmed me in". He had become engaged to a daughter of a Hawick girl, a tailoress, Joanna Miller. Following the wedding of his brother James, in August 1913, at which Francis was best-man, the engagement was broken off. There were thus several grounds for his depression.

His doctor recommended a move to the seaside, preferably to the West coast. Scott obtained a post at Dunoon Grammar School.

Among his Dunoon friends were the Lauder family. The Scots comedian Sir Harry Lauder had built himself a handsome house on the Innellan road.[5] Scott was a frequent visitor, being a close friend of the comedian's son, John, who was killed in the 1914 war.

While at Dunoon, Scott crossed the Firth of Clyde one evening to attend a concert at Greenock, where some of his earliest songs were being performed. One of these songs, the composer later remembered, was a setting of some verses by his friend George Reston Malloch, 'Rebellion'. In thanking the artists, the Chairman described the songs they had just heard as being "as good as Strauss himself could have done".[6] This trivial, rather tactless remark, provided the shock which altered Scott's whole attitude. "I didn't want to write songs that seemed to educated people to imitate Strauss," he said. "I wanted to write songs that would obviously be by Francis George Scott, and equally be Scottish."

In May 1914 he moved to Glasgow, a move that was to mark the end of his long creative apprenticeship.

REFERENCES

1 According to report, the older generation of the family believed one reason to be not unconnected with his fondness for the ladies, although the records of Edinburgh University show that he failed the mandatory Latin examination at the end of the first session, and apparently failed to put right this omission in the Autumn re-sit.

2 In *Men of Mark: Francis George Scott,* a BBC Scotland radio feature broadcast in 1957, a cassette of which is in the National Library of Scotland.

3 Actually his third.

4 Cassette in the National Library of Scotland.

5 Later a hotel. It was destroyed by fire and subsequently demolished.

6 In view of such masterpieces as Strauss's groups of songs Opus 10 (1883), Opus 17 (1887) and Opus 29 (1894), a wholly ridiculous comparison.

Chapter 3

FIRST WORLD WAR AND EARLY TWENTIES

The First World War aroused similar, if less eloquently articulated, feelings among Scots to the "now God be thanked who has matched us with this hour" heroics of England's Rupert Brooke; a mood that was soon to give place under pressure of realism to the bitter sense of futility reflected in the poetry of Sassoon, Owen, Grenfell, Rosenberg and the Scot, D. S. MacIntosh. The novelist Neil Munro records in his autobiographical sketches *The Brave Days:*

> On Sunday 2nd August, 1914, two days before our declaration of war, rural telegraph offices were kept open all day and night . . . I am ashamed when I recall now what silly patriotic and romantic elations were stirred in me when I found that already there were armed guards on every railway viaduct, on reservoirs, and the Loch Long torpedo testing station. All along the Callander-and-Oban and West Highland railways, the fiendish ubiquity of German spies, and their readiness to start immediately blowing up culverts and railway bridges, of poisoning us at our own kitchen-taps, were already taken for granted . . .

> Nowhere in these islands could the illusion of fear and false rumour have been more ludicrous than in the West of Scotland, where never an enemy spy was discovered nor a single shot of the enemy heard. The men in the shipyards, engine-rooms, and munition factories of the Clyde, working through all those war years with more passion for their job than ever they knew before, were suspected by London of a tendency at any moment to sedition and Bolshevism . . .

Just before the outbreak of war, Scott fell in love with a fellow teacher of Dunoon Grammar School, Burges Gray, the daughter of William Gray of Fraserburgh, a deceased timber merchant. One of the pupils in his 1913 Senior 3 class, Helen MacGregor, recalls the great interest that the pupils took in the courting couple when, "at discreet intervals . . . singly, not collectively, they would come to the empty School Board Room". This was the signal for Sarah Coutts, an eccentric fellow-teacher from Aberdeen, who must have had acute hearing, to retreat from her rostrum and go to her glass-topped door. There she would remain until the two left again, but as Sarah's back was to us and we weren't interested in the courting couple, we were able to enjoy ourselves". Helen MacGregor remembers Scott then as being "very good looking . . . his hair longer than that of the other male teachers. I seem to remember that he wore a velour hat". She also recalls an occasion in Dunoon Pavilion — from the ashes of which arose the present Queen's Hall — "on Friday June 13th 1913, when there was a 'grand production of 'Pearl, the Fishermaiden' by the senior pupils . . . Who was the conductor but Mr Francis G. Scott Mus. Bac. . . . My father did the limelight effects. Of the boys who took part, many were killed in the 1914 war . . . The adult me wonders what a Mus. Bac. was doing . . . acting as singing teacher in a cockeyed school like ours".

The possessor of a fine mezzo-soprano voice, Burges Gray had studied singing at Glasgow's Athenaeum School of Music (now the Royal Scottish Academy of Music). She and Scott spent some time in Paris together, where a daughter — Francise (1914-1977) — was born to them in the winter of 1914. According to the entry in the Registrar's Office, St. Nicholas House, Aberdeen, they were married by the Rev. J. A. Campbell on 4th September, 1915 in the Bellslea Hotel, Fraserburgh, where a year or so before Burges Gray had been the bridesmaid at her sister's wedding, when the train-bearer had been "Master George Bruce, nephew of the bride, exquisitely garbed in pale blue satin embroidered in cream". The *Fraserburgh Herald* for 7th September, reporting a marriage which "united two highly gifted musicians", stated that Mr Scott had "entered upon what promises to be a brilliant career as a composer" while "Mrs Scott is a charming singer and as a soprano vocalist vies with her sister".

Three other children were to be born to the couple: Lilias (1918), George (1925) and Malcolm (1927).

In addition to the satisfactions of family life, F.G. (as he became known about this time to his friends, and remained so to the end of his days) and Burges explored together the rich literature of the German Lied, including the songs of Hugo Wolf and Richard Strauss, as well as the songs of the Russians,

Mussorgsky and Rachmaninov. Once the 1914-18 war was over, they gave recitals together in different parts of Scotland, introducing several Scott's songs that had been written with the characteristics of his wife's voice in mind. Nevertheless, in spite of what seems to have been a performing triumph in the Scottish context, Scott increasingly felt a sense of personal frustration. There is little doubt that in the years immediately after the war, the urge to break free from teaching, to embrace wholeheartedly the career of a composer, was a constant torment. But Scott's practical nature, his desire for an assured and steady income, his enjoyment of the security of family life, perhaps also a certain inherent Calvanism and Conservatism, held him back. He therefore set himself deliberately to limit his ambitions and stay in the teaching profession.

Those in later years who blamed the insensitivity of the Scots people for failing to appreciate Scott's gifts were apt to overlook the fact that in all probability he had at that time neither sufficient technical capacity nor self-confidence to meet the risks a composer's life then demanded. Indeed, all he had to offer was a handful of songs. As a serious songwriter rightly unwilling to compromise with commercialism, he was already set on too narrow a course to be likely to succeed as a professional musician of real standing in a country where the few opportunities for the kind of career that sustained, for instance, that other part-time composer, the Austrian Gustav Mahler, were inevitably filled by foreigners with behind them a varied and practical life-long music training. Even Rimsky-Korsakov, originally a naval officer, displayed while still in the Russian navy a varied and constant creative flow that Scott simply did not possess. To what degree an upbringing in a country with well-established musical traditions might earlier have resolved Scott's conflicting leanings towards both music and letters is an open question, but pointless now to ask. The fact is that, all things considered, Scott probably took the right decision, even although it left him with life-long regrets; regrets that, as the years passed, were to turn to bitterness.

Scott volunteered for war service, but was rejected on health grounds. Throughout his life his stomach gave him trouble. He settled down to the routine of teaching schoolchildren English. The war brought new friendships. At Kennedy

Street School, Glasgow, there arrived in 1916 a young student teacher of art, William McCance (1894-1970), later to mature into a distinguished Scottish painter, and the most interesting of the Scottish disciples of Cubism. McCance and Scott formed a friendship that was to last for many years.

During the war years and those immediately following, Scott devoted himself to a thorough study of musical nationalism, particularly the folk-music of his own country.

He began his studies with the recently published volumes *Songs of the Hebrides* (1909-1917, 3 volumes) by Marjory Kennedy-Fraser (1857-1930), the butt of much high-sounding ridicule by later folk collectors, but hailed by no less a critic than Ernest Newman, who wrote of her Hebridean songs: "Schubert and Wolf would have knelt and kissed the hands of the men who conceived them". Certainly they opened out the world of Hebridean song to thousands who would never have come to know it through the cracked-voice recordings of authentic folk-crones, of interest to sociologists rather than musicians. Most important of all, Scott studied closely *The Songs of Robert Burns* by James Dick, the monumental work that first categorised and systematised Burns's contributions to Scottish folk-song as song-writer, arranger and editor. Dick's publication, which first appeared in 1903, has remained an accurate and scholarly account that has not been surpassed, and, indeed, has been republished in America (1962).

The problem facing Scott was how to evolve a personal style that would both be his own and yet also clearly Scottish. In Scott's day, the by no means undistinguished heritage of early polyphonic music and Jacobean Court Music, recently unearthed and edited for performance by Dr Kenneth Elliott and others, was to all intents and purposes lying forgotten in libraries. In spite of the apologists for Calvanism, there seems little doubt that the socially narrow and imaginatively inhibited regime forced upon Scotland, like permanently pinching shoes, after the Reformation of 1550 eventually rendered music either a privileged Court prerogative or drew it underground to survive purely as a folk-art. After the Union of the Crowns in 1603, there could no longer be even a native Court art. The achievements of subsequent foreign-trained composers like William MacGibbon (1695-1756), Charles MacLean (c.1700-c.1773), and the remarkably gifted Sir John Clerk of Penicuik (1684-1755) — all pupils, or at least disciples, of the Italian Arcangelo Corelli (1653-1713) — and Thomas Erskine, 6th Earl of Kellie (1730-1781), a pupil of Carl Stamitz (1749-1809) in Mannheim — were inevitably reflections, or re-creations of alien styles, with varying degrees of personal intensity.

While Henry Purcell at the end of the seventeenth century, and J. C. Bach in the middle of the eighteenth, were either inventing their own 'Scotch Airs' or, as in Bach's case, incorporating genuine folk airs in their compositions ('O saw ye my Laddie?' and 'The Yellow-Haired Laddie' in two of his Opus 17 set of Piano Concertos) the concentration upon the renewal of interest in things Scottish after the threatened engulfment of all that was national by the Union of Parliaments of 1707 rested mainly on folk-poetry and the attempted revival of the Scots tongue. Allan Ramsay (1686-1758) and his friends did something to retrieve the airs for the songs that they wrote down and usually gentilified. But it was left to Robert Burns, his musical associate Stephen Clarke and his publishers, James Johnston (*The Scots Musical Museum* 1787-1803, 6 vols.) and George Thomson (*Selected Scottish Airs,* 1793 to 1841), seriously to collect and publish the old airs.

Other collectors carried on his work into the nineteenth century. Lacking Court life, a music-orientated national Church and even any serious professional theatrical life, there was simply no market for serious 'composed' Scottish music.

Revival came indirectly, through the English Renaissance led by Sir Charles Hubert Parry (1848-1918), a movement that in time was to produce Elgar, Bridge, Holst, Delius, Walton and Britten, among others, but in its early days included the Irishman Sir Charles Villiers Stanford (1852-1924) and the Scot Sir Alexander MacKenzie (1847-1935), soon to be followed by Greenock-born Hamish MacCunn (1868-1916). MacKenzie studied in Germany, and in such works as his *Scottish Piano Concerto,* his cantata *The Cotter's Saturday Night,* his tone poem *Tam O' Shanter* and his *Pictish Suite for Violin and Orchestra,* grafted Scottish pseudo-folk melodies on to his post-Mendelssohnian Germanic style, sometimes, as in the Piano Concerto, by no means ineffectively. Although a pupil of Parry and a determined setter of Scottish texts, as MacCunn's once-

popular cantatas *Lord Ullin's Daughter, The Lay of the Last
Minstrel, Queen Hynde,* and *Bonny Kilmeny* (to words by
Campbell, Sir Walter Scott and in the last two instances Hogg)
testify, MacCunn fell too completely under the compelling influence of Wagner, who adversely influenced the style of his
opera *Jeanie Deans,* a good enough piece of stage-craft though
musically in no real sense particularly Scottish.

MacKenzie and MacCunn, together with another Greenock
man, William Wallace (1860-1940),[1] an opthalmic surgeon by
profession, were the most distinguished members of this gallant,
if stylistically rather forlorn, Scottish band. In addition, there
was a whole host of arrangers, most famous among them Sir
Hugh Roberton (1874-1952).

There was thus no living tradition for Scott to base his style
upon. The tide of musical nationalism that had surged so
gloriously over Europe flung only a few eddying sprays on Scotland's shores, Mendelssohn's *Scotch* Symphony and *Hebrides*
Overture, Gade's *Ossian* Overture, Berlioz's *Waverly* and *Rob
Roy* Overtures and Bruch's *Scottish Fantasy* for Violin and
Orchestra among them. Scott had therefore to start virtually
from the beginning, building for himself out of our heritage of
folk-music and our rich and varied store of poetry a personal
idiom that would create the illusion of growing out of a non-
existent continuing art-tradition that could be infused with contemporary sensibility. The astonishing thing is not so much that
he sometimes failed, lapsing into banality, as that so often in
his finest songs he succeeded triumphantly.

Some of his earliest publications were part-songs, for which
there was a demand among school choirs and adult amateur
bodies. Although he continued writing such pieces for many
years, in a curious way none of these usually unaccompanied
choral pieces fully reflects the characteristics of his style, except
perhaps his melodic invention. In 1919 Scott published his first
part-song, 'Ay she kaimed her yellow hair', which won first
prize in a competition organised by Hugh Roberton, the conductor of the Orpheus Choir.

By the early 1930's, Hugh Roberton's world famous
Orpheus Choir had built itself up an international reputation
for the production of precisely-fashioned and tonally rounded
choralism. This fine instrument, however, was never deployed

on major choral works, but concentrated entirely on small-scale, often sentimental choral pieces, many of which were arranged by the Conductor himself; "bon-nie wee tusheries" I was to describe them, years later, when, as the youthful Music Critic of the Glasgow newspaper *The Bulletin,* I was poking fun at the Choir's tendency to over-articulate consonants.

The Orpheus Choir's magazine *The Lute* for September, 1919, comments on the "feature, as gratifying as it was unexpected", of "the discovery of (to us) a hitherto unknown Scottish composer — Francis George Scott. When his envelope was opened and we saw, against the *nom-de-plume* 'Teri' an address within sprinting distance of our own, we looked up. Mr Scott, we learn is a Borderer . . . His prize setting 'Ay she Kaimed' is a beautiful, haunting bit of work". (Scott put this Hawick *nom-de-plume* at the top of several of his earliest compositions).

Roberton, who was to be knighted in 1931, organised a second part-song competition in 1924. Scott again gained the first prize with an early version of 'O Jesu Parvule' (later re-written as a solo song), though by rather unusual means, apparently arising out of an incident that occurred between the competitions. One day the conductor called at Scott's flat in Woodville Gardens, Langside, which was indeed within "sprinting distance" of Roberton's own home, when the composer was out. Received by Mrs Scott, Roberton announced that if Mr Scott would like to submit some of his compositions, he would be pleased to consider them for performance by the Orpheus Choir. Mrs Scott, nettled that Roberton was apparently unaware that her husband's work was already published, replied that if he wished to consider her husband's songs, all he had to do was to go out and buy them.[2] The door was closed, and Roberton went off in perhaps understandable annoyance.

There are two versions of the story of what followed, one remembered by the composer's daughter, Mrs Lilias Forbes, the other by his son George, and by his nephew by marriage George Bruce. In the former version Scott, feeling that Roberton would now be unlikely to look with favour on an entry from himself, had the idea whilst on a visit to William Burt, his old Langholm friend now teaching at Linlithgow, of entering the song in Burt's name. Burt was not, of course, a composer, and

C

advised strongly against this ploy, but Scott persisted, entering the part-song 'O Jesu Parvule' as being by his friend. Soon afterwards, Burt was dismayed to receive a telegram telling him that "his entry" had won the prize. He at once wired a disclaimer, revealing the name of the real composer to Roberton, who, not unnaturally, was furious, thinking that underhand methods were being tried out on his judging committee, or that his own impartiality was being questioned.

The more colourful, but perhaps less probable, version has Scott submitting two songs: a good song under his own name and a bad one under Burt's. The bad song won (but 'O Jesu Parvule' is emphatically not a bad song) and Burt was duly notified. Burt thereupon made an alarmed phone-call to Scott, who proceeded to Roberton's house to explain the matter. The conductor, however, was then in London. On explaining the "mistake" to Mrs Roberton, she replied: "But *you* are mistaken Mr Scott. You did not win the competition. My husband has discovered an entirely new composer."

The Lute for March 1924 has its version, explaining perhaps why no further competitions of the sort were held.

> The Prize Competition initiated by the Choir for compositions and arrangements was only a modified success. Many were called, but few were chosen. In fact, there was just one ewe-lamb in the bunch — a very sensitive part-song by Francis Geo. Scott, entitled 'O Jesu Parvule'. The subject is that of a mother hushing the christ-child to sleep, and is written in the rich Buchan dialect (sic.) The composition, for what reason no man knoweth, was sent in under another name. As a result, the name of an innocent person has been flourishing in the musical journals as the composer . . . The final result was one prize of thirty pounds and three consolation prizes of three guineas each.

Another of Scott's part-songs, 'New Corn', came into the Choir's repertoire in 1934, and remained there for many years.

Of Scott's published unaccompanied part-songs, the most spirited are settings of Burn's 'There was a lad was born in Kyle' and 'The deuk's dang o'er my daddie o' '. 'There was a lad', dating from 1924, is surpassed so obviously by Burns's admirably chosen original tune that no other version would have any chance of ousting it in popularity. The other song, a vigorous six-eight piece published in 1937, is in Scott's happiest folk-vein. There are two TT BB pieces, respectively 'The

Three Fishers' and 'Pretty Nell', also both imaginative and effective. There are also several part-songs with piano accompaniment, notably a setting of Helen Cruickshank's 'Sea Buckthorn' (1932) and settings of three Chinese poems, translated by Arthur Waley (1932) — 'There grows an elm-tree', 'New Corn' and 'Plucking the rushes' — all chorally and musically successful. Such pieces may be clouded by changes of fashion, but do not ultimately disappear.

Scott was always a natural and inventive melodist, and one whose lyrical sense in maturity derived closely from his long acquaintance with Scot's folk-songs. Even the MacDiarmid settings, his most adventurous songs, for all their other essential qualities, reflect Scottish influences in their vocal lines.

'Three Short Songs for Medium or High Voice', his first collection, appeared in 1920, settings of poems by Wilfred Gibson, Seumas O'Sullivan and Walter Wingate. They hint at Scott's natural melodic gift, but are harmonically unadventurous and now and then lapse into conventional trivialities of a sort that were the stock-in-trade of drawing-room balladists of the Edwardian period, though never of Richard Strauss.

In 1922, at his own expense, Bayley and Ferguson published the first two volumes of Scott's *Scottish Lyrics,* the title chosen perhaps in emulation of Parry's *English Lyrics* (1881-1920). Of the eight songs in Book One, six were settings of poems by Burns, one of a Scots poem by Burns's Edinburgh publisher William Creech, and one of an anonymous folk-poem of the kind Burns so often re-worked for Johnston and Thomson. Though the melodic folk-influence is obvious in all of them, they often show a highly personal rhythmic energy and a sense of characterisation, frequently sustained by the accompaniment. Book Two was made up of nine songs, six to poems of Burns, the others to words by John Imlah, Allan Cunningham and an anonymous lyric, like the other two, firmly in the Burns tradition. Broadly speaking, these Burns and Burns-related settings fall into two categories: those that are essentially lyrical, the melody rising from the rhythmic flow of the words, like 'Ay Waulkin O' ' and 'Mary Morison'; and those robustly humorous, like 'Last May a Braw Wooer'.

Scott held strongly to the view that in some cases Burns's traditional tunes were either banal or downright inappropriate.

He also felt that the inevitable strophic nature of words set
to a folk-tune meant that dramatic nuances in the text could
not be given a musical counterpart. One of the difficulties
that for long militated against wider popular acceptance of Scott's
earlier songs is that the Burns-loving public simply did not
agree with him. It is one thing to provide a setting for a song
the folk-tune for which is a near unsingable and unknown
fiddle dance-tune, like that for 'The Lovely Lass O' Inverness'.
It is quite another to challenge such choices by Burns as the
airs for 'Of a' the Airts' and 'The Red, Red Rose'. Beautiful
as they are in both these cases, Scott's settings failed to displace
the affection in which the folk-airs were held. Neil Mackay,
the Editor of the centenary edition of Scott's *Selected Songs,*
has commented that in certain cases where Scott's Burns settings
are concerned, "Scott's compositions seem to have as their
basis an act of criticism, a personal reaction to music already
written. In a sense he was writing 'music about music', offering
a musical commentary on musical tradition, and coming to terms
with a tradition."

There are several examples of this among the seventeen
songs in Books One and Two. Twelve of these are settings of
Burns poems. Book One, for female voice, includes 'The Carles
O' Dysart', Ay Waukin O' ', 'Last May a Braw Wooer', 'The
Wren's Nest', 'The Lovely Lass O' Inverness', and 'Hey, the
Dusty Miller'. Book Two, for male voice, includes 'Wha will
buy my Troggin?', 'O merry hae I been teethin' a heckle', 'Mary
Morison', 'The Weary Pund O' Tow', 'Crowdie' and 'O were my
love yon lilac fair'.

Of those in Book One, two of the finest, 'Ay Waukin O' '
(which impressed Roger-Ducasse) and 'Last May a Braw
Wooer' exemplified the two contrasting types of Burns settings
Scott composed. The former represents Scott's lyrical vein, the
second his humorously dramatic category.

Burns matched 'Ay Waukin O' ', the expression of a girl's
hopeless sense of longing for lost love, to a melody remarked
on by Dick as being notable for its brevity and simplicity (Ex. 1).

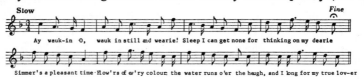

Scott's flowing melody matches the speech-rhythm of the lines. Though it maintains some of the basic internal characteristics of the original — the falling third and the rising fourth — it has no more than a basic kinship to Burns's tune. The flattened seventh in the fourth bar underlines the girl's yearning (Ex. 2).

With his dislike of strophic settings, Scott uses a melody derived from the refrain for verses two and three, the piano interlude between these stanzas being the melody from stanza one.

The accompaniment sets the melancholy mood in the first bar, with its dejected thirds. A B flat pedal point in the refrain, and again, three octaves high in the third stanza, when it supports arpeggiated chords in the high register of the piano — a favourite Scott device for depicting loneliness or eerieness — suggests the single-mindedness of the girl's longing. The various chordal uses to which the pacing octave figure, implied in the first bar, is put should be noted.

Also in the category of 'yearning' songs are 'O were my love yon lilac fair' and 'Mary Morison'. Burns's air to the former has an undistinguished simplicity (Ex. 3). Scott's modal

air is much more beautiful (Ex. 4), but it is supported by a rest-

less accompaniment some have thought inappropriate. If the song is to succeed, the composer's overall indication, 'Andante con delicatezza', must be remembered, and his direction to the pianist 'sempre teggierissimo' strictly observed. In my view, the broken arpeggios, falling then rising to the words 'And I mysel' a drap o' dew/Into her bonnie breast to fa'' should sound like the tremble of an Aeolian harp. (Scott uses a similar device to match Dunbar's 'clear sun whom no cloud devouris' in the later song 'Rorate Coeli').

Burns provided 'Mary Morison' with a slowed-down strathspey of no great effectiveness (Ex. 5).

Scott's melody carefully adjusts to the word-rhythm of the poem (Ex. 6). The composer even went so far as to indicate

in a footnote: "In this song the pulse-rhythm should be felt as
— — ⌣ in 3-pulse sections
and as — — ⌣ ⌣ in 4-pulse sections

The song is a fine one, but may reasonably be criticised for the weight of hysteria which breaks out in the accompaniment (Ex. 7) overburdening the melodic line.

Of the humorous character songs Scott fashioned from poems by Burns, 'Last May a braw Wooer' is not only one of the earliest, but in fact the second longest text Scott was to set. The tune chosen by Burns, though a good one, does become tedious with repetition (Ex. 8).

Scott here achieves considerable breadth of treatment, as was so often his practice, through the accompaniment. The melody is a family relation of the Dick tune, and subjected to a few variations, including augmentation, does duty for each verse. The opening of the accompaniment presents a figure that is a kind of inversion of the singer's first bar, and pictorial touches abound. The dotted rhythm stresses both the darts of the girl's 'bonnie blue e'en' and their effect on her suitor (Ex. 9).

The suitor's ponderous caperings are also taken care of (Ex. 10).

The chromatic augmentation and rather mocking repetition of the word 'warlock' made Neil Mackay wonder if this was a dig at the leading English song writer of the day, Peter Warlock, whose work Scott thought "insipid", though he admired 'Captain Stratton's Fancy' enough to pay it the tribute of imitation in his unpublished 'Admiral Benbow', written in 1934.

Of the songs in Book One, 'The Carles o' Dysart' revels in Scott's characteristic energy to a cheeky tune that catches the almost arrogant self-assurance of the words. 'I'll gar our gudeman trow' has always been one of Scott's most popular songs with women singers. 'The Wren's Nest' is feather-like, only twenty six bars long. 'Hey, the Dusty Miller' — to be performed "as light and quick as possible" — has the girl rushing out her protestations in triplets, against the jogging octaves in the bass of the accompaniment (like the turning of the mill-wheel). From this rhythm the melody in due course takes its cue. The explosive high spirits of this song have a decidedly dance-like flavour.

It has some similarity in rhythm and feeling to 'Wha will buy my Troggin?', the first song in Book Two (though wrongly placed in the Contents List). In addition to the songs already described there is the flowing folk-like setting of John Imlah's 'Weel I lo'e Mary' — the nearest Scott came to creating what sounds like a genuine folk-air, though its strophic use is varied by the accompaniment — and a group of what might be called songs in Scott's vigorous "trotting" manner. These include 'My Wife shall hae her Will', assertive octaves in the piano's opening bars making quite plain the truth of the title.

During the war, in addition to his friendship with the young McCance, Scott made other friends who were to remain close to him, Edwin Muir and Denis Saurat. The earlier of these friendships was probably that with the bi-lingual Denis Saurat (1890-1958), from 1918 to 1921 Lecturer in French at Glasgow University, before becoming Professor of English at Bordeaux University. Saurat returned to London in 1924, where he settled as Director of the French Institute. In 1926 he became Professor of French Languages and Literature at King's College, London.

It was Saurat who, in the April 1924 issue of *La Revue Anglo-Americaine,* wrote an article, 'Le groupe de la Renaissance Ecossaise', thus giving the revival of Scottish letters of the 'Twenties and thereafter the title of 'Scottish Renaissance', a title that has adhered to it. The erudite Saurat wrote many books, including studies of Milton, Blake and Victor Hugo. *La pensée de Milton* (1921) is generally regarded as his most important work. He held strong views on the importance of occult thought in English literature, and, influenced by the theories of Robert Fludd, found a source-link in the works of his three authors. Saurat set out his philosophical system in a series of Dialogues under the title *The Three Conventions* (1926), dedicated to Scott.

Scott probably met Saurat when attending an evening lecture given by the Frenchman at Glasgow University. Scott, who always leaned towards French rather than German culture, had good French. His interest in French culture and his special regard for the poetry of Paul Valéry was probably strengthened by his friendship with Saurat. Scott also found much to attract him about the characteristic clarity of the French musical tradition. More important perhaps, Saurat encouraged Scott's belief that the creation of a musical style both personal and national was the surest way to make an international contribution to music.

Long afterwards, Saurat described the nature of Scott's search for a personal style.

> What he was looking for was *forces,* which were perhaps in a Scottish garb and came out of Scottish nature, but which were universal. He felt that in Scottish literature, and in Scottish music, some element of human nature which was universal, and which had never been given a real hearing before, could now be brought to the fore, and be the foundation of a new future for Scotland, because then the separation between Scotland and England would be quite clear, although he wished it to remain friendly, and the originality of Scotland, which was what he felt most deeply, would be brought forth triumphantly.[3]

These were the days when the Scottish Renaissance movement and the Scottish National Party were both coming to birth. Saurat's words make somewhat ironic retrospective readin half a century later. The steady growth of Scotland's sense of nationhood has been confined to cultural matters. Unfortunately, her industry has been steadily diluted by take-overs, incorporations and 'rationalisations', and while Scotland's political will for a stronger say in her own destiny has also advanced, characteristically it appears to falter and fall back as soon as there seems some hope of its achieving practical significance.

Scott's nationalism found expression in his setting of Burns's 'Scots wha hae'. Scott maintained that the original tune chosen by Burns resembled a dirge. His own assertive tune, however, has also a drag at its rhythmic feet, which perhaps accounts for its failure to be adopted as a national anthem. Although Scott never joined the Scottish National Party (or any other, for that matter) he made the S.N.P. a present of the manuscript, though the song remained uncollected until the appearance of Book Five of *Scottish Lyrics* in 1939.

The second of Scott's wartime friendships was with the poet Edwin Muir (1887-1959), a gentle Orcadian by birth, who after working for seven years in a Glasgow beer-bottling factory moved to a bone factory at Greenock (the 'Fairport' of his *Autobiography*), where he survived unhappily from 1912 to 1914. In 1912 Muir was thus living in Greenock when the incident of the Straussian song occurred, although there is no evidence that the two men met during this period, or that Muir was at the concert. Muir's next job was with the shipbuilding firm

of Lobnitz of Renfrewshire. He moved there shortly after the outbreak of war, and travelled to work daily by train from Glasgow.
According to the recollection of Willa Muir's cousin, Betty
Anderson, it seems likely that Muir and Scott first encountered
each other at a meeting in Glasgow of the Guild Socialist Movement.

Guild Socialism, supported by the *New Age,* the publication
run by A. R. Orage (1873-1934) to which Muir became a regular
contributor, was devised by men who feared that State Socialism
would merely substitute absolute centralised bureaucratic control
for absolute control by individual employers. Their alternative
was to have industry in its various forms owned by the Nation,
but controlled by the Guilds made up of those employed in them,
the basis for the structuring of which, it was felt then, already
existed in the Trade Union Movement.

Scott, who strongly upheld the right of the small shop-
keeper to develop his own business, also admired the early
pioneers of the Co-op movement. He adhered broadly to the
idealist sharing and caring principles on which the theory of
Socialism is based, and might well have attended a Guild meeting. At any rate Muir, in his *Autobiography* (1954), recalls that
he met at a time when he was writing his 'aphorisims', —
1916 to 1918 — under the pseudonym of 'Edward Moore'. These
'aphorisims' first appeared in the *New Age,* and were published
in book form as *We Moderns* (1918). Scott was later to refer
to Saurat and Muir as his "greatest pals during the war".[4]
Muir wrote of Scott:

> He and Saurat were fast friends, continually visiting each other
> and discussing music and Saurat's system of ideas . . . Both
> accepted me warmly into their circle, and two worlds, the
> world of music and the world of intuitive speculation, opened
> before me.

Later, Muir recorded:

> My first impression of Scott is very difficult to give. The
> extraordinary energy, a rather brusque manner sometimes,
> extreme violence in debate, and a sort of fire and lightness
> when he was either discussing music or singing his songs at
> the piano . . . He inclined towards the French school at that
> time, rather than the German, and we had many arguments
> on that point. He was interested most of all in applying
> modern techniques to Scottish sentiments and Scottish music.

In his *Autobiography* Muir recorded further impressions:

> I was struck from the start by the contrast between Scott's explosive vitality and the extreme delicacy and grace of his songs. Like some of the people from the Borders, he had a fine Caesarean head, cut so vigorously that you thought you could still hear the thud of the hammer on the chisel. He was blunt and uncompromising, yet delighted by the most fantastic notions, which he carried to wild lengths out of sheer enjoyment then, without warning, he would make some remark which brought the whole structure down, while he listened with delight to the crash. Along with this he had the finest delicacy of feeling, which he showed to those who knew him well; but usually he was as explosive as Landor, whom he resembled in some ways, particularly in the combination of great vitality with the utmost perfection of form: I mean the exquisite Landor of the poetry, not of the prose writings. There was no musician in Glasgow with whom he would have deigned to discuss music; so he had to be content with Saurat, who knew a good deal about it, and myself, who knew very little, but was eager to learn. These days in Glasgow with Scott and Saurat were too delightful for me to attempt the impossible task of analysing their fragrance.

Muir's description of Scott's tactics in argument is borne out by the testimony of Betty Anderson, who remembers an evening when his sister, Dora, and Mrs Scott were also present. The discussion turned on feminism, inspired by talk of Lawrence's *The Plumed Serpent*. Betty Anderson asked Scott if he had read Virginia Woolf's *A Room of One's Own*. As he had not, she lent him her copy. "A bedsitter to herself and a cup of cocoa is all she wants," was Scott's scornful criticism. Betty Anderson recalls, too, that however fierce the argument, at the end of it all Scott would stand up and say: "That was a very good evening. Come back soon."

I can still recall an afternoon, during which I vigorously defended Byron and Yeats — unlikely bedfellows — against Scott's fiercely derisive attack. Having roused me almost to fury, he suddenly grinned, leant forward in his chair and conceded: "All right, I'll admit they're not bad poets, but they're no use to me. I can't set them." Delighted at having outraged then astonished me, he threw back his head the better to let out the great roar of his laughter.

A year or so after meeting Muir, Scott was introduced to

the poet's newly-married wife, Willa Anderson. She remembered Scott as: "A very vital, stimulating person, enveloping and warm and exciting. I *enjoyed* him so much. I enjoyed his company, I liked being with him, and he gave me a feeling for all sorts of small emotional nuances in the songs, which I hadn't thought of. It wasn't only his vitality, you see, it was his sensitivity, his sensibility, and it was all carried along in the terrific drive and surge of excitement, and whatever the song was, he was *full* of it".

Willa Muir preserved her 'enjoyment' of Scott's vitality for the rest of her life. Years later the composer's nephew, George Bruce, remembers accompanying Scott to call on the Muirs. Willa opened the door and cried out: "Scott, you old bugger! ", rushing forward to embrace him, while Edwin stood quietly in the background until the demonstration was over, then held his hand out and said: "How do you do, F.G.?"

Through Saurat, Scott met the French composer and teacher, Jean Jules Amable Roger-Ducasse (1873-1954), a pupil of Fauré, who, in 1935 suceeded Dukas as Professor of Composition at the Paris Conservatoire. Scott was introduced to Roger-Ducasse in the summer of 1921, and Saurat later recalled what happened.[5]

It was in Bordeaux lived a man who was considered the most acute critic of French music, Roger-Ducasse. He lived in a small village which might be considered a suburb of Bordeaux, and it was frightfully hot. Nevertheless, Scott and I went, and we took to him some music of Scott's, being very keen to get his opinion. Particularly, we took 'Ay Waukin O' ', and — well — he began making some remarks, after he played perhaps two or three minutes of it. Then gradually, as he went on playing, his remarks became softer and softer in tone, and before the end he had given up. He had given up the position of being a teacher, and he became a friend and colleague.

Being myself an impartial spectator, I was very impressed by the effect of a single piece of music on a great critic, and it gave me a high opinion of Scott as a composer and Ducasse as a critic. Later on, when Scott was out of the way, Ducasse — and this was, mind you, about 1921 — Ducasse said to me that here we had found the Scottish Mussorgsky.

Saurat's account is slightly misleading, in that other meetings

with Ducasse followed on succeeding days, and the Frenchman
saw more than one song. 'Ay Waukin O' ' would certainly not
suggest Mussorgsky, although one of Scott's explosive character
songs might well have done so.

Scott's own account of the Roger-Ducasse encounter is
contained in a letter to me dated 20th May, 1945 (referred to
hereafter as the 'Autobiographical Letter'), the original of
which is now in the National Library of Scotland. Incidentally,
in the matter of the wartime friendships, it is noteworthy that
Scott names Muir first, suggesting that his was the earlier friendship, which the date of Saurat's appointment to Glasgow University appears to substantiate.

> During the war my greatest pals in Glasgow were Edwin Muir
> and Denis Saurat, and having spent many holiday months in
> France before the war — the setting 'Twist ye, twine ye' is
> dated from Paris in 1914. I had the opportunity of a meeting
> (about 1921) with Roger-Ducasse in Bordeaux, where Saurat
> was then English Professor. This meeting with Ducasse gave
> me the first bit of assurance that what I was writing was
> of value. Ducasse insisted on my visiting him every day at
> his small estate outside Bordeaux, to let him hear the MSS
> songs I had brought with me: said he would have them per-
> formed at a coming contemporary music concert in Paris
> if translations of them could be made (Saurat tried this!)
> and finally invited me to settle in Paris and work with him for
> nix, nought, nothing as fee! It was a tempting offer, for I
> knew Ducasse was right in the Conservatoire inner circle,
> which included Fauré, Debussy, Ravel etc.[6] But I couldn't
> take the chance. I had married and had two daughters by
> 1921, the whole quartet entirely dependent on holding down
> a school job in Glasgow.

Clearly, Scott found his contact with Roger-Ducasse
creatively stimulating, and through him Scott met Gabriel Fauré,
then an old man.

The most important of the friendships formed by Scott at
this time, creatively at any rate, was that with his former pupil
C. M. Grieve, now the poet Hugh MacDiarmid. There are two
accounts of how this reunion took place. In his book *The
Company I've Kept* (1966) MacDiarmid writes:

> Scott was a School Teacher of mine at Langholm Academy
> when I was a boy of fourteen or fifteen. I lost touch with him
> completely from about 1906 to 1922, when he happened to

see one of my early MacDiarmid lyrics in *The Scottish Chapbook*[7] and wrote to me, not knowing, of course, that the
pseudonym of 'Hugh MacDiarmid' covered an old Langholm
pupil of his. We met, found that I had reached independently
(for up to then I knew nothing of Scott's work as a composer,
though he had already been setting Scottish songs when he
was one of my teachers at Langholm) a position very close
to his own with regard to Scottish Arts and Letters, and
realised that we had a great deal more in common — a deep
community of insight. We were both Borderers — Scott belonging to Hawick, only twenty miles from Langholm. After
that we became the closest of friends and there can be few
cases of closer collaboration between a poet and a composer.
Scott is one of the few men, perhaps the only man, for whom
I had an unqualified respect. Simply because he so clearly
and completely understood that ability of any kind depends
upon self-respect and was incapable of losing his on any
account. I think the world of him . . .

Scott's account of the reunion with Grieve is contained
in the Autobiographical Letter. It is broadly similar, but gives
more detail. The "former colleague" referred to was, of course,
William Burt. Wrote Scott:

It must have been somewhere in 1923 that a former colleague
of mine in Langholm Academy sent me a copy of the *Scottish
Chapbook,* published in Montrose by Mr C. M. Grieve, on
the staff of the *Montrose Standard,* and who on further
enquiry proved to be the young hopeful we both had taught.
A meeting of all those was arranged and conversation naturally turned to memories of Langholm, and of what we had
been doing since we left it. From that day to the publication
of *Cencrastus* in 1930, I should say that practically every
poem Grieve wrote was sent to Glasgow for my consideration
(vide the author's note to *Sangschaw* (1925), *Pennywheep*
(1926) and *A Drunk Man Looks at the Thistle* with dedicatory
poem, 1926). During this spate of creative activity, Christopher spent as many weekends in Glasgow as he could
manage, and the Scott family took its month's holiday in
Montrose, with lots of conviviality needless to say, as Willa
and Edwin Muir were sometimes to be found there when
not abroad, Willa being a Montrose girl.

MacDiarmid's early lyrics appeared in the two collections
referred to by Scott, *Sangschaw* and *Pennywheep*. Most of the
poems had previously been published in magazines and newspapers. According to Scott, the poet had been experimenting

in various styles and under different pseudonyms during the early 'Twenties. "No one was more surprised than Chris", Scott maintained, "when *Sangschaw* was so well received". The *Glasgow Herald* of 3rd December, 1925, thought MacDiarmid's achievement "quite unheralded". *The Times Literary Supplement* commented on the poet's "unusual sense of movement and changing aspects of the earth in its diurnal round, a gift for seeing things from new angles and illuminating poignant situations by flashes of imaginative insight . . ." Edwin Muir, equally impressed, carried the analysis of these remarkable lyrics a stage further, commenting, with particular reference to "Country Life", on the "fantastic economy, a crazy economy which has the effect of humour and yet conveys a kind of horror which makes this poem so original and so truly Scottish. It is pure inspiration; nothing could be better of its kind, and the kind is rare".

Saurat, writing of the lyrics in 1924, when they were still uncollected, said:

> MacDiarmid must take the place of Burns. I do not mean that he is a new Burns. That would be a calamity. But as Burns began something new, MacDiarmid is beginning something new — consequently, something which is not Burns. And yet which is Scottish, but at the same time Burns was European only in his platitudes.[8]

Scott approved of Saurat's assessment, at any rate as regards MacDiarmid.[9]

Up to the time of the reunion with his former pupil, Scott had shown himself to be a highly talented song-writer, harmonically conventional, a master of rhythmic characterisation with a strong sense of lyricism. His style, broadly speaking, was that of a late Romantic, although by the time he came to publish Books One and Two of *Scottish Lyrics,* national overtones and influences had been firmly absorbed.

It was the stimulus of his contact with MacDiarmid's early lyrics, however, that transformed him from being a highly gifted Scottish song-writer to a significant international one, albeit through a comparatively small handful of songs perhaps not much greater numerically than the slender fifteen which keep alive the reputation of the French composer Henri Duparc.

A picture of MacDiarmid and Scott together at the height

of the partnership has been preserved by 'A. T. Cunningham' (John Tonge): [10]

> Before going any further, said F.G. we'd to listen. He sat down at the piano, legs crossed, and with a smile — *dolce* — slowly sang:
>
>> As the dragonfly's hideous larve creeps
>> Oot o' the ditch whaur it was spawn'd
>> And straight is turned to the splendid fly,
>> Nae doot by Death's belated hand
>> You'll be changed in a similar way.
>
> The poet hugging the arm of the sofa, as Scott continued serenely with the accompaniment hinting at its satirical commentary — *sempre dolce* —
>
>> But as frae that livin' flash o' licht
>> The cruel features and crawlin' legs
>> O' its former state never vanish quite
>> I fancy your Presbyterian Heaven
>> 'll be haunted tae in a hellish leaven.
>
> Scott had reserved to the end the hellish dissonances proper to such a superbly concentrated little hate poem. And by then MacDiarmid was curled up with delight. There was no need to ask. 'You like it Christopher?'.
>
> I was to find the episode typical of the encounters between Scott and MacDiarmid — never as frequent as both would have liked — for on most occasions when they foregathered in the 1930's there was a setting of yet another MacDiarmid lyric on the piano.

Scott's collaboration with MacDiarmid was to last for approximately ten years. It began in 1923 with a setting of 'Country Life' (though it was not published until 1949), and included 'Moonstruck' (1929), which shows Scott's awareness of Schönberg's *Pierot Lunaire,* 'Wheesht, Wheesht, Foolish Hert' (1924) — perhaps the most adventurous of all — 'The Eemis-Stane' (1924), 'The Watergaw' (1927), 'Milk-wort and Bog-cotton' (1932) and 'An Apprentice Angel' (1933), songs that assimilate contemporary European musical trends. Scott had studied Schönberg's harmonic treatise some years earlier. Scott's experience of modernism was thus merely aurally confirmed at the series of International Contemporary Music Festivals in Salzburg which he began to attend during the summer of 1923,

D

when Muir was his companion. These MacDiarmid songs first internationalised Scottish music, rather as MacDiarmid's early lyrics internationalised Scottish poetry, absorbing French Impressionism and Symbolism.

Scott had also studied Bartok's music in the post-war years. He was to meet the composer a decade later on one of the two visits Bartok paid to Glasgow under the auspices of Erik Chisholm's poorly supported but highly enterprising Active Society. The Bartok influence is perhaps most obvious in the setting of 'Country Life'. Scott himself said that the setting was "atonal . . . the voice and piano parts have little to do with each other. There is no melody in the usual sense of the word." As in so many of Scott's songs, there is nevertheless a secure pedal anchorage, in this case on D. The jagged percussive style of the piano part made it seem to one critic "a study in grotesquerie". By its avoidance of the contrast in the text between 'outside' and 'inside', it is perhaps also a deliberate and subtle stressing of the uniform transience of all sensory experience.

'Crowdieknowe' (1924), with its vigorous, striding piano writing full of pictorial effects, in contrast to the ironic hint of an 'urlar' of a pibroch in the vocal line — or perhaps, as Neil Mackay suggests "a hymn-like ecclesiastical suggestion" — makes mocking gusty comment on the absurdity of the traditional Scots view of physical resurrection.

Just as the finest of these early lyrics "push through", as David Daiches put it, so Scott pushes through the literal meaning of the words in order to recreate a purely musical meaning. In a sense the poetry of words is inevitably destroyed as soon as a composer sets any text. Thus in Scott's folk-like setting of MacDiarmid's 'Reid E'en' — which both relates to folk-belief and underlines the poem's literary ancestry with its use of the reprise, 'Hey nonny nonny' — the sound-effect of the words is lost, but an additional underlining dimension is added by the music. On the other hand in 'Wheesht, Wheesht', 'The Eemis-Stane', 'The Watergaw', 'Milk-wort and Bog-cotton' and 'An Apprentice Angel', voice and piano go their own way yet complement each other to form a whole new self-contained musical entity. The great MacDiarmid lyrics do not make their impact merely on the plane of literal or imagist meaning. David Daiches wrote of the poet's "seeking for words to contain an

experience whose reality is wholly independent of the poem".
Commenting on his setting of 'Wheesht, Wheesht', Scott claimed
that music was really "bi-planal" — to emphasise the point
visually he gave the piano and the voice part different keys —
the vocal line "still quite clear, the voice of an old man crooning
by the fire-side, the piano part very remote, swinging like 'Eemis-
Stane' to a sort of metaphorical rhythm of its own". Speaking of
this group of MacDiarmid songs, Scott observed that "there
was nowadays practically no region of the unconscious that
music does not attempt to explore. Thus we could have music
that could be described as literary, realistic, objective, subjective,
or on the purely physical side as one, two, three or four dimen-
sional, polytonal, or atonal", drawing the image of "one plane
differing from another as horizontal does from vertical". Thus
when MacDiarmid produced his poems in what was then rather
unhappily called "synthetic Scots" (because the poet had run
together words from any and every dialect and age, for good
measure adding some obsolete words culled from *Jamieson's
Dictionary*) the composer "felt it was his duty to say something
in half a dozen dimensions about them". Of 'The Watergaw',
Scott rightly said that it was "a veritable masterpiece of consumate
expression in twelve lines which I think it would be difficult to
match in any language. The music is polytonal (viz, it seems
to be in several keys at one and the same time) and endeavours
to carry over into music the tremendous emotional power behind
the words". In this aim Scott certainly succeeds.

Scott frequently pointed out that 'Milk-wort and Bog-
cotton' was influenced by pibroch. Pibroch (or Piobaireachd, to
give it its Gaelic name) consists of a theme, the urlar, and a
series of variations, usually about eight, each increasing in
rhythmic complexity, an effect secured by the complications of
the grace-notes. No other form of development is possible in
bag-pipe music, the chanter having eight notes and three fixed-
interval drones. The vocal line of 'Milk-wort and Bog-cotton'
does, indeed, resemble the urlar of a pibroch. Many pibroch
urlars have a certain hymn-like quality. This may in part be
due to the serious "great music" tradition of the form which
perhaps suggested Calvanistic religious associations to the Gael.[11]
There is also the fact that the gathering complexity of the variations generates its own increasing physical momentum and pace.

The urlar of the pibroch also sometimes bears a resemblance to the musical device of recitative (in its pre-eighteenth century Italian opera form), defined by Eric Blom as "declamation in singing with fixed notes, but without definite metre or time". Scott secures control of the metre, but in 'Milkwort and Bog-Cotton' implies a sense of timelessness by writing the song without bar lines.

Arising from his interest in Gaelic Scott had, in fact, made a close study of pibroch, intending to write a book about it. He got no further than the production of a fascinating lecture. Many years later, with his permission, I began to edit it for publication in a short-lived music magazine of the 'Forties, *Con Brio*. Unfortunately, the magazine ceased publication before the lecture article could be printed. It sums up however so admirably the nature and structure of the pibroch form that it is printed here as Appendix B. In preparing his notes for the lecture, Scott used Tonic Sol-Fa notation, and had the assistance of a piper. The Principal of the College of Piping in Glasgow, Seumas MacNeill, has kindly re-edited Scott's lecture, filling out Scott's illustrations in piping notation.

Of the five 'bi-planal' MacDiarmid songs mentioned, the vocal lines, though tailored to match the spoken rhythm of the words, all possess a pentatonic pibroch quality. The 'Scotch snap', often slowed-up, is another recurring feature. Thus for all their European harmonic connotations, the Scottish influence still shows through.

The terseness of MacDiarmid's finest lyrics, their remarkable visionary qualities — I know of few, if any, other poems in English or Scots that match them in this respect — and their simultaneous movement on several planes of thought and feeling, enabled Scott to find a contemporary European voice as an inspired miniaturist of a high order.

By the end of the decade of collaboration with MacDiarmid, the supply of lyrics had dried up. While we can only guess how much Scott's criticism at his weekend meetings with the poet influenced the contents of *Sangschaw* and *Pennywheep,* Scott, the literary critic, acknowledged what was to be his greatest contribution to Scottish literature by stating plainly the part he played in helping MacDiarmid to shape and consolidate his long masterpiece, *A Drunk Man Looks at the Thistle.* This

sequence of satirical comment on the Scottish ethos, punctuated
by intuitive lyrics relevant to the context, uses the device of
the temporary liberation caused by drunkenness to consider
the Scotland of the middle 'Twenties from the widest possible
imaginative viewpoint, a viewpoint orientated to the values of
world literature.

During the late 'Forties, Scott took part in several broadcasts, in some of which I interviewed him. Lamentably, BBC
Scotland destroyed all these recordings except the last, made
when Scott was in his seventies. One of the earlier interviews,
however, was of such unusual interest that immediately afterwards I took notes of what the composer had said, publishing
them, with Scott's agreement, in Volume 3, 1950 of the Saltire
Review under the title 'Talking with F. G. Scott'. Scott claimed
that he had put together *A Drunk Man Looks at the Thistle,*
while on a visit to the poet in Montrose, from a large number
of scraps of paper with the various sections scribbled on them.
Several critics, notably Kenneth Buthlay, treated Scott's story
with scepticism, remarking in his otherwise admirable little
study of MacDiarmid:

> We have the authority of Maurice Lindsay for the story that
> Scott, who had been making musical settings of many of
> MacDiarmid's poems, received a telegram in Glasgow and
> rushed to Montrose, where he found the poet 'surrounded by
> innumerable bits of paper, about six inches long', on which
> were written the lyrics out of which the poem was finally made
> up. According to Scott, there was no arrangement about the
> squares of paper. The aid of a bottle of whisky was invoked
> and after some hours of picking and choosing they 'got the
> thing into order', and Scott thought up the brilliant stroke
> of giving the last word to the protagonist's wife, after Mac-
> Diarmid had come to an end with the line 'O I ha'e silence
> left':
> > — 'And weel ye micht',
> > 'Sae Jean'll say, efter sic a nicht!'

To this diverting anecdote must be added the fact that six
samples of a poem already called *A Drunk Man Looks at the
Thistle,* and described as 'a complete poem, in over 600 lines,
deriving its unity from its preoccupation with the distinctive
elements in Scottish psychology which depend for their effective expression upon the hitherto unrealised potentialities of
Braid Scots', appeared in the *Glasgow Herald* for 13th
February, 1926. And these extracts, although self-contained,

clearly present the same key-symbols that are developed
throughout the poem as published, in about 2,500 lines, in
November of that year. Also it should be remembered that
MacDiarmid himself when confessing his 'inartistry' and his
consequent great debt to Scott, said of the latter's help with
the *Drunk Man* manuscript that 'he was not long in seizing
on the essentials and urging the ruthless discarding of the
inessentials'. This is a very different matter from there being
'no arrangement about the squares of paper'.

Buthlay's main point, however, is arguable, as will presently
be seen.

In *The Company I've Kept,* published eight years after
Scott's death, MacDiarmid admitted Scott's influence:

> When I wrote the *Drunk Man* working on my own I had got
> to the point when I had ceased to be able to see the forest for
> the trees. I found the necessary imaginative sympathy in
> F. G. Scott and handed over the whole mass of my manuscript
> to him. He was not long in seizing on the essentials. I had no
> hesitation in taking his advice and in this way the significant
> shape was educed from the welter of stuff and the rest pruned
> away.

> Drastic treatment of this kind is particularly necessary in
> literary work. Musicians and artists do not require it to the
> same degree, but in writing it is fatally easy in the absence of
> such consultative and co-operative correction to forget that the
> essence of art is presentation. I was, of course, particularly
> lucky in having at my elbow such a determined artist as Scott
> who in his own practice was wont to eliminate to the last
> degree and concentrate, at no matter what sacrifice of pet
> material, upon the highest ordering . . . While Ezra Pound
> did something very similar to Eliot's *Waste Land,* what hap-
> pened in my case has been widely misunderstood. All it
> amounted to was that Scott read the great mass of verse
> I'd written, advised me to scrap a good deal that he thought
> repetitive or inessential, and suggested a more effective placing
> in order of what remained.

Characteristically, the poet then quotes a story from *Le
Chant de la Resurrection* in which its romantically-minded
author, Romain Rolland, claims that when an unspecified sonata
of Beethoven's was completed, "Beethoven himself repeatedly
failed to realize (sometimes for a long period) that certain
ideas belonged not to this or that work for which he had conceived them but quite somewhere else . . ." What Beethoven,

on occasion, did — as in the "Eroica" Symphony and elsewhere — was to re-use in expanded and enlarged form material already set out in earlier works, themselves still extant. There is thus really no parallel between what Scott did for the *Drunk Man* and what Ferdinand Ries may or may not have given by way of advice to Beethoven.[12] Nobody ever doubted Beethoven's ability to handle large-scale artistic construction. In any case MacDiarmid's views on music have always been suspect. George Bruce recalls that when he was leaving the funeral of William Soutar in Perth to catch a bus back to Dundee, where he was then teaching, MacDiarmid and Scott 'walked him' to the bus stop. As they stood waiting, Scott suddenly said to Bruce: "D' you know who the greatest music-critic in the world is?" "No", said the surprised Bruce. "Chris here," said Scott, "he's tone deaf!" The poet, who never outgrew his pupil-teacher relationship with Scott, said nothing.

Fortunately, Scott's own straightforward account of his part in shaping the *Drunk Man* has come to light. It forms part of the Autobiographical Letter, received by me in 1946, then laid aside and forgotten about, until it was acquired with part of my archive by The National Library of Scotland, who 're-discovered' it and supplied me with a photographed copy. Wrote Scott:

I outlined the plan and supplied the title of the poem during a rainy hike and a night in Glen Clovis Hotel. Christopher usually wrote his poetry in snatches: he never had any sense of form and after some months of scribbling on the back of envelopes and odd bits of paper, he sent to Glasgow an urgent call for me to come for a weekend and see the litter (and mess!) he'd been making of my bright idea, as Blackwood's were asking for the MS and there *was* no MS. It was late at night when I reached Montrose and after his wife and youngsters went off to bed, we sat down to a table, a great heap of scribbled bits of paper and a bottle of whisky.[13] I can still see Christopher's face when I was indicating the shape the poem, or for that matter a musical composition, ought to take — he was literally flabbergasted either by the extent of my knowledge or by the whisky — it's anybody's guess! We spent until day-break sorting out the items worth keeping, Christopher arranging them on the table like a pack of cards in the order that I indicated as likely to give the best sequences, climaxes, etc. My plans necessitated a pianissimo close, after so much bustle ('The Stars like Thistle's Roses

flower') to be followed by ('Yet hae I Silence left, the croon
o' a' ') and I'm pretty certain I supplied the last two lines
to bring the thing to some kind of conclusion.

Such is the real story. The best laugh I got from the published book when it arrived was the effrontery of the author's
note with its reference to 'sections' and 'hand-rails'. His
dedicatory poem is quite a good one and I have often thought
of setting it to music, if only as a remembrancer of a 'very
special occasion' . . .14

In the light of Scott's explanation, added significance is
given to the fact that when MacDiarmid's first *Collected Poems*
appeared in 1962, the poet broke up his long masterpiece,
turning it back into short poems, giving each a title, a misguided
dismemberment corrected by David Daiches, with the poet's
approval, for the second edition.
    Scott continued:

Christopher's next call for a visit was before the *Cencrastus*
MS was sent off to Blackwood's. Again I went through to
Montrose but he was very disappointed that I couldn't give
my approval of the poem and he was still more disappointed
when the MS was returned to him. I know that for some
time after this he was very unsettled and gladly went off to
London to assist Compton Mackenzie in running a new radio
paper called *Vox,* pottered on the *Cencrastus* MS for a few
months and it finally appeared in 1930, but Blackwood's
dropped him, I fancy after completing the contract, and when
he wrote me from London enclosing the book, he asked me
never to discuss it with him.

I have rehearsed in some detail my more than brotherly com-
panionship with Grieve — which by the way continues
unalterable — not that I wanted to speak of it, but because
you asked for definite information and because if the story
of the Scottish Renaissance ever comes to be written the story
ought to have something more than hearsay and guesswork
to support it.

Scott adds that, "Christopher . . . more than ten years ago
. . . proclaimed to a P.E.N. gathering met to discuss the use of
the vernacular that 'he might have become a poet without
F.G.S. but would never have become a *Scottish* Poet . . .'".
    No doubt Scott's claim to have thought out the idea of the
Drunk Man will surprise some readers, but there is supporting

evidence that could be interpreted as backing up his claim in part
of a letter from Scott to the painter William McCance. Only
the middle section of the letter has survived.[15] However, it
contains a reference to an article McCance was about to write
for the *Socialist Review*. Scott tells McCance that he has asked
Grieve to send on material that might be useful. Grieve's subsequent letter to McCance[16] has also survived. In it he refers
to Scott's request as the motive for writing from Montrose on
12th March, 1926. MacDiarmid tells McCance that he has
three books coming out that year *"— Pennywheep,* a companion
volume to *Sangschaw,* this spring; and in the autumn *Contemporary Scottish Studies;* and the *A Drunk Man Looks at the
Thistle",* of which he enclosed for McCance a column of extracts
that had appeared in the *Glasgow Herald.* The poet wondered
if McCance might do him "either a frontispiece or some cuts
or something", promising to send "the thing in full" before a
decision was expected. MacDiarmid explains "it isn't quite
ready. I want to touch it up here and there and add a little
yet."

Allowing time for MacDiarmid to react to the letter from
Scott, it seems reasonable to date Scott's fragmentary letter
to McCance about the end of February, 1926. The theme of
some of the sections presumably of the unfinished and still
unassembled *Drunk Man* are paraded by Scott to McCance for
some undefined purpose:

> I have put forward a suggestion that we do the seals Mrs
> Kennedy Fraser speaks about popping up and singing Hebri-
> dean airs with some of the Orpheus Choir people in their
> purple hoods in the offing. A few more items meant sarcastic
> should make quite a decent beginning so I suggest you set
> your brain-pan to simmer on both plots and designs and let's
> make a collection of the choicest specimens in our Scottish
> life suitably *pinned* down so that they'll cease to annoy in the
> future. I'm thinking now of the Harry Lauder ilk and the
> crooked nibby and the London Scottish, Caledonion Societies,
> etc., not omitting Kirkwood and the politicians, nor J. M.
> Bullock, Will, Barrie, and the Kailyaird generally.

Scott then went on to give an account of "our Symposium
held a fortnight ago".

> Grieve going great guns on Synthetic Scots (it reminds one of
> synthetic rubber!) and an equally tough proposition. To let

> you, as a privileged person, into the know it's a compound
> of all the most outlandish polysyllables to be found in Jamie-
> son's Scots Dictionary with any others Grieve can remember
> or invent duly served up for the confounding of the intelli-
> gentsia of present Scotland. It is proving mighty efficacious
> and I fancy Grieve is strong enough to work it off so that
> in another 100 years' time folk will be writing theses and heaps
> of explanatory notes about it. To put it shortly, your line is to
> damn and deny anything that currently passes as Scots in
> London, and to proclaim that we are making affiliations with
> all continental movements without asking London about them.

This event provided the occasion for Peggy Grieve, the
poet's first wife, to write to Helen B. Cruickshank[17] in somewhat sharp terms. The poet, we learn was scarcely visible under
an accumulation of books and papers, and not in too amiable
a frame of mind, being in the middle of "hatching out *Cencrastus*
— and, it seems a worse process than producing babies. Scott
was telling us of the Dunbar Symposium but I did not gather
whether he really was taking part or not. He's lazy and too
fond of the ladies to do any real hard work — or not fond
enough" — an odd comment from a married woman with two
children who, in the same letter, observes that she keeps "falling
in love a dozen times a year" and singeing her fingers in the
process.

MacDiarmid left Montrose to go to London in 1929. The
disasters that befell him there, including the break-up of his
first marriage and his subsequent experiences in Liverpool and
Edinburgh, do not concern us here. A few years later he did,
however, contract a serious illness the cost of the treatment of
which, according to what Scott later told me, was borne, at
least in part by him. Writing to Helen B. Cruickshank on 9th
September, 1935, William Soutar sheds some light both on the
seriousness of the poet's condition and of the concern of his
friend:

> Yesterday Tonge drove Scott up to Gilgal, came down to our
> place for half an hour and then collected F.G. again —
> returning here. Scott thought there was a slight improvement,
> though not much to build on yet. Certainly not enough to
> warrant Christopher's removal for quite a time. F.G. said he
> was still very shaky on his legs. However, he is submitting
> quietly to the treatment . . .

From the time of that illness, MacDiarmid's lyric impulse

appears to have dried up. He turned increasingly to constructing in English what he called an "extended poetry of fact", an all-embracing structure of ideas, evolving a rocky landscape with vast wordy wastelands and the shifting sense of other people's quotations, above which only fleeting glimpses of the great poet he had been were still now and then to be sighted. Writing to George Bruce after reading a broadcast review in which Alexander Scott had claimed that MacDiarmid had written some of the worst as well as some of the finest poetry ever produced, the poet said: "My job, as I see it, has never been to lay a tit's egg, but to erupt like a volcano, emitting not only flame but a lot of rubbish."[18] Obviously major organised creative possibilities somewhere between these two extremes have been successfully realised by most of the world's greatest artists. But, as MacDiarmid said also of himself in the *Drunk Man:* "I'll hae nae hauf way hoose, but aye be whaur/Extremes meet — it's the only way I ken." This later work of MacDiarmid, often shot through with Communist propagandising (though even here he was by no means consistent) was of no use to Scott, the composer. Nor, it must be admitted, had Scott, the critic of literature, much time for it either.

During the 'Twenties, the Scott family had formed the habit of holidaying in Montrose. There, the composer could enjoy the company not only of MacDiarmid, but of Edwin and Willa Muir.

Scott also paid several visits to the International Festival of Contemporary Music at Salzburg. Edwin Muir accompanied him in 1923. On the way to Salzburg for another such visit in the summer of 1926, Scott arrived in St. Tropez for a fortnight's holiday and to see the Muirs. Willa relates that his arrival was closely followed by that of "Mary Robertson, now Mary Litchfield, for whom we found a room in the village. These two visitors, whose Scottish temperaments got free rein on holiday, led us a gay dance. More and more St. Tropez was filling up with artists from every quarter, including some from Scotland, and we found ourselves caught up in what Edwin denounced as 'the exclusive gregariousness of artists'. I was both startled and amused to discover that Mary's seven years in London had turned her into a siren capable of annexing at once any man she wanted, and still more startled to observe her effect upon

Scott. One evening, when Mary had vanished with a new man, Scott raged up and down our sitting-room shouting: 'Such a damned tangential bitch I never did meet!'."

Of the eventual break-up of the Montrose trio, Scott was to write: "As with other movements, a time came when 'personalities' began to count for more than the principles from which the movement originated. A case in point was Compton Mackenzie, that facile play-actor, who saw himself as the Prince Charlie of a neo-catholic Alba and whose intrusion was, in my opinion, a disastrous blow, leading to lots of log-rolling in the political field, and to great confusion and misunderstanding in every other". Scott recalled to me that at this time he had often said to MacDiarmid: "Christopher, you will have to make up your mind whether you want to be a poet or a politician", thus showing an acute awareness of the irreconcilability between the truth of the artist and the rhetorical pragmatism of the politician. "It was this turn in affairs," Scott went on, "that kept the Muirs always at a distance, and it explains why I never saw my way to become a member of the National Party but kept strictly to my job of writing music, for I had no faith that a true renaissance would be brought about by political propaganda from loud-speakers", a view which must have been shared by Muir, who, according to his wife, near the end of his final illness kept reiterating: "There are no absolutes, no absolutes".

A vivid picture, not only of F.G. but of the relationship of the Montrose trio, one to another, has been preserved in Willa Muir's own autobiography, *Belonging* (1968):

> Christopher and his wife Peggy were living in a council house on the fringe of the town, where Peggy cooked the meals and washed and ironed Christopher's shirts. I noted her efficient ironing with some ruefulness, for I was the world's worst ironer. She was then pregnant with their second child; we thought her most attractive as she stood clinging to Christopher's arm, the day we first met her, looking up shyly through dark eyelashes, with a daisy-like white collarette round her neck, apparently an embodiment of the 'wee wifie' loved by Scotsmen. We noted that she did not care for the housing estate in which they lived: she complained that she had to put extra net curtains across her windows to keep neighbours from peering in. Nor did she like Christopher's susceptibility to whisky.
>
> It was not that Christopher drank a lot of whisky, a very small

amount being enough to over-set him, but as the local editor he had to attend farmers' dinners where whisky was the only drink. This inconvenient fact set off domestic crises, one of which we helped to cope with. Calling by chance one evening we found Peggy at her wits' end, Christopher having come home from some farmers' junketing and locked himself into the bathroom, since when there had been neither sound nor movement from him. Peggy was sure he had passed out. Edwin managed to scramble from outside through the high, narrow bathroom window, found Christopher lying mother-naked, cold, insensible but alive in a completely dry bath, and unlocked the door at once. We lugged the poet into the living-room where we laid him on the hearthrug by the fire, covered him with blankets and left him to Peggy's ministrations in that respectable council house.

This respectable background of Christopher's was something we took for granted, but it represents a strand in the lives of each of these wild Borderers, Scott and Grieve, in strong contrast to the rest of the pattern. Scott, belonging to an older generation, was the more firmly attached to an ideal of respectability, and it was a Victorian ideal. Whenever he had to make an appearance in society he put on a mask of formal Olympian gravity which sometimes did not survive an outburst of his demoniac temperament. At home he was a bit of a tyrant, especially to his wife and daughters whom he expected to be conventionally respectable, more so than his sons. He did not approve of 'his' women drinking beer in public, for instance.[19] When Edwin and I lunched with the Scotts in a restaurant Mrs Scott did not dare to have a lager like the rest of us. He much enjoyed being an *enfant terrible*. Yet he was also a man of most delicate sensibility as appeared in the settings he made to Christopher's lyrics and in his response to all nuances in music and poetry.

Christopher was nearly as pugnacious on paper, and had as delicate a sensibility for poetry, but although still influenced by Scott was not so much swayed by the illusion of respectability. He and Peggy had both been conditioned by serving in the armed forces towards the end of the 1914 war, and had shed a good many conventional inhibitions. Yet at this time Christopher was holding down a respectable steady job and Peggy seemed to be doing all that could be asked of a respectable steady wife. The shock of yellow hair standing on end above Christopher's impressive brow, the restlessness of his eyes, suggested that he might be somewhat unpredictable, but not more so than could be looked for in a poet. Peggy was more completely camouflaged; despite her intelligent-looking forehead one would never have guessed at her future career. No one could have predicted that her 'wee wifie' charm would be so effective as to secure for her a coal business in London, after divorcing Christopher, so that in time she became an authority in the next wartime Ministry of Fuel and Power. Neither Edwin nor I had any inkling of what was to happen to this young Scottish couple, or of the influence Christopher was to wield as political agitator and poet of Scottish Nationalism. And certainly it never dawned on any of us that Scott and Grieve and Muir were all going to become honorary doctors in the course of their lives.

These two Borderers, Scott and Grieve, had a make-up quite unlike Edwin's. He had no wish to fight or 'show off' or score over other people: he had passion, but in him passion aspired towards ecstasy rather than domination; he preferred simplicity in his conduct as well as in his writings, and could never have become a publicist. This difference in temperament separated him from Scott and Grieve's campaign as much as his difference in attitude towards the English language.

The 'Twenties ended with MacDiarmid in London, most of his finest poetry already written — though some still continued to appear in new collections up to his *Second Hymn to Lenin* (1935) — while the Muirs had embarked once again on their foreign travels.

For Scott, the latter half of the decade brought an important change. In 1925 he had applied for, and been appointed to, the job of Lecturer in Music at Glasgow's Jordanhill Training College for Teachers. Soon after he moved to what was to be his final home, 44 Munro Road, a grey sandstone terrace house within easy walking reach of the college. For the first time he was now earning his living out of music, even if not by composing. Since the flow of what Scott regarded as settable poetry from MacDiarmid had dried up, Scott turned his thoughts in other directions: to writing for orchestra, and to setting some of the poems of William Dunbar, the mediaeval Makar who, with Burns and MacDiarmid, is the earliest of the triumvirate of Scotland's greatest poets.

REFERENCES

1　His symphonic poem *Villon* is worthy of occasional revival.
2　The composer's son, George, and daughter, Lilias, both think their mother's action uncharacteristic, and feel that their father probably exaggerated "to heighten a good story".
3　BBC Programme *Men of Mark: Francis George Scott* (1957).

4 Autobiographical Letter.
5 *Men of Mark: Francis George Scott:* BBC 1957.
6 Debussy, however, had died in 1918.
7 A magazine then being edited by MacDiarmid from Montrose.
8 *MacDiarmid: A Festschrift* (1962).
9 Scott never underrated Burns as Saurat does here. In one sense, only Burns's 'platitudes' — if such memorably enshrined proverbial wisdom can be so described — are translateable. It is as impossible to translate effectively Burns's Scots 'virr' as to catch in another language the Scottishness of MacDiarmid's lyric concentration.
10 *MacDiarmid: A Festschrift.*
11 No pibroch of proven pre-Reformation vintage has come down to us.
12 Scott was told by letter of the supposed Beethoven parallel, the revelation being described, almost in schoolboy terms, as "a marvellous joke . . . but only for the cognoscenti".
13 Actually Scott drank very little. His son, George, "never saw him even slightly drunk".
14 In that same year Scott was the dedicatee not only of *A Drunk Man Looks at the Thistle,* but also of Saurat's *The Three Conventions* and Muir's book of essays, *Transitions.*
15 The McCance Archive, Massie University, Canada.
16 In the possession of Mrs Margaret McCance.
17 Letter dated 'Easter Sunday' in Edinburgh University Library.
18 Anticipated however, by Romain Rolland's much earlier comment on Richard Strauss ". . . his art is torrential, producing at one and the same time gold, sand, stone and rubbish . . ." *(The Life of Richard Strauss:* Alan Jefferson).
19 According to Lilias, her mother "hated beer" and F.G. could never have persuaded her to drink it, had he wanted to.

Chapter 4

THE THIRTIES

When MacDiarmid, taking a title-cue from Saurat, openly set his course upon establishing a Scottish Renaissance, one of his battle cries was "Not Burns, Dunbar! ". If this is interpreted as a suggestion that the fifteenth century Scottish Makar was a greater poet than Burns, it could only be regarded as obviously ridiculous. The slogan, however, did have the beneficial effect of drawing renewed attention not only to the achievements of the earliest of Scotland's trio of greatest poets, but to the entire group of Makars from Gavin Douglas to Sir David Lyndsay, Alexander Montgomerie, and the first Alexander Scott, thus re-awakening interest in a then neglected part of our heritage. The effect of MacDiarmid's exhortation on his fellow Renaissance worker-in-music was to turn Scott's attention to the possibility of setting Dunbar texts.

William Dunbar (1460?-1520?) was a minor cleric, diplomat and courtier at the Court of James IV, a mediaeval Scot of strong and dark passions, and a poet of seemingly effortless metrical skill, obviously not unfamiliar with the strict traditional bardic rules of Gaelic verse. In his day, Gaelic-speaking Scotland formed a larger component in the linguistic pattern of the country than it has done since, and was a closer and more vocal neighbour to the Lowland Scots tongue. With the exception of his only surviving love lyric 'To a Lady' (the original air for which has been lost), Dunbar's ferocious energy could rarely be compressed within a short space. Even with judicious cutting, Dunbar was not therefore a noticeable suitable poet to partner a composer like Scott, who required compressed texts.

Scott's first and most successful setting of a Dunbar poem, 'Rorate coeli desuper', was made in 1922, just before the beginning of the decade of close association with MacDiarmid. Like its Easter counterpart, 'Done is a battle on the dragon black', 'Rorate Coeli' is a great organ-peal of praise fashioned from words: an affirmation that sings itself into a triumphant climax; a celebration of Christmas almost pagan in the brightness of its colours, being concerned not with the grey shades and colds of a Scottish December, but with the metaphorical "clear sun whom no clud devouris".

Scott's pentatonically-flavoured melodic line to his cut version of the poem is not one of his more memorable tunes, yet it allows him not only to indulge his taste for pictorial reference in the accompaniment, but also to achieve an exciting build-up of complexity through which words and melody soar to a mighty climax. To some critics the illustration of the "balmy shouris" has suggested Brahms and Wolf; to others, a piano accompaniment almost organ-like or orchestral in its implications. Yet there is nothing unbalanced about it. Indeed, this is not only one of Scott's greatest songs but, in my view, one of the most unsentimental and uplifting celebrations of the Christmas legend in any musical tradition.

Like the other songs in Book Three of *Scottish Lyrics,* which appeared in 1934, the smaller type-face of 'Rorate Coeli' reveals that its first publication was in the pages of an impressive quarterly journal of the times, *The Modern Scot,* which an enthusiastic and wealthy American supporter of the Scottish Renaissance issued from St. Andrews between 1930 and 1936.

'To a Ladye', Scott's next Dunbar setting, was written in 1928, though it did not appear in print until it was published in the Saltire Society volume of 1949. Again, there is a modal quality to the melody, but in this case a grace and clarity in the piano part that underlines the irony of the poet's love for one so "merciless" as the subject of the poem. The Editor of the Centenary edition of Scott's songs, Neil Mackay, felt that it vaguely resembled an English lute song. In 1923 a new edition of H. Lane Wilson's 1899 anthology, *Old English Melodies,* appeared. This seems to have inspired Scott, ever conscious of his need to "make his own tradition", to provide a Scottish counterpart. 'To a Ladye', 'Cupid and Venus', a setting of the sixteenth century Ayrshire poet Mark Alexander Boyd's one surviving sonnet in Scots, and that of Drummond of Hawthornden's 'Phillis' (described by Scott as "a Pastoral in the manner of the English Renaissance"), are companion pieces in a similar vein. Though lighter in style than anything else he published, they are all in their different ways both characteristic and delightful: a nod, perhaps towards the mood of the "silver" 17th century

E

poets, of whom Drummond was the only Scottish representative.

Dunbar's 'Airlie on Ash Wodinsday', set by Scott with the title 'The Twa Kimmers', is a discussion during Lent between two women who complain as they drink wine that Lent and fasting make them thin: a pre-'Womens' Lib' protest at the dual standards of a male dominated society. Scott's vocal line runs along to a robust modal fiddle tune, punctuated by a contrasting section which uses a kind of recitative style to carry the dialogue. The heavily accentuated first beats in the bar of the accompaniment and the use of the 'Scotch Snap' provide detached ironic comment. For some reason this song never seems to have achieved the popularity of either 'Rorate Coeli' or 'To a Ladye'. Dunbar was to take up his women's viewpoint theme in his much racier and longer tale of 'The Twa Marriet Wemen and the Wedo'. Scott, for his part, was to do better with it in his setting of Burn's 'Wha is that at my bower door?'.

Scott's next Dunbar setting, 'Of Ane Blackamoor', is one of the least successful of his published songs. It describes a mock tournament the prize for which was to be the so-called 'favours' of a female negro slave. The poem itself might be regarded as an unpleasant one, reminding us of the survival of barbaric standards even among the comparative civilisation of a Stuart Court.

It was sometimes Scott's practice to provide his singers with programme notes about his songs, notes which had often originated in his own lecture-recitals. Writing to the baritone W. G. Noble about this song, Scott shows that he either missed Dunbar's point, or decided to evade it:

> This is the first time, says the poet, he has written anything about *black* ladies. He had on previous occasions, as every reader knows, said a great deal about white ones . . . In Dunbar's time blackamoors of the Spanish type were not known in Scotland, but whoever stood for the picture painted here must surely have been a fully mature African beauty. In the final stanza he imagines a tournament in her honour.

Suffering rape as prize-flesh hardly seems an 'honour'! But Scott used a text that was both cut and bowdlerised. The lines describing the fate of those competitors who might lose their "knychtlie nerve" in the contest — they would be required to kiss the slave-girl's hips, from behind, and "nevir to uther comfort claim" — seem to have been too much, even for him. The air of the mock-tournament is created through the piano's martial gestures, but the quality of Dunbar's scurrilous energy is not matched, and because of the use of this cut version the purpose of the poem is obscured.

The nearest Scott came to matching in musical terms Dunbar's daemonic personal energy is in 'Ane his awn Enemy', in Book Five of *Scottish Lyrics* (1939). Here, the composer is content to set the text to a vigorous folk-like tune, while the accompaniment adds weight and breadth to the sentiments. The song, marked 'Giovale', belongs to the category of what Neil Mackay calls "composed folk-songs", but is none the worse for that. The last lines of the poem enshrine convivial sentiments which sometimes lead to them being used as a secular grace.

> Now all this time let us be mirry.
> And set nocht by this warld a chirry,
> Now, while there is gude wine to sell,
> He that does on dry bread wirry,
> I give him to the Devil of Hell.

There exists a vigorous unpublished setting for solo voice of 'Amends to the Tailors and Soutars' and an unpublished part-song, a setting of Dunbar's 'Welcome of Scotland to the Queen' for S.A.T.B. It was probably inspired by the first visit of Queen Elizabeth to Scotland after her coronation. It is a fresh and wholly charming setting. Like the solo song, it should certainly be published.

Scott's only other setting of a Dunbar poem involved the orchestra: 'The Ballad of Kynd Kyttock', for baritone and orchestra. Dunbar was also the inspiration behind Scott's ballet suite *The Dance of the Seven Deidly Sins*.

Books Three and Four of *Scottish Lyrics* contain many of Scott's greatest songs. In Book Three, which carries both a glossary and a prose summary of what the texts of the songs in Scots are about, there are settings of seven MacDiarmid songs, Dunbar's 'Rorate Coeli' and Mark Alexander Boyd's 'Cupid and Venus'. There is also a setting of some rather weak verses by Jean Lang, 'St Brendan's Graveyard'. A relation of the historian, essayist and poet Andrew Lang, she is best remembered for a topographical book on the Border country. Her lines appeared in the *Glasgow Herald* on 28th April, 1931, and Scott set them almost at once. What appealed to him was probably the thought expressed in the final line of the first stanza:

> High up they rest, their long day's work done,
> Above the rocks that bastion the shore.
> They are drench'd by rain, warm'd by the sun,
> Awaiting the day when Time is no more.

Scott's interest in pibroch had been fully stimulated in the 'Twenties, although as early as 1917 he was already noting Gaelic airs from a Gaelic song collection made in 1908 by Malcolm MacFarlane, *Bardic Melody*. The influence of pibroch's 'timelessness' can be seen in the vocal lines of the MacDiarmid settings, but in most of those already referred to it may be less immediately obvious to the ear, the transmogrification combining it with other elements being highly concentrated.

In 1933, Scott first met the Perth poet William Soutar (1898-1943). In the early 'Twenties, Soutar developed a form of spondylitis which was neglected, and for which in any case there was probably then no cure. By 1924 he was moving with increasing difficulty and by 1930 he had taken to his bed, his life shrunk "to a view from a room and the small family circle of his parents"[1] until his death. Walled up in his parent's house, with the aid of a mirror to find the books he wanted, he read extensively, wrote the bulk of his poems and diaries, and talked with his friends.

On June 26th, 1933 Soutar received a letter from James Whyte in St. Andrews:

> My Dear Soutar. I am only just back from London a day or two, so I hope you'll forgive me for not writing sooner. It was very kind of you to send a copy of 'Seeds in the Wind' to me and Cunningham[2] and we were greatly touched and flattered by your kind inscriptions. I have been reading the poems over several times with great pleasure . . .
>
> I was showing the volume to F. G. Scott, the composer, who was staying with me last week and he was greatly interested. He is thinking of coming over to St. Andrews again for the month of August and is anxious to come and see you. I think you would enjoy meeting him, as he, even more than Grieve, is the man who is responsible for the whole idea of a 'Scots Renaissance'. I hope he will be able to play some of his songs when he comes over: that is a sight which I should go — and have gone — many miles to see!

The entry in Soutar's diary for 28th August[3] subsequently reads:

> Whyte phoned to say he'd bring F. G. Scott along . . . I enjoyed Scott immensely: his mentor-relationship with Grieve very interesting: a psychological touchestone: granting Scott's imaginative insight — why does Grieve depend so much upon his criticism: the reflex in Scott's case — as it seems to me is to patronise Grieve: however, perhaps the relationship keeps Grieve more balanced: I don't think Scott is a big man — his penchant for song-setting rather suggests that — but he is a very interesting type. I like his straight, rather sardonic blue eyes: he is keenly alive.

Soutar, of course, was right in one sense, although there is nothing "little" about being a song-writer, and indeed Mac-Diarmid is at his greatest as a poet of short lyrics. In any case, Scott was at that time more interested in Gaelic music and in his new-found preoccupation in writing for orchestra than in the poems of William Soutar, although he was to turn to them increasingly towards the end of the decade.

An article on Pibroch by Scott caught the eye of Neil M. Gunn, then still an Excise Officer, living in Inverness. On 29th December, 1932, Gunn wrote to the painter William McCance:

> Thank you for your fine card, with its iron bells, strong bells, bells for Nationalists, not tintinnabulating Nationalists, but iron-throated men, with beams strong enough wherefrom to hang white-throated parasites! Cheers! Enter F. G. Scott, playing piaobaireachd! I must get in touch with Scott. What's his address? I could talk bagpipe all night. And that rhythm and timelessness; ah, my dear fellow, not the little bits of stick you set up in your staff notation, but timelessness, like the peals from your bells, peals that are both earth tremors and acts of God.

Almost certainly Gunn did meet Scott, his fellow-contributor to *The Modern Scot,* but there is no evidence that they either corresponded regularly or became more than acquaintances. Gunn was much more interested in the poetical and mystical qualities of pibroch than in its technical construction and manipulation, which certainly fascinated Scott. Scott, however, likened his own researches into Gaelic music to an extension of his artistic embrace "to include the Celtic North; much as Sir Walter Scott strove to do": a dream of Scottish wholeness no artist has so far achieved.

Because pibroch consists of an urlar, or theme, and rhythmic variations of increasing complexity and ornamentation, pibroch themes are of necessity usually slow in tempo. The gathering accumulation of ornamentation has also given rise to a practical tradition allowing for a certain amount of rubato, or 'robbed time'. All this has the cumulative effect of creating a sense of continuous texture, like early polyphonic music untrammelled by regular feet marked off by bar lines. Scott's employment of the blurring effect of pedal-held sound, said by one writer to suggest "allegiance to French impressionism", was often used to create a feeling of remoteness or timelessness; subtly in 'The Eemis Stane', less so in Jean Lang's 'St. Brendan's Graveyard', where a low G softly reiterates like a single bag-pipe drone. The melody's Mixolydian modal flavour contrasts with this firmly-rooted G feeling that refuses to be shifted, except to make way for a few chords and an arpeggiated clarsach-like sweep in the piano coda. This confirms in the final bars the apparent double tonality between mode and scale that has prevailed throughout. The composer's performance instructions are "like pibroch — *impersonal and without nuance*". The accompanist is told to play the "piano part as if independent of the voice", and the bars are indicated only by dotted lines, as if the composer put them in merely in response to printing convention.

'St. Brendan's Graveyard' is not a very successful song in performance, the effect being one of tonal muddiness rather than of timelessness. Since we are all inevitably so strongly enchained by time, nothing is more difficult to convey in music than timelessness. The composer who fails to do so usually creates, paradoxically, boredom, the strong desire for time to move on.

A year later, employing no bar lines at all and with far less studied contrivance, Scott did succeed in mastering pibroch's a-rhythmic timelessness in his setting of MacDiarmid's 'Milkwort and Bog-Cotton'. Here, the melodic line undulates as if being fingered on a chanter, the poet's contrast between dark and light providing a magical momentary lift from minor to major. (Ex. 11). The gently drumming triplets at the close

remind us that for humans, timelessness can only be conceived in the context of time, the poet's eternal dream of shadowless perfection ultimately no more than an expression of man's time-bound longing for immortality.

In addition to the songs already mentioned Book Three of *Scottish Lyrics* is filled out with Scott's Paris 1914 setting of 'Twist ye, twine ye', Meg Merrilee's song from *Guy Mannering,* one of the great Scottish novels by Scott's great earlier namesake, Sir Walter Scott. The accompaniment runs like a spinning wheel and the voice introduces a lilting figure in six-eight time, vaguely reminiscent of Sir Arthur Sullivan. But Scott has been attracted by the doom-conscious madness of Meg as she describes the ingredients that "mingle human bliss and woe", so he builds up a dramatic and romantically-conceived structure in which the accompaniment bulges with muscle and the lyric all but sinks beneath the weight of this musical superstructure.

The Burns disciple Patrick Birnie's 'The auld man's mear's dead', composed in 1918, describes the demise of an animal suffering from "the fierce and the fleuk/The wheezloch and the wanton yeuk", along with other ailments, in spite of which the poet expresses surprise that she has succumbed. It is not a very good poem. The phrase "The auld man's mear's dead" is declaimed by Scott dramatically, "Adagio assai", contrasted with a "Doppio movimento" section, a folk-like tune in strathspey rhythm, when the farm jobs once done by the mare are described, and, second time round, to a heavily stressed four-square rhythm as the diseases are recounted, in detail. A ponderous quotation from the "Marche Funèbre" slow movement of Chopin's B minor Piano Sonata No. 2 may have seemed amusing in 1918 but to-day merely sounds banal.

Book Four of *Scottish Lyrics* (for Baritone voice) was given over entirely to settings of Burns (eight songs), Dunbar (two songs) and Drummond of Hawthornden (one song).

Burns's 'The Tailor fell thro' the bed', marked by the composer "very rude", is a folk-like setting of an amusing lyric about a lassie who "lay still" since "she thought that a tailor could do her nae ill!'' The accompaniment makes much of staccato octaves, often used by the composer to underline energetic irony. It is a little less ebullient than 'Scroggam', the tale of an auld wife in Cockpen who "brew'd guid ale for gentlemen". But when her "daughter fell in a fever" and "the Priest o' the Parish fell in anither", the cure was obvious and simple.

> They laid the twa i' the bed thegither,
> That the heat o' the tane might cool the tither,
> Scroggam, my dearie, ruffam.

The slightly ridiculous opening folk-phrase, supported when it first appears by an 'oomph-pah' accompaniment, is put through various guises but with such good-humoured energy that the song admirably catches the mood of the poem, reflecting in musical terms that indescribable and untranslateable folk "virr" of some of Burns's earthier pieces; in fact, the very essence of a central aspect of Scottishness.

The humorous and the bawdy come together equally openly in 'My Wife's a wanton wee thing', the poet observing that: 'She play'd the loon e're she married/She'll do it again e're she dee'. The accompaniment is full of pictorial suggestion. Heavy triplets reflect the husband's observation 'She winna be guided by me', descending octaves emphasising his treatment of her — 'I took a rung and I caw'd her' — and a heel-kicking figure in the last four bars, ending in a chordal shift beneath the singer's sustained B on the word 'she', leaving the listener in little doubt that in this poetic case, even the old Scots pastime of wife-beating would probably not prove an effective 'cure'. 'Amang the Trees' is a rather fussy setting of an extract from a Burns poem, neither self-contained nor self-explanatory. Musically, it is little more than a pleasant enough exercise in some of the composer's mannerisms. 'O dear minny, what shall I do?' is a slight but immediately attractive folk-like setting that prances along to a toe-pointing dance-rhythm.

The remaining Burns settings are couched in Scott's lyrical mood. 'Of a' the Airts the wind can blaw', a strophic setting, flows beautifully, and would most surely win our affection were not the slowed-up strathspey tune by the eighteenth century fiddle-composer William Marshall originally chosen by Burns at least an equally beautiful melody. There is obvious kinship between Marshall's melody and Scott's.

'O were I on Parnassus Hill', another strophic setting, does not have this social disadvantage. It is, in fact, remarkably like a folk-setting in every respect, its fairly conventional accompaniment supporting the warmth of feeling both of melody and poem.

'My Luve is like a Red, Red Rose' reflects the yearning quality characteristic of much of Scott's lyricism, here partly achieved by the use of the Dorian mode for the melody, partly by the fact that the accompaniment frequently rises above the vocal line, a quality also found in such other Burns settings by Scott as 'Mary Morison' and 'O were my love yon Lilac Fair'. 'My Luve is like a Red, Red Rose' is by any standards a beautiful and deeply expressive song, the 'seamless' melody and the markedly linear writing flowing, so to say, out of themselves. Once again, unfortunately for Scott's song in public regard, it is a beautiful traditional folk-air that Burns associated with the words. Nevertheless, a culture that is sure of its strengths and limitations should find ample room for both.

The anonymous but Burns-like 'When I think on the happy days' is a pleasant, composed folk-song, reflecting the characteristic Scots theme of regret for the change time works on the poet's beloved. The Dunbar songs and 'Phyllis', already commented upon, complete this collection.

Writing to Sorabji on 16th September to thank him for his favourable review of the volume in the *New English Weekly,* Scott told him:

Such understanding must surely be the only kind of recom-

pence one ever gets — and yet how few in any sense deserve
to be understood. I have long since not cared a straw about the
appreciation or depreciation of the daily journalist (having
had personal acquaintance with not a few), so that now I
find a kind of sadistic amusement in watching the poor devil
try to say something.

I sent copies to Newman,[4] Bax,[5] Evans,[6] and Dent[7] — Tovey[8]
spent a night over them with me just before the date of
publication, when, by the way, there was a good deal of talk
of yourself and *himself*. What a queer fish he is — You've
seen his latest published Oxford essay on Musical Form or
something. I treat him very suspiciously as a master of
apologetics, now become purely verbal. Newman and Evans
and Fox-Strangways[9] so far have said nought — Bax replied
immediately that he thanked me for the volume as he had
appreciated the previous volumes 'so keenly': Dent was going
on holiday, would go into them when he returned and would
endeavour to get them sung during the winter. That's about
all I've had so far, excepting of course our local penny-a-
liners, who have beaten their own best in saying the wrong
thing.

In 1932 a group of MacDiarmid's friends raised a sum of
money to enable the poet to move up to the 'dry' Island of
Whalsay, in the Shetlands. Separated by four hundred miles,
a continuing close association between MacDiarmid and Scott
thus became impossible. In any case MacDiarmid's preoccupation was increasingly with a verse that concentrated on trying
to associate and assimilate the facts of different aspects and
disciplines of life, and on poetical Communist propaganda.
Neither of these aspects of literature or life had any real appeal
to Scott, who often said that he "no longer knew what Christopher was about," and that "whatever it was he was producing,
it wasn't poetry."

Even before reaching Shetland, MacDiarmid had ex-
perienced the difficulty of struggling to exist without a fixed
income. He wrote to Helen Cruickshank in dignified yet fairly
definite terms setting out his urgent need for a job. She at once
wrote to Scott, who, apparently taken by surprise, replied to
her on 19th December, 1936:

It is a curious thing how seldom in all the correspondence
that has passed between us he has not so much as hinted at
financial difficulties . . . As for advice, I really can't think
of any, except to continue being as kind to him as you have
always been.

Scott added that he would be sending the poet a Christmas hamper, and promised to "take a hand" if Helen Cruickshank went ahead with her plan for raising "£20-£30 by subscription".

The yearly Montrose summer holidays had come to an end in 1929, when the Grieves left for London. For the Scott family there was a holiday at Kilcreggan, on the Clyde, in 1930, but bad weather made Scott resolve in future to go East again. While at Kilcreggan he sketched out thirty-three bars of a pentatonic melody which he called 'Heroic Chant'. A decade or so later he made a version of it for violin and piano. By February, 1941, it had found its effective final form as an attractive piece for string orchestra, 'Cumha nan loach' (Lament for the Heroes).

Summer holidays thereafter were taken at St. Andrews, where friends still came to visit, and there was a useful patron. Around 1930 a wealthy American whose father was of Hebrew origin and whose mother was Scottish, James H. Whyte, came to St. Andrews, where he remained until 1939. He had adopted his mother's surname, and become passionately involved with the idea of a Scottish Nation. He bought an old building, then derelict, number three South Street, converting the vaulted ground floor into the Abbey Bookshop and the upper floors into a house for himself. There he lived from 1931 to 1938, when the bookshop closed and the property was sold to the University. It was the meeting place of those interested in what was regarded as 'modern Scottish', and a haunt of, among others, the youthful Douglas Young. In 1931 Whyte also acquired the old coast-guard building, numbers five to eleven North Street. Employing a Dundee architect, he had it constructed into two houses with an art gallery on the upper level in between, the new edifice being locally referred to as 'the Moorish monstrosity'. The first tenants of the houses were in number five, W. MacAusland Stewart, a Lecturer in French at the University and subsequently Professor at Bristol, and in number eleven, Whyte's close friend the journalist, John F. Tonge. Number five later became the home of the composer and first professor of Music at the University, Cedric Thorpe Davie.

While in St. Andrews, Whyte founded probably the most sumptuous review ever to be published in Scotland, *The Modern Scot,* which he edited from 1930 to 1936, when it was absorbed in another magazine, *Outlook,* of which he became literary editor.

Ronald G. Cant, then a St. Andrews lecturer who knew Whyte, described him as "an odd and not particularly attractive person" but one whose "intentions were, probably, sincere and timely" for "the patronage extended through *The Modern Scot* to C. M. Grieve, F. G. Scott and others". Whyte went back to Washington D.C. at the beginning of the war, and opened a book shop there, disposing of his St. Andrews properties to the University (after military occupation) in 1945. He paid a return visit to Scotland in the early 'Fifties, and died soon afterwards in America. All the songs in Book Three of *Scottish Lyrics* made their first appearance in Whyte's *Modern Scot*.

Friends also visited the Scott home in Glasgow, among them, in April 1932, Edwin Muir. Muir, then living in Crowborough, Sussex — he and Willa were to move to St. Andrews in 1935, making their home there for some years — sent Scott a copy of the beautifully produced *Six Poems* which had just been brought out in a limited edition by the Sampson Press of Worlingham,[10] remarking of them that they seemed to have more of the "craftsmanship you were speaking about than any of my former work, which was sadly deficient in it". Muir went on:

> It was a great pleasure to see you again, though for such a short time, and to listen to the very beautiful work you have been doing. The sonnet moved me more than any music I have listened to for a long time, and still teases my mind with its combined strangeness and firmness, its formal perfection and its vocation of strange and beautiful things. It was the thing that overcame me most, and that's why I am writing about it in particular, but, unlike myself, you have a great surge of mood, and technique, it seems to me, that can deal with anything you conceive, and if I could only analyse music as authentically as I feel it, I should like to be a music critic simply for the sake of being able to write about your work as it deserves. By one means or another you will have to be published — not merely for your own sake, but for other people's. I wish you would do something about it; I certainly shall (with or without your permission!) if I ever get the ghost of a chance.

About this time William Johnstone, Scott's cousin — a painter and teacher who was eventually to become head of London's Central School of Art, before retiring back to the countryside near Jedburgh and in old age establishing a high reputation as an artist — painted an apocalyptic portrait of the composer. Scott had been helpful to Johnstone during the painter's student days as a young man in Edinburgh. Muir wrote to Johnstone in July of the same year:

> Yes,[11] F. G. Scott has often mentioned your name to me: but F. G. is a very bad correspondent, much worse even than myself, and I don't think that I've had more than two letters from him in the last four years. One of them, strangely enough, came only a few weeks ago. He is in the middle of a new productive period and is doing very wonderful work. I know this for we were up in Scotland last Whitsun, and heard a great many of his new songs.

Scott seems to have found his work at Jordanhill reasonably satisfying. But twice, at the beginning and at the end of the decade, he made efforts to take himself off elsewhere. On 11th May, 1930, he was writing from 103 Woodville Gardens, Langside, to the painter William McCance, then living in London:

> I have taken your injunction to come to London so much to heart that I have just filled up a form of Application for a post of *Inspector of Music under the L.C.C.* It looks a fairly good crib (though I hope there's not too much work attached to it) and at any rate there's the prospect of more money and the opportunity in it of watching you hustlers at work. While telling Grieve about it in a pub last night (you'll know he's on his way to Liverpool) he at once suggested getting in touch with Mitchison and Naomi[12] who he swears have all kinds of social, political, educational and other varieties of 'pull' in the London milieu. He thinks Mitchison must know several influential members of the L.C.C. in more than a business capacity — and Naomi's connections with the history of education should also count for a great deal. The post as advertised is for an Inspector of Music (District Rank) in the Education Officers' Department, The County Hall, Westminster Bridge, S.E.1. beginning at £700 per annum and going to £1000. ERGO: if you really want to see my physog, you'll phone or wire the Mitchison's *at once,* (applications not later than tomorrow the 12th May), and get them to 'pull' like Old Nick while observing the commandment — Canvassing disqualifies.

> There's another matter which ought to interest you which I knew while in London but only divulged to Grieve last night in my cups. It's this: that the British Institute in Paris (of which august body Saurat is a member) are setting about holding an exhibition of *Scottish Art* in Paris in *1932.* Saurat

has carried, in addition, that while the Exhibition is running,
a concert of *Scottish Music* be given, and since returning to
Glasgow he has informed me that *I've been placed in charge*
with Roger-Ducasse, a former teacher of mine, responsible
for the Paris arrangements. ERGO again I must be up and
doing — in fact I suspect this is Saurat's little way of circum-
venting my proverbial laziness. Apart from that however 'twill
be glad' news for Agnes[13] and you to hear of such an opportunity, to pulverize London and incidentally Scotland by creating a sensation in Paris. No doubt you'd already have guessed
why I didn't breathe the matter to Grieve and yourself when
in London — I feared Christopher wouldn't be able to contain
himself with such a bit of information and I would ask you in
turn not to mention it at all till we've got the right people,
J. D. Ferguson, Duncan Grant and folk like yourself so
deeply entrenched that there'll be no room for any others.
If the thing became coloured with anything like an 'entente'
whitewash it would of course be a wash-out right away. That's
why Saurat waited till he'd got me recognized as chief agent
here — the Franco-Scottish Society in Glasgow are to take
their instructions from me and not vice versa. So get busy
you dear people and see that you land me the London job and
we'll all set out for Paris together. I add a wee note specially
for Agnes — I hear her name and fame are leaping sky high
and I wish you both heaps of luck with your present exhibition.

That attempt to widen his horizons came to nothing. Again,
in 1938, he applied for the post of Gardiner Professor of Music
at the University of Glasgow and Principal of the Scottish
National Academy of Music (a double post in these days that
had just been vacated by W. Gillies Whitaker, but which was
eventually divided into two appointments). Scott's printed "Statement of Qualifications" includes the information that he is
"under contract with Messrs George Routledge, the London
Publishers, to write an authorative book on 'Piobaireachd' ".
It also defined his duties at Jordanhill as "the giving of Lectures
in Theory of Music and Musical Appreciation to the following
categories of students: Non-graduates, Graduates, and Honours
Graduates; teachers taking a diploma in the 'Further Training
of Teachers' Course, and candidates for the Froebel Certificate
(Music in the Infant School)", adding: "All these classes have
practice in Choral Singing". His referees were George J. Burnett,
Director of Studies at Jordanhill, and H.M.I. Dr A. F. Hyslop,
of the Scottish Education Department. From Denis Saurat came
this testimonial: "I have known Francis George Scott since

1919, and I have pleasure in stating that, to the best of my judgment, he is a man of extraordinarily wide culture and interests, one of the soundest and most penetrating judges of men and things and art and literature that I have met.

It may be of interest that the French maître Roger-Ducasse, after several days of close work with F. G. Scott has told me personally that in his opinion F. G. Scott's musical work is of the very highest and most original order." Saurat appended his name as Professor of French Literature at King's College, London, (formerly) Professor of English at the University of Bordeaux, Directeur de l' Institut Français du Royaume Uni (Universités de Lille et de Paris) and External Examiner in French to the University of Glasgow.

It may, in fact, be doubted if Scott's absence of experience in practical music-making and the marked limitations of his musical sympathies would really have fitted him for the double post, which in any case would have left him with little enough time for composition. In the event, the appointment went to the Organist of Westminster Abbey, Ernest Bullock, and Scott remained at Jordanhill until he retired in 1946.

For his students he wrote occasional part-songs, now and then successfully entering choirs for classes at the competitive Glasgow Music Festivals. He also trained a small orchestra. His sociable nature made him popular, if always perhaps a little distant. "Be in the crowd but not of it", was a motto he impressed on his own family. One student, Margaret Macfarlane, of the 1933/4 session, remembers him daily striding towards the College from his home, his hair flowing beneath his velour hat. Another recalls his habit of addressing the wall above the back row of students in his lecture room, as a good way of ensuring that the voice carried (though it is also a means of keeping one's listeners firmly in their place!). Once, as Mrs Catherine Ironside remembers, when giving a recital with his wife at the College, Burges had to make a difficult entry. To make sure that she got it right, Scott "counted aloud 1, 2, 3, 4, before she started to sing, and then turned and said to us, with a twinkle in his eye 'I'll pay for this when I go home! '."

Another former student, Ronald Calder, who became Assistant Head of Music, BBC Scotland recalled:

After we had settled into the room, the door burst open, and

> F.G. breezed in — there is no other word to describe his
> arrival — within a few moments he had us singing our heads
> off at the National Anthem, and what's more . . . in two keys
> at once. I'll always remember how, after a few moments of
> this, he leapt from the piano, clutched his head and cried:
> 'My! what a dreadful noise!'. From that moment he had us
> in the hollow of his hand. And from that 'dreadful noise'
> he got us to see how we might help our future classes to
> sing with at least reasonable tone and, even more interesting,
> to see something of the reasons behind the elementary
> harmonic rules. It was a real lesson to us all in *teaching*, and
> of the importance in teaching of something that Scott always
> had: personality.

One of Scott's lectures, written out in pencil, has survived
in its entirety, probably because it was also intended for an
extra-mural student audience. It is on Wagner, about whom
Scott concludes:

> No other artist has so exerted his influence on the general
> cultural outlook of his time, and even today almost every
> musical phenomenon is determined directly or indirectly by
> that influence.

With easy clarity, Scott traces Wagner's development from the
early 'Overture for Grand Orchestra' to 'Parsifal'. Though most
of what he is explaining is common knowledge to mature music
lovers, this lecture for young people and extra-mural students
contains several examples of his concentrated perception.

> It is a fairly simple matter to follow the three divergent
> streams in European music from the year 1600 to the present
> day. It is perhaps helpful (though not strictly accurate) to
> remember that the musical side of opera (bel canto) has been
> the concern generally of Italian composers and others who,
> like Mozart, wrote to Italian models; that the dramatic side of
> opera owes much to the Germans, Gluck, Weber, Wagner; and
> that ballet and stage spectacles are the special provinces of
> the French and Frenchified Russians.

In view of his own creative retreat from the harmonic
exploration of his MacDiarmid settings, it is interesting to find
him restlessly expressing himself on the side of the *avant garde*
when writing to Sorabji on 2nd March, 1932:

> . . . To me the ultimate goal of all present day music is an
> entirely new form that will contain it, just as in turn fugue

and sonata were the outcome of endeavour to write in independent parts and to contrast themes on a basis of diverse keys. I ask myself therefore, what is this new form that we must be moving towards? Is it fugue? or sonata? or what? Of the moderns, I feel (rather than think) that Schönberg is almost alone in his understanding of the problem . . . In my opinion it isn't going to be solved along either fugue or any other line we *know* of. I have an incurable suspicion of what we *know* of from the past, and an inherent disability to accept solutions once valid, whether recommended by Tovey, Busoni or the whole gang of neo-classicists — who, in short, want to keep us on the gold standard.

During his period at Jordanhill College, Scott also served as an Inspector of Schools, touring every year through Central and South West Scotland. Scott's H.M.I. notebooks have survived, and from them we can gain some idea of the poor state of education in remote Galloway at that time. After such a trip in May 1931, Scott recorded:

From Doctor Ross the Medical Officer for the County, I learned the following particulars. Drink and sexual immorality are in flourishing condition and affect both Headmasters and Education Committee, with the result that seldom is a teacher sacked, unless under the most extreme provocation.

At Wigtown, both Headmaster Edwards and his Assistant-in-Qualifying Class, Mr Irving (a Yorkshireman) are well-known boozers. Edwards used to do a round of the four pubs in Wigtown (a 'haf' in each) at every play interval and dinner interval. Irving has a lurid past. Was for twenty years on the Variety Stage — became Headmaster — drank himself out of the post and had to accept an assistantship at Wigtown. At present, Edwards and Irving are watching each other, and there's been a marked improvement in the conduct of both of them.

Birch . . . is a simpleton (he has a useless wife and a large family) and is really in desperate straits to make ends meet. His Newton Stewart pupils have gradually left him on account of his inefficiency . . . At 41 years of age he is unlikely to change into an efficient teacher.

Smith, at Douglas Ewart (High School, Newton Stewart), is a suave creature that promises a lot but doesn't *do* much. Ross called him a 'jessie'.

The notebooks for 1934 are also in the Scott Archive

F

at Glasgow's Mitchell Library. From them we learn that at
Rothesay Academy, "Gregory blethers all the time — always
telling them something — keeps yattering on about things and
I fancy nobody pays any attention to him. He's a bit woolly-
headed and jumpy": while at Greenock High School Scott
records the Headmaster's opinion "against Cuthbert-Foster, who,
though supervisor for the district is a bit of a dud. He hasn't
any initiative: just keeps on doing the same thing from day
to day. He's no disciplinarian."

Praise was also meeted out in his notes, though usually not
defined. When Scott discovered a highly effective teacher who
had come late into the profession and was worried because under
the rules of the day he would not qualify for a pension, Scott
noted: "Must speak to Hyslop about him."

It was while he was on one of these circuits in June 1936
that I first encountered Scott. To complete the practical side of
the Higher Music Leaving Certificate Examination, for which
I was the Glasgow Academy's first ever candidate, I had to play
a prescribed piece on the violin in the presence of, indeed
accompanied by, the examiner. Eight years after the event I
described the encounter in a BBC Overseas Broadcast.

> One of the pieces was Raff's 'Cavatina'. At the appointed
> time, with my violin-case under my arm. I knocked at the
> class-room door. A hearty voice ordered me to enter. The
> class-room was in one sense empty, in another sense full. For
> there beside the piano was a fierce-looking man with a mag-
> nificent face and a shock of greyish hair.

> After I had left the presence, I asked my music-master the
> name of the examiner. 'Don't you know?', he said: 'That's
> Francis George Scott, the composer'.

> I was overawed and a little surprised. It was, in fact, the
> first time that I had ever been in the presence of a real com-
> poser, and a composer one of whose songs our school choir
> had sung.[14] What surprised me was that the song we had
> sung was so exquisitely tender a lullaby.

After the broadcast, the script of which I had sent to him,
Scott replied: 'It was interesting to read that I acted as examiner
for your Higher Music, and gratifying to see what good use you
have made of it since: there would be good hopes for Scottish
music if all the entrants followed your lead.[15]

Though his students, and at least one of his school examinees were in no doubt either about his abilities as a composer or his originality and forcefulness as a teacher and lecturer, his songs did not make consistent progress with the wider public during the 'Thirties. When Erik Chisholm founded the Active Society[16] in Glasgow, bringing Bartok (twice), Hindemith, Casella, Florent Schmitt and others to the city, a few of Scott's songs were performed at the opening concert, and a larger group on a subsequent occasion. On the first occasion, an anonymous critic in the *Glasgow Herald* decided that of the six songs by Scott, four of them being performed for the first time, the "most beautiful . . . were 'When I think on the happy days' and 'Phyllis' . . . another clever piece of writing. Mr Scott's terse style is emminently suited to the Scottish verse he delights to illustrate." The programme included excerpts from W. B. Moonie's opera 'The Weird of Colbar' and music by Cedric Thorpe Davie. The more extended recital, the first of three entirely devoted to Scottish music, and given in Glasgow's Stevenson Hall, took place in 1932. On that occasion the singers were billed as Miss Boyd Stephenson, Mr Logie Annand ("whose intonation was rather uncertain", according to *The Bulletin*) and Mr George Burnett. But Mr Burnett took ill and could not appear. As another anonymous critic put it: "The group which Mr Burnett should have sung was undertaken by the composer himself, although it was announced that he had no pretensions of having a voice. He was too modest. His voice proved to be more than average quality and his brilliant characterisation amply compensated for any vocal defects, real or imaginary". *The Bulletin's* H.K.W. thought: "Mr Scott's modern touches . . . inclined to sound over sophisticated . . . On the other hand, there is a danger of lapsing into the conventional, which did happen once or twice — possibly in the case of earlier compositions." The *Glasgow Herald* music critic felt that there were times "when the piano was called upon to furnish, while the voice rested, material that did not really advance the expression." The columnist of the *Evening News*, 'Looker-on', who was present at the concert when Scott deputised for Burnett, was one of the first to react to a difficulty that was to disadvantage Scott for the rest of his life. "Mr Scott is one of C. M. Grieve's 'white hopes'. Whether Mr Grieve has enough musical taste, knowledge and experience to act as a musical Rhadamanthus I do not know. But his persistent and often petulant boosting of Mr Scott was distinctly unfortunate for the composer himself: it raised undue expectations and evoked a hyper-critical attitude."

The critics of the evening papers, rarely if ever musicians or even musically trained, were thus politely appreciative. The popular daily picture paper *The Bulletin* then had as music critic the elderly Herbert K. Wood, whose father entertained Chopin in Glasgow. Wood, whom I succeeded as music critic of *The Bulletin* in 1947, consistently praised Scott's Burns settings, but thought that some of the other accompaniments were elaborate.

The critic who counted for most with music-loving readers was Percy Gordon of the *Glasgow Herald*. He remained obstinately suspicious of the national characteristics of Scott's songs. Typical of his comments are those following an Active Society concert of 3rd February, 1933. Next day, his notice said of Scott:

> There is individuality in his work, but it is not sufficiently controlled while he is setting his poems; and expressive mannerisms make themselves felt when, as last night, a number are heard in succession.

> The music often suggests that he became too absorbed in the pleasant task of composition for its own sake . . . and overlooked for the time being his responsibilities towards the text. The result is sometimes a fragmented quality in the music and, especially in settings of a lively mood, a spasmodic utterance. It is debateable whether, in songs like 'A luvin' woman is a licht' (MacDiarmid) Mr Scott does justice to the Scottish temperament. The sudden outbursts he indulges in are not characteristic of our nature, but reflect more the mercurial and almost volcanic natures that are to be found in eastern Europe. The true Scot makes his meaning clear in more subtle ways, and can be, for that reason. more impressive because more controlled.

Casting one's mind over Scottish history to Bruce's impulsive murder of Comyn in the Greyfriars Monastry at Dumfries, through the long succession of treacherous killings that mark our progress from Mediaevalism to the Reformation and on to more modern times, Gordon's conception of the restrained and subtle behaviourism traditionally manifested in the Scottish character seems strange indeed! His notice continued:

> The piano accompaniments generally underline this tendency to be over-expressive, and add, by their hint of impoverished effects, to the rhapsodic quality of the whole.
>
> The part-songs were much more satisfying. The absence of a piano and the need to knit together the sections of the choir into a texture of sufficient substance induce more control, and the results are free from those touches of momentary effects that disturb the balance of the songs. The part-songs are effective chorally and attractive musically.

So, indeed they are: but most of them lack the originality, the effective stamp and energy which alone belong to Scott's songs for solo voice. The critic wound up by praising Sir Alexander Mackenzie's then recently re-published Piano Quintet of 1875, which Gordon found "delightfully fresh and genial in all its four movements" and 'well worth reviving", since it provided "many little surprises of the most pleasant kind".

The Mackenzie Piano Quintet is certainly a pleasant enough work, and very possibly still "well worth reviving", almost half a century on. But it is cast firmly in the post-Mendelssohnian school of conventional German Romanticism, of which Gordon himself was a product. He was a kindly man and a good musician, but his sympathies were limited. Between 1936 and 1938 I was myself a pupil of his, studying harmony and counterpoint. My father had a holiday home at Innellan, my teacher a little white-washed cottage that sat on the sea-washed rocks almost at the foot of nearby Toward lighthouse, two or three miles further to the west. One Sunday afternoon I cycled along to Toward. On approaching the cottage I was astonished to hear the sounds of an ironic brassy polka blaring over the summer air from his gramophone. "What" I asked, "was that music? It sounded fun." "Fun?" snorted Gordon. "It is simply youthful bad taste. It won't do." The piece was a movement from Shostakovich's ballet suite *The Age of Gold,* which still "does", in spite of having been succeeded by a series of mighty symphonic masterpieces from its composer. (Incidentally, Shostakovich was one of the few contemporary composers for whom Scott frequently expressed very considerable admiration).

Gordon returned to the charge two years later, incorporating a review of *Scottish Lyrics,* Book Three, in one of his weekly *Herald* articles, entitled "Scottish Music. Is there a National Idiom?". His conclusion was that there was not. Furthermore, such an idiom could not be created by shutting "ourselves out from what is being done in other parts of the world . . . It is no compliment to the Scots character to hint that in musical matters it can be neutralised from outside". He reminded his readers that:

> Mr Scott is strongly national in his sympathies and ambitions, and his imaginative and enterprising work is well known to many people. His wish is to create art songs that are definitely Scottish in feeling, and can claim to be described to be descended in spirit from our folk-music.
>
> In spite of the resource in composition that his songs display, he often introduces effects, and expresses himself along lines that defeat his object . . ."

Gordon then quotes a powerful genuine ballad-stanza, and compares it with a feeble imitation by Burns, concluding that the ballad is "truly Scottish in feeling", whereas Burns merely represents "the conscious poetic cultivation . . ." One aspect of "the Scot's character is the habit of speaking with such directness and concentration that the listener must meet the message half way".

A similar pre-occupaion with ballad directness was to become the very credo of a poet who had by then entered into Scott's life, William Soutar, although the composer had not yet become deeply interested in the poet's work. It was seriously to mar Soutar's achievement in English, since Soutar, like Gordon, had failed to realise that the ballad tradition belonged to an age whose circumstances were wholly different from our own. For one thing, the ballad tradition evolved out of the need to employ oral transmission, to some extent acting as a news-carrying medium. Each age must re-interpret its inherited traditions and adapt them in poetry to the speech-rhythms of the times, in music to the current state of expressive sensibility. Gordon simply did not apprehend the power and subtlty of the great MacDiarmid songs, nor sense that in these songs at least, Scott showed himself to be aware of what was going on musically in other parts of Europe. Oddly enough, had Gordon survived long enough he might have taken delight in such late Scott settings as the songs to poems by George Campbell Hay, where the utterance is direct.

It must have been depressing for Scott to have to steel himself to ignore such a sustained and locally influential attitude of disapproval. No doubt it played some part in what was to prove a more or less disastrous step in the 'Thirties, the decision to devote a large part of his creative energy to the composition of music for orchestra.

However, if the critics were cool, his friends praised him in print whenever the opportunity arose, often in terms so extravagant as to be counter-productive. Kaikhosru Shapuri Sorabji (b.1892),[17] a wealthy Essex-born composer and critical guru who kept most of his music from the public for forty years[18] but was more liberal with his musical pronouncements, wrote a regular column of what is sometimes called "trenchant criticism" for *The New English Weekly*. He got to know Scott in the early 'Twenties,[19] meeting first at the Chingford, Essex, home of George Reston Malloch. On 13th October, 1934, reviewing the same volume of *Scottish Lyrics* that so displeased Percy Gordon, Sorabji showed a much greater understanding of what Scott was really about.

> One is first of all struck by the superb shape and design of the songs; next . . . the firmly convincing vocal line, observing the exigencies and inflections of the verse with exquisite and loving, but never exaggerated nor laboured care. Idiomatically one is at once struck by the marked independence, the freedom from any sort of harmonic *parti-pris* . . . and the subtle way in which the composer modifies the harmonic vocabulary to suit the needs of each poem.

So far, so good. Had he left it at that, Sorabji might have made useful contact with his musical readers, but he could not resist going on to denigrate another composer, claiming that Scott's harmonic adaptability was "unlike that of people of the Schönberg kidney, who have one and one only very constricted vocabulary, which they apply with impartiality", whatever the nature of the poem. Although, personally, I am not a great admirer of the music of the Second Viennese School, and see what Sorabji was getting at, the absence of wisdom in praising the work of an unfamiliar composer at the expense of that of a better known and well-regarded world figure, is obvious.

Sorabji's trait of musical over-sell was to become yet more absurd and damaging to Scott. Writing in *Scottish Life and Letters* No. 1 (1934) he shouts: "How different is Scott's treatment of the love lyric, or rather how different his *points de départ* from those infinitely boring, revolting wishy-washy, sexless and eunochoid 'Frauenliebe und Leben', 'Schöne Müllerin', and all the rest of the stock-in-trade and claptrap of German sentimentality".

By 8th July, 1948, reviewing a recital at the Institut Français that had taken place in London on 19th June, this critic announces that Scott's songs stand up to the test of "a one-man recital, a test that few composers can stand up to, not even many of the Masters of the Lied, of whom it is the custom to inflict upon audiences words of inspissated amorous sentiment of that glucose and tacky texture to which Schubert and Schumann have accustomed — but not inured us".

Such absurd coat-trailing in order to air a highly personal prejudice was regularly repeated by Sorabji in other journals, until finally it was enshrined in his second collection of autobiographical essays *Mi Contra Fa* (1947). Inevitably, all this did much to prejudice Scott's chances of being taken seriously within Scotland, and even more so furth of his own country. It was further hindered by the continuing extravagances of his old friend and collaborator, Hugh MacDiarmid.

In *The Modern Scot*, MacDiarmid had "dealt with" Percy Gordon[20] — "the sort of booby that comes between the Scottish artist and the Scottish public" — and by way of comparison cited the already quoted review of Sorabji, at whose "amazing gifts" the poet marvels in his autobiography *Lucky Poet* (1943). By the time he reached its pendant, *The Company I've Kept* (1966), we are expected to accept MacDiarmid's preposterous contentions "that F. G. Scott is . . . a great man, a finer artist, and more distinguished personality, than, say, W. B. Yeats", and that "Kaikhosru Sorabji is a greater musical genius than say, Delius or Elgar . . .". The total irrelevance of the first comparison, coupled with the complete absence of musical judgment of the second, would leave one gasping if one could take it seriously. To celebrate Scott's 75th birthday, MacDiarmid put together a pamphlet, an essay alternating uneasily between

extravagant over-praise and the by now all too familiar mani-
festations of his own megalomania.

While probably few enough people bothered to taigle
seriously with the turgid prose of the propagandist who had been
a great poet in the 'Twenties and early 'Thirties, MacDiarmid's
avowed Communism not only held back serious recognition
of his own best work throughout several decades, but, by
association, did much to discredit the notion that Scott could
possibly be a serious composer rather than simply another Scottish Renaissance nationalist in need of special pleading.

The irony of the situation was that not only did Scott
consistently stand back from dogmatic extremisms and propagandising in any form, but positively disapproved of many of his
former collaborator's extreme pronouncements. In his letters
to MacDiarmid he frequently stated his distrust of Marxism
and dialectical materialism in practice, usually drawing from
the poet a defiant defence of his own position. When I presented
Scott with a copy of *Poetry Scotland Two*, a wartime anthology
I edited, carrying the first publication of MacDiarmid's poem
'Talking with Five Thousand People in Edinburgh', Scott
quipped: "You've made a mistake here. There's a nothing too
many. Chris never talked to five thousand people at one time
anywhere in his life! "

Throughout the 'Thirties and early 'Forties, MacDiarmid,
writing from Whalsay, constantly tried both to impress his friend
and former teacher, and convince him that only urgent daily
business prevented the production of further lyrics suitable for
Scott's attention. Much effort was being expended by the poet on
his *Autobiography* which, Scott was told, was 500,000 words
long, but "has had to be cut to 150,000 words". It was "the
goods", and Scott heard that he had "a treat" coming to him.
On 20th November, 1939, the poet was still reiterating his
eagerness to "turn out some lyrics of the right sort for you",
claiming that his *Autobiography* had been holding him up. Scott
was told that this book was "not only exciting but encyclo-
paedic", a book going far beyond anything ever produced in
Scotland before".

However, a major source of contention had erupted in
1932. It drove a fricative wedge between MacDiarmid and Muir,
and to some extent eventually coloured even the relationship

between MacDiarmid and Scott, at any rate on Scott's side. This was the publication of Muir's book *Scott and Scotland* (the Scott in this case being, of course, Sir Walter).

In this book Muir, the critic, advanced the thesis that when Scotland was an independent kingdom with a distinctive culture and two languages of its own, Scots and Gaelic, (though Muir did not deal here with the latter), writers could express the whole mind of the nation. Furthermore, there was a living relationship between the language of the Court and of the subjects. After the Reformation and the Union of the Crowns, the educated turned increasingly to English, and Scots failed to develop to meet the linguist needs of a changing world. English became the language of thought for most people, Scots the language of feeling. Thus, in neither tongue could the ethos of the whole nation any longer be expressed. Even Burns and Scott could not avoid being affected by the resulting dichotomy.

Only linguistic bigots today would feel disposed to quarrel with that analysis. But Muir went on to advocate the abandonment of Scots, urging the "necessity" of turning to English, though neither arguing his case convincingly nor taking sufficient account of the great work produced by MacDiarmid in the 'Twenties, his high praise of MacDiarmid only resulting in the conclusion that MacDiarmid had left "Scottish verse pretty much where it was before". As Muir's biographer, Peter Butter, points out, Muir may have been "a 'too quick despairer' with regard to the possibilities of the Scottish language". On the other side of the argument, he certainly acknowledged that by 1932: "for a large and increasing proportion of Scotsmen, English, with some tincture of a Scottish accent and the addition of a few Scottish words, was the mother tongue, and broad Scots virtually a foreign language. For them, English is the only natural language to write in, and there is no reason why they should not, . . . , achieve a fusion of thought and feeling in it. The situation can be altered, if at all, only by political action". And there is absolutely no sign whatever of such action materialising. During the half-century or so that has passed since Muir's book was written, Scottish writers have continued to make use of whatever language comes most naturally to their temperament though, undeniably and inevitably, English is making steady in-roads as the most widely spoken language of Scotland. Today, it is difficult to see what all the bother Muir's book created was about. Neil Gunn reviewed it in a balanced way, and so did some others; yet when George Bruce arrived on a visit to St. Andrews that summer, he found Scott in a rage over Muir's somewhat extreme conclusion that nowadays "Scotland could only create a national literature by writing in English". "What will Chris say to this?," F.G. roared. Bruce then called on Muir, who thought that these fellow Borderers, Scott and MacDiarmid, would naturally feel more hostility to England than himself. He was apparently totally unaware of the furore he was about to unleash. MacDiarmid, who had himself then just finally abandoned Scots in favour of English (for a variety of reasons, one being the drying-up of his lyric flow, but another suspiciously like a work-out of the very theories advanced by Muir), saw the book as a betrayal of the whole Scottish Renaissance movement. He was to attack Muir, furiously and bitterly, in newspapers and magazines for the rest of the Orcadian's life; an onslaught which the gentle Muir made no attempt whatever to counter.

Bruce expressed his own doubts to his Uncle as to whether a genuine contemporary art could be built on a national foundation any longer. He forgets now the details of the onslaught he thus drew upon himself, but remembers an ensuing evening when, in the presence of the Muirs, James Whyte and his young friend, the Scottish critic and journalist John Tonge, they listened to "the composer at the piano rendering among others his . . . setting of poems by William Dunbar. Here were applied the musical resources of one versed in contemporary techniques, so that the individual qualities of the works were realised . . . 'a psychological notation' was what the composer said". Bruce felt then that the "idiom was secure".

The new ambition which Scott's connection with Dunbar was to fire, however, was far from secure. In the late summer of 1934 (16th September), Scott wrote to Sorabji:

> I am spending the few remaining weeks before College reopens on some larger scale stuff for voice and orchestra, and reading all the old authorities on orchestral combination and balance, but so far I've come out by the same door as in I went, and I'm convinced once more that each one of us has ultimately

got to find salvation within himself — that really nothing can
be taught that's worth knowing. So much for a member of
an Educational College Staff!

Scott was, in fact, engaged upon a setting of Dunbar's
The Ballad of Kynd Kyttock for baritone and orchestra, which
he completed later in the year.[21] Scott did not think naturally
in terms of orchestral colour. It was his practice to make a
piano sketch first, then orchestrate it. But he had no practical
experience of scoring for the orchestra, although he kept a
notebook in which he analysed the orchestration used in a wide
variety of works — Elgar's Symphonies, Stravinsky's *Petrouchka*
and *Le Sacre du Printemps,* Strauss's *Don Juan, Tod und Ver-
klärung* and *Symphonica Domestica,* Florent Schmitt's *Palais
Haute,* Schönberg's *5 Orchestral Pieces* and works by Honegger,
Debussy, Holst, Reger, and Roger-Ducasse. Scott also noted the
details of Sir Henry Wood's suggestion "for an *ideal* festival
orchestra some 100 strong! ". For his setting of Dunbar's poem
about the ale-house lady who ended up selling her wares outside
St. Peter's gate, and whom the poet asked us to patronise as we
pass by, Scott chose a large orchestra that included two tenor
trombones, bass trombone, bass tuba and a percussion section
made up of timpani, cymbals, big drum, triangle, tamborine,
bells, xylophone and glockenspiel. Scott's major faults of
orchestration are his tendency to use the instruments of the
ɔrchestra as if they were voices, and also to produce passages
where the sound is likely to be so thick as to be ineffective with
regard to the individual lines. While he was scoring this piece,
he carried on a correspondence with Nicholas Gatty (1874-1946),
an English composer who had some success with his operas,
notably *Prince Fenelon* (1921), and whose *Haslemere Suite for
Strings* is still occasionally to be heard. He was for some years
music critic of the *Pall Mall Gazette,* and in 1928 completed
Schubert's unfinished song, 'Gretchen's Bitté'.[22]
Gatty made some suggestions from sketches which Scott
sent while his work was still being written. The Englishman's
final verdict came in an undated letter written at the end of
1934 or early in the New Year:

> Much of your score will, I think, sound well. But there are
> some passages I feel need revision. I have indicated these in
> some explanatory notes . . .

I am doubtful about the voice part; it will not be heard very well occasionally, partly because of the amount of orchestra and partly because it seems to me too much in the lower register. If possible I should try to get alternative notes well up.

Another suggestion I should like to make for future guidance. I rather think that the vocal line should be closer-knit; there are longish gaps and there are some long-held notes which suggest a delay in expression.

Scott had attended the Cramb lectures at Glasgow University in 1926, when Gustav Holst had dealt with the composition of the Wagnerian orchestra, laying special stress on the trombone (as befitted a former trombonist with the Scottish orchestra). Scott had noted down Holst's description of Wagner's use of the trombone in "Tristan" as " a deeply emotional instrument, giving wonderful orchestral colour".

Dunbar was to provide the inspiration for Scott's next orchestral piece, a ballet suite based on the poem 'The Seven Deidly Sinnis'. The plan follows that of the poem, Pride, Ire, Envy, Cuvatice (Avaris), Sweirnes (sloth), Lechery and Gluttony, giving place to a reel representing Satan's culminating Highland Pageant, in which the Devil produces a cloud of smoke to smother all dancers (Ex. 12, pages 94 and 95). The suite begins with a Prologue and ends with an Epilogue, both of which feature a trumpet solo that made its first appearance in 1924, in a sketch for an incomplete MacDiarmid song, 'Grey sand is churning in my lungs'. (Ex. 13).

The weakness of the score is its episodic construction. Scott shows himself unable to develop extended ideas architectonically. However, the music is by no means without interest, and should not be consigned to the silent oblivion of the library. A Scottish ballet company, looking for a national theme and a

score that lends itself to contrasting choreography, need search no further than *The Seven Deidly Sinnis.*

Scott's most successful orchestral piece, however, was his Overture *Renaissance,* written during the winter of 1936/37. It sets out in the space of 6½ minutes to evoke both Dunbar's Scotland of the Makars and that of the Scottish Renaissance movement of Scott's own time.

Scott sought Roger-Ducasse's help with the orchestration. At first the Frenchman hesitated.

"I'd be delighted to help you — but how? It is very difficult (1) to send a manuscript (2) to make written comments when verbal ones would do (3) to guess your intentions or at least to understand them. So what can I do?"

These difficulties were overcome, however, for Roger-Ducasse in due course looked over the score of the 'Renaissance' overture, and sent detailed comments. He summarised his views in a general observation.

> I read your score with great interest. From the point of view of composition I have nothing to say! As far as the orchestration is concerned, the main fault, my friend, lies in your exaggerated use of trombones and trumpets, which, if I'm not mistaken are rather deafening. You should first of all attend to the balance of your sounds and make sure that the melody, that's to say the part that above all one should hear, is not swallowed up by the accompaniment. Moreover the violins sound much better in loud forte passages at the octave than in unison and again too often you treat the cellos as double bass which sometimes have time to 'take a walk'. Furthermore, when you have a rhythmic pattern it would be better not to make it heavy by backing it as you do. Finally, remember that one always puts in *too many* instruments. Study the first movement of Mozart's Symphony in G minor and see how discretely he uses backing and even harmony support. The first pages have none and it sounds marvellous. It is difficult to enlarge upon by letter but the pencilled strokes which I've written across your score will shed light on the criticisms in this letter.

Scott accepted his advice and twice revised his score.

It was first performed in St. Andrew's Hall, Glasgow, by the Scottish Orchestra under Issy Dobrowen, and was well received, even by the "auld enemy", Percy Gordon, writing in the

Glasgow Herald on Monday 14th January, 1939: "Mr Scott's overture 'Renaisance' was the opening number of the programme. That is not the best place for a novelty, but it is difficult to see how, in the circumstances, any other position could have been given it." The rest of the programme consisted of Schumann's 'Spring' Symphony and Chopin's E minor Piano Concerto, itself then still something of a novelty, so far as Glasgow was concerned — "Mr Scott had the satisfaction of a practically full hall, ready assembled to hear his work, and *Renaissance* was well received.

It begins very forcefully — allegro feroce — and is noisily scored. But the effect is sufficiently arresting, even if its chief value is to prepare a welcome for the succeeding moods. These are well set forth, and offer a growing interest for the listener. The close of the overture is well devised".

On 28th January, 1937, Roger-Ducasse wrote from the Gironde:

> It is quite unusual for a new work to be so well received by the Press and especially one's own country where, as you know, no man is a prophet. That is something that must encourage you to continue and to work harder. The first step, the most difficult one, is now taken.

MacDiarmid pronounced this short piece the "crown of Scott's work — which is to say far and away the finest composition by any Scottish composer (for there is no comparison between Scott and any other composer Scotland had ever produced; he stands on a plane of his own, immeasurably removed from theirs), this great overture is a magnificent challenge to all the suppressed and latent potentialities capable of creating a distinctive culture in Scotland on a level in keeping with all the best traditions in the whole range of our national history . . ."

It is an immensely exciting work, dynamic to a degree, even dynamitic; a superb summation of all the vital elements in our national past, ordered in the most masterly fashion and projected vertically into the future by a single horn on its topmost note . . . "

The overture, which plays for six and a half minutes, is constructed from five main ideas, the last being the germ figure

G

of the melody for Scott's setting of 'Scots wha hae'. Ex. 14).

The characteristic modal flow and the use of the Scots 'snap' are present. The piece is, indeed, thoroughly effective, and has enjoyed several subsequent broadcast performances. It is quite as attractive in its different way as MacCunn's much-played *Land of the Mountain and the Flood* overture, and certainly does not deserve neglect.

Whether or not the staid and conservative Manager of the Scottish Orchestra, Glasgow lawyer Joseph Barnes, was put off by MacDiarmid's outpouring after the Scottish Orchestra performance, or by the newspaper controversy in which an ill-advised scribe suggested that Mr Dobrowen might have insufficiently prepared the work (only to be attacked by the composer in defense of his conductor) there is now no way of knowing. Barnes was reputed not to like publicity of a contentious nature. Years later, writing to me on 3rd December, 1948,[23] Scott recalled:

> The Renaissance Overture was performed after Tovey recommended it to Szell, but actually it was conducted by Dobrowen during Szell's absence. What I *do* recall is that I had to pay for having the parts copied out and received nothing but the applause of the audience. I suggested the *Seven Deidly Sinnis* to Barnes. His comment, that the title didn't indicate anything very interesting, annoyed me quite as much as the fact

that he didn't ask me to submit the work to the Committee. In other words the 'Scottish' in my experience expect something for nothing, and the only approach I would adopt would be Susskind's — 'the committee and Barnes are just a set of dead heads'.

If Scott ever contacted Susskind, nothing came of this approach.

Scott's interest in the music of the Gael continued to develop, perhaps stimulated in 1930 by one of his early admirers, the collector and arranger of Hebridean folk-songs, Marjory Kennedy-Fraser, who, though terminally ill at her Edinburgh home, sent him a pamphlet on the Pentatonic scale as found in Breton music, writing that she hoped she could be carried down to her music-room to hear Scott sing his own songs (a hope not destined to be realised).

Once Scott had worked his way through what seemed to him the suitable poems of Dunbar, his search for Scottish poems that caught his musical fancy continued. Unlike a composer of the first order, Scott always had to have a text that gave him a literary as well as a musical 'lift'. He was to find several such poems after meeting the young Gaelic poet, George Campbell Hay, in 1937 at Taynuilt, which had succeeded St. Andrews as the Scott family's holiday centre. The first Hay setting appeared in Book Five of *Scottish Lyrics*.

This last book of *Scottish Lyrics* was published in 1939. It contained thirteen songs, most of them the product of his fruitful period during the early 'Thirties. Although it is true to say that Scott did not 'develop' after the MacDiarmid songs in Book Three, during the next fifteen years he went on to produce many songs that are among his loveliest and best. Several of these are in Book Five. There are six Burns settings, and one to words by a Burns disciple, James ('Balloon') Tytler, 'I hae laid a herrin' in saut'. It is a flowing folk-like air. As the ardent protestations of the lover listing his goods and achievements grow more urgent, the accompaniment neatly underlines the little drama. The coquettish staccato figure that links the stanzas gives place to rising octaves and heavy chords to match the lover's appeal to 'tak me noo', though, like the lover in real life, we are left in some musical doubt as to the final outcome.

'Wee Willie Gray' has always been among Scott's most popular songs. The lightness of its accompaniment emphasising and matching the verbal speed of Burns's portrait in miniature of a nursery-rhyme character from the Scots folk-tradition. Scott himself said that the character in the song "could hardly be wee-er: a veritable Lilliputian, but the words carry affection rather than malice in them".

The setting of an anonymous lyric by some 17th century 'silver' poet, 'Since all thy vows, false maid', is one of Scott's finest melodic triumphs. The beautifully flowing vocal line has hardly a break. (Ex. 15). Though the melody is strophic, the

accompaniment varies the lover's mood, the prospect of his ghostly return being written in the higher register of the keyboard.

'The Discreet Hint', in which Burns's lover tried to get admittance to the bosom of the beloved only to be told "The way to me lies through the Kirk/Young Man, do ye hear that?" is a delightful dialogue situation song. Scott uses a kind of parlando style for the young man's words, the piano underlining his dream of bliss with conventional harmonic progressions, the shriller but more realistic response of the girl matched by more open treble writing and a wry variation of the melodic line.

In 'Oh Wha my babie clouts will buy?' Scott far surpasses Burns's original tune. Both in the melodic line, in the minor key, and in the flowing accompaniment, Scott wonderfully catches the uneasiness of the girl's yearning, the move from minor to major when the girl answers her own doubts with the thought of love perhaps to come, 'The rantin dog, the daddie o't', meanwhile stressing the strength of her pride in her man and in the motherhood his sexuality has brought her.

'Wha is that at my bower-door?' is a variation on the theme of 'The Discreet Hint', except that in this instance the lady complies with her lover's demand under a promise of secrecy. It is Scott's most extended dialogue song, except for his setting of the ballad 'Edward'.

Burns uses a reel tune with a modal flow. Scott retains this modal double-tonic effect, again using a parlando style (the marking is "recitando"). The setting is extremely pictorial, catching such details as Finlay's knocking in the first three bars and the immediately following ascending figure, and Finlay's persistence in boldly swaggering chords.

'Rattlin', Roarin' Willie' is a spirited setting of a Burns poem in which a domestic relationship is neatly presented. There is a particularly effective pictorial touch in the last six vocal bars, where tenderness and a welcome home to the wanderer are suggested by means of a diminuendo, a rallentando and a safe slide back to the home tonic.

'Scots Wha Hae', dating from the 'Twenties, is a strong and stirring setting. Psychologically, it adumbrates a self-confident Scotland woefully different from the reality of her recent history. Burns wrote his poem inspired as much by the French Revolution as by Bruce's struggle for Scottish independence. Scott thought Burns's tune a dirge. So it is, though a fairly forceful one. A nation that has come to regard the escapist nonsense of 'Scotland the Brave' as the nearest thing it possess to a national anthem would scarcely be likely to welcome the proud assertiveness of Scott's patriotic hymn.

Of the MacDiarmid settings 'Wheest, Wheest', only twelve bars long, is a miniature masterpiece. Though there are hints

of Debussy and Schönberg in the piano part, "shot through with
sudden placings of triads" as Neil Mackay observed, the music
is anchored on D. There is an ironic hymn-like Plagal cadence
to round-off the poet's final injunction. 'A' lust o' lovin' by,/
Wheest, wheesht, ye fule'.

'The Watergaw' is constructed out of the six-note bag-pipe
scale in the quasi-recitative style to be found in pipe music, as
described by Scott himself in his Pibroch lecture, and as such
is perhaps not really a 'tune'. Scott called the poem "a veritable
masterpiece of consumate expression in 12 lines which I think
it would be difficult to match in any language. The music is
polytonal . . . and endeavours to carry over into music the
tremendous emotional power behind the words".

'The Love-sick Lass', by comparison, is a simple setting,
stretches of high piano writing suggesting, as so often with Scott,
the quality of eerie wistfulness. 'Empty Vessel', MacDiarmid's
enrichment of the folk-song fragment 'Jenny Nettles', has a
gently rocking tune and an accompaniment that echoes the
rhythm of the melody. The tragic implication of the line 'Singin'
till a bairnie/That was nae langer there' is underlined with a
bleakly empty accompanying figure on the piano.

Apart from the Dunbar song already referred to, Book Five
also contains 'To a Loch Fyne Fisherman who keeps to the
old ways' by George Campbell Hay, finished in June 1939.
Hay — son of the author of the powerful novel *Gillespie* (1914)
— fundamentally a Gaelic poet, was not only a virtuosic translator into and out of several languages, as may be seen from his
one non-Gaelic collection, *Wind over Loch Fyne* (1941), but also
a master of the difficult art of expressing in a timely manner the
'feel' of the Gaelic idiom in English. This was a gift plentifully
possessed by Anglo-Irish writers from the time of James Clarence
Mangan and Sir Samuel Fergusson onwards, but singularly
lacking in their Scottish contemporaries like John Stuart Blackie
and others, whose original verses and Gaelic renderings alike
have cooled upon the page. Hay did not really so much 'invent'
his Scottish-Gaelic idiom (as some writers have suggested) as
adapt it from the Anglo-Irish example established a century
or so earlier.

Scott, with his interest in Gaelic, responded enthusiastically
to Hay's work. The composer felt that in Hay he had at last

found a new and promising collaborator. In his first Hay song, 'To a Loch Fyne Fisherman', the composer is striving after the sort of timelessness of the pibroch he had effortlessly attained in 'Milk-wort and Bog-cotton'. In 'To a Loch Fyne Fisherman', the vocal line of the first stanza is repeated with only slight variations for the other stanzas. From the slow soft opening chords — the song is marked "like a pibroch, impersonal and aloof" — the accompaniment evolves harmonically, bursting into a momentary *forte* at the image "to go like a broken branch in the grip of a torrent", subsiding again to die away into silence, *morendo pp.* The song reads well enough on the page, but in my experience is apt to sound a little monotonous in performance. Sibelius, whom Scott rather loftily despised (or at least affected to in old age, when cynicism sometimes coloured his view) was a master of held stillness, even on the largest symphonic scale. The volatile Scott was not.

When the 1939-45 war finally broke out, Scott seems to have had anxieties about the security of his Jordanhill job, anxieties that fortunately proved unfounded. But although Scott himself was not directly affected by the fortunes of war, many of his old friends were. In February, 1942, it brought MacDiarmid down from Shetland to work, first as a fitter in a Clydesdale engineering firm, then two years later to serve as a deckhand, eventually promoted to First Engineer, on the Norwegian M.F.U. *Gurli,* employed servicing naval ships in the Clyde estuary. Muir, whose American literary market had collapsed, found himself for a time a clerk in the Food Office in Dundee while doing evening duty as a Home Guardsman at St. Andrews Telephone Exchange. After a serious illness forced him to give up these tasks, he joined the British Council to organise programmes for the Polish, Czechoslovak and French Houses set up by H. Harvey Wood in Edinburgh. Saurat continued his teaching in London, much involved with de Gaulle's Free French, but in July, 1944, was in his home, 33 Cromwell Road, when it was demolished by a flying bomb. As he told Scott on 28th October, when his hand had recovered sufficiently to allow him write:

> By a miracle, only my left leg and my right hand were injured, some providential material having protected my body. I was dug out within two or three minutes by the brave young fellows of the French Air Force, who rushed into the house

> while it was still in the process of falling down. Then hospital, two operations etc., North Wales for recuperation . . .

> Did you get my *Soldat Romaine* which meanwhile came out? I also sent a copy for Grieve. Could you now send this one on to Muir? I have lost his address in the wreckage . . . Now it is up to you to write a symphony about *le soldat romaine*.

Scott and Muir wrote in appreciation of the book, though Grieve had not done so when Saurat's next letter, dated 18th November, arrived together with another copy of the book to be sent to William Burt.

Saurat prophesied:

> We are at the most dreadful period of the war, as the fighting settles, problems emerge, and crush the men that were good enough for victory but not good enough for common sense, so we have a battle of interests that can have no good issues at all.

He had recovered the use of his left leg, thought he thought that one of the fingers of his right hand might remain crippled.

> Though it is a small price to pay: the house that did it by falling on me saved my life from the blast, since at that short distance the V.1 pulverises, and the walls that tumbled down actually kept the blast from my body. So who is who in that battle?

Scott was nearing his 60th birthday when the Second World War broke out. Although he had never been a pacifist, his humanitarian spirit resented the brutality and senselessness of it all. Years of luke-warm support from critics and public alike may not have made him bitter, but they had certainly sharpened his aggressive instinct towards other Scottish composers. He knew that at least in his own field of song he was good, and that most of the others were not. Like all artists, behind the outwardly scornful demeanour sustained by his Borderer's pride, he must have longed for some measure of recognition.

REFERENCES

1 *William Soutar:* George Bruce (1978).
2 Pseudonym for Whyte's friend the journalist John Tonge, who was not permitted by his employers to write other than for them.
3 *Diaries of a Dying Man:* William Soutar, ed. Alexander Scott (1954).

4 Ernest Newman (1868-1959), Music critic of *The Sunday Times* and author of a definitive *Life of Richard Wagner.*

5 Sir Arnold Bax (1883-1953), British composer of Irish extraction who became Master of the Queen's Music.

6 Edwin Evans (1874-1945), Music critic of the *Pall Mall Gazette, Musical Times* and *Daily Mail.*

7 Sir Edward Dent (1876-1957), English Musicologist and Professor of Music, Oxford.

8 Sir Donald Francis Tovey (1875-1940), Professor of Music at Edinburgh University. Author of *Essays in Musical Analysis.*

9 Arthur Henry Fox-Strangways (1859-1948).

10 All but one of the poems later appeared in *Journeys and Places* (1937).

11 *Selected Letters of Edwin Muir* edited by Peter Butter (1974).

12 Naomi Mitchison, Scottish novelist, and her husband George, a Member of Parliament.

13 McCance's first wife.

14 Probably the choral version of 'O Jesu parvule'.

15 Letter in National Library for Scotland, dated 20th September, 1946.

16 Scott served on the Committee, but by September, 1934 he was reporting to Sorabji: "Erik, I fear, is having a bad time with his Active Society and I'm getting S.O.S. calls to attend committee meetings, and help decide whether or not the thing has to go on during the coming season. I'm afraid I'm lukewarm about it all, and yet I'm willing to stand by him in any effort."

17 Real name Leon Dudley Sorabji, son of a Parsi father and a Spanish-Sicilian mother.

18 Highly virtuosic in style. From the little I have seen or heard of it, much influenced by Alkan, Debussy and Ravel.

19 Scott corresponded with him for many years, addressing him with great respect. By 1934, however, Scott was becoming more critical of his friend's music, writing of the dicffiulty found in understanding it.

20 Years later, MacDiarmid consoled Scott with the information that in the small role of Scottish musicians of any calibre, the "very objectives and qualities" Gordon used in objecting to Scott's work had been "used in almost all the cases, and most notably that of the Earl of Kellie, as the very qualities always characteristic of Scottish composers". MacDiarmid did not disclose his source of this somewhat surprising information.

21 Dunbar's authorship has never been proven, but those who deny it must establish the contemporary existence of a poet as metrically and imaginatively gifted as Dunbar, with a similar style and technique, yet with a different name.

22 *Music and Letters,* special Schubert issue.

23 Edinburgh University Library.

Chapter 5

THE FORTIES

The early days of the war deepened Scott's acquaintance with Soutar into friendship, and brought a new friendship with one of the leaders of the group called by Eric Linklater "the Second Wind" of the Scottish Renaissance, poet, scholar, traveller, polymath and Scottish Nationalist, Douglas Young. Young was soon to refuse to be conscripted by the British Government on the grounds that for such a body to conscript a Scot was a violation of the act of Union of 1707. His wittily argued trial eventually resulted in his imprisonment, although he could have secured exemption immediately on account of his bad eye-sight simply by submitting to medical examination.

Young first wrote to Scott on 2nd October, 1940, enclosing some verses, "experiments in Scots, synthetic or what you will, more or less on Gaelic models . . . the attempt . . . made to imitate the Gaelic assonance scheme, where a stressed vowel in the first halves of the 2nd and 4th lines echoes the terminal stressed vowel of the 1st and 3rd respectively". The verses enclosed foreshadowed Young's Scots version of Sorley MacLean's great Gaelic sequence *Dain do Eimhir*.

MacLean also corresponded with Scott about this time, and indeed Scott suggested that a wordless song he had produced might form the basis of a Scottish National Anthem, if MacLean could provide the words. MacLean, however, was never able to write "to order".

The last paragraph in Young's letter must have distrubed Scott:

Hay writes to me today, he is still at large, though as long ago as July 19th the Appellate Tribunal registered him for military service. The government seems to let sleeping nationalisms lie as Welsh non-compilers with conscription also are so far unharried. He is much better writing Gaelic than spitting and polishing buttons.

George Campbell Hay spent the early months of the war

'on the run' in Argyll. But he was not to remain free for long. After evading the authorities for eight months, Hay was caught, incarcerated in Edinburgh's Saughton jail for a few days, then taken for a medical examination. Writing from Catterick Camp a little later, Hay told Scott:

> Not a very glorious business, but I said I would defy them and I did my poor best . . . I have been in the Army since June and am now getting hard boiled (I hope) . . . So far I have found it impossible to write either prose or verse. I am not in a frame of mind conducive to creation. After all I damned well said I wouldn't let them get the better of me. But here I am in khaki. Yet the Germans are a very pestilence in their doings, and perhaps one should be in khaki.

Hay's war experiences were effectively to silence him as a poet, frustrating Scott's hopes for a sustained collaboration.

From Shetland MacDiarmid,[1] in August, 1940, was feeling "hellish cut off". But he found energy to tell Scott[2] how contemptible he found Edwin Muir's delicate and moving *The Story and the Fable;* a book MacDiarmid called a "ridiculous autobiography", describing Muir's "little personal psychological whipsnade, where, indeed, it's brilling all the time", as "a beastly book in every sense of the adjective". In March, 1941 MacDiarmid's spirits had risen, as he wrote jokingly to Scott: [3]

> I notice Dollan is thinking of a penny in the pound rate for the encouragement of music in Glasgow and am expecting every next 'Bulletin' I see to contain your photo kissing Lady Dollan's hand on your inauguration as Municipal Music Director at a few thousand p.a.

Until his departure for Glasgow and heavy war work, MacDiarmid kept reiterating to Scott his confidence in his *Autobiography* and detailing the difficulties caused by its great length. Occasionally he lectured Scott, in a tone of respectful defiance, on the "need" to suppress Christianity, or on some point of Marxist dogma which Scott had evidently been challenging.[4]

Meanwhile, William Soutar had sent Scott a copy of his book *In Time of Tyrants,* privately printed in 1939. On 5th January, 1940 Scott wrote:

> I was delighted to have your Christmas gift *In time of Tyrants* — both the book itself and what it contained. Musical com-

position has been engaging my attention so much during this
holiday season that I've had time for little else, but any delay
there has been in acknowledging your book has given me all
the more time to read and re-read the many lyrics it contains
that are really of excellent quality. You will know me well
enough I hope to believe that I am not saying flattering words
when I make a statement like this, for I have read viva voce
most of the best items to the whole family and even to one
or two who have visited us lately. As author you will no doubt
feel the truth of Nietzsche's aphorism — 'I listened for
criticism but heard only the echo', so perhaps you will accept
my considered opinion and choice.

Scott then goes on to select his favourite pieces, adding:

I occasionally feel that your *very* short lyrics are overweighted
with 'thocht', as Grieve calls it, and this perhaps explains why
I feel more at ease in some of the longer ones like the Sonnets; but on the other hand 'In Time of Tumult', and
especially the very last one in the book, 'To the Future', are
extraordinary good, in both instances the expression of a single
idea in direct speech. These two are so good in *my* opinion
that I feel tempted into music on their behalf — in other
words, I believe I could hear them as music.

So much for what is my genuine response to your latest
poems. The Introductory Note on Pacifist Faith and Necessity
is also very good, though pacifism isn't a faith I can feel in
my bones, though I have been opposed to the present war all
along. But then how can we define our faith in such a welter
of contrary opinion? What if it turns out that all faiths are
bogus and that we're just the animals we were at the beginning of time? You and I prefer to cling to 'pious hopes' in
humanity, and they are something no doubt to be thankful
for — but enough — here's wishing you and your Mother
and Father all the best of everything.

This confession of Scott's scepticism is one of his few
recorded opinions on religion, in his attitude to which he perhaps
shared something of Burns's ambivalence. Soutar responded with
some manuscript poems, and on 7th September, 1941, Scott
wrote again, this time from his holiday address, Brolas, Taynuilt.
He tackled head on the problem that the bulk of Soutar's output
in English presents to readers; a problem caused not only by the
poet's mistaken belief that the ballad form would carry poetry
to a wider audience, but by an absence of ear for 20th century
speech-rhythms. It is a good example both of Scott's outspoken

and frequently accurate literary criticism and of his curious insensitivity to verse not susceptible to the attentions of his own Muse.

I confess right away that I find, and have always found, difficulty in evaluating your work. Your standard of writing is a high one and you maintain a consistently high level of, shall I say, accomplishment in the working out of each idea. The ideas, too, are generally good honest ones — kindly, generous, reflective ideas that essentially are the man behind them. A strong vein of the traditional runs through most of them — country sights and sounds, country folk and their ways of life — in fact Scottish life as it was and, at any rate in rural areas, still is. This of course is the work of memory, the 'something' which has been handed down by our past, of which we are the heirs, the background of our thinking.

Whether or not this is the best approach you can make to Scottish poetry I am not so sure. Unless the traditional is seen from a new point of view or put into a new language or passes through a new kind of mind, it is apt to look like just another effort to restate a familiar theme — an old song on a new fiddle. To my way of looking at Scottish verse there is a sad, very sad lack of impulse, the compulsion that brings both feeling and the expression of it. All the Marion Angus, Muriel Stuart, Helen Cruickshank, William Jeffrey, Lewis Spence gang were *'literary'* folk trying to make bricks without straw, hoping that by doing their damnedest they would do their best. They have (or had) no belief in their own powers, were quite pleased with faint praise, and no doubt were surprised to find themselves taken notice of by anybody. Now I can't call these people poets; they are versifiers, manipulating words like any addict to crossword puzzles and like them, awfully pleased if they find a solution of some kind to their problems. To me, their solutions are generally wrong ones, conclusions that don't follow from what has gone before, wandering makeshift with no feeling of certainty in them. This inconclusiveness comes, of course, from the plain fact that nothing can't be turned into something; if there was 'in the beginning' no original idea, it is just a waste of time to expect the new world to take shape. I hate the current phraseology 'creative thinking', but I must make use of it here, for I reckon all the above verse addicts knew nothing about it. They could all think (far too well in fact) but they couldn't think 'creatively'. (I see I should have listed Edwin Muir among the damned).

While there is some truth in Scott's general point, he seems not to have noticed the slight but genuine lyrical note of regret for woman's lost opportunity in Helen Cruickshank's one successful lyric, and in two or three of Marion Angus's. Nor is he surely right in 'damning' Edwin Muir, although some critics, including myself, feel that, for all his excellence, there is often a 'bookish' quality about much of Muir's poetry, as if his Muse had never had mud on its boots. Scott went on:

> But I have dwelt too long on contemporaries in a letter supposedly dealing with yourself. Perhaps my rambling will be of use if it hints a slight reference to your own work, which very occasionally smacks a little of the literary coterie I have referred to. Maybe this feeling of a certain literary complacency, in your case, comes from reading through one of the volumes at a sitting and trying on the strength of this to assess its value rather than the merit of the poems taken separately. This reading in bulk may nevertheless reveal certain weaknesses an author may himself fail to notice when he thinks of the poems as units in separate creations. Curiously enough I got more deeply interested in the Scottish Lyrics volume than in the other two — I can't exactly say why. Maybe the reason was simply that I found myself working out the poems (the lyrics, I mean) in my own way and finding in so doing that I could make alterations that look like improvements. This foible of mine has become such a habit that I seldom read a poem nowadays without immediately casting about, altering phrases, altering rhythms, re-arranging stanzas etc, all to my own complete satisfaction.

Then follows detailed criticism of the poems in English Soutar had submitted. Of Soutar's amusing 'Whigmaleeries' Scott makes his choice, adding "I found some of the other pieces rather slight and wasn't interested. Personally, I'd cut out everything in a volume that doesn't pull its weight — but tastes of course differ".

Of Soutar's lyrics in Scots, Scott complained that he found what he thought was a good deal of repetition, in the manner if not in the matter.

> The total effect of the volume is of a high standard of competence rather than of achievement. I am puzzled to find the right expression for what I mean, but the main impression left on me is of poem after poem that isn't sufficiently lyrical in manner to transform and recreate its subject matter. As I said above, with quite a number of the pieces I had a go at

improving them and invariably this was in the direction of
substituting *direct* speech for indirect, which for me means
direct thinking for indirect. I remember once upon a time
telling Jeffrey that I wasn't pleased with a lyric of his that
began 'What songs the sirens sang', because what I wanted to
hear wasn't reflections on the theme but the actual songs
themselves. Maybe this comes as near as I can get to those
weaknesses I find in some of the 'Lyrics in Scots'. To me a
lyric is before anything else a direct utterance — not a
reported utterance, no second or third hand information. The
author is (for the moment) the person speaking and he is
speaking for himself. Take 'Song', and ask yourself who is
speaking and who is being spoken to, (both stanzas finish
with question marks — they should be exclamation marks!)
. . .

Then follows further criticism.

'Scotland' . . . is one of a type I can't find much use for.
There is nothing of the trumpet call in it — it is a notion,
a bit of reflection, a 'wee think' about a great theme. That's
maybe a bit brutally stated but I've tried to get Grieve so
often to write a new 'Scots Wha Hae' and got nothing from
him that I am prejudiced against anything entitled 'Scotland'.
'Heritage' . . . is another of the same kind — I'm looking for
a poet in whose breist the stane has already broken! Ye'll all
have to go back to oratory and rhetoric! T. S. Elliot's desic-
cated finesseings have been a curse all along the line, and
as I've told Christopher time without number our present-day
poets are neither born nor made — they just make themselves, by hook or by crook. In this time of revolution and
tyrants we need nothing but the plainest of plain words —
words with a breath of a new life in them to clear the fog
from our minds — in short, a people's literature and art.
So I welcomed your Churchill poem more than any other. It
has relation to the needs of the hour — it is relevant. The
poetry of the future will, to my way of thinking, get down
(or up!) to the general heart of mankind — it will be personal
only in so far as it expresses the thoughts, aspirations and
feelings of whole masses of people who would otherwise be
inarticulate; viz., the poet will be truly the vox populi;
certainly not the masturbating perverts of the present —
they'll be the deadest of dead wood in the very near future.
And Scotland requires a very thorough overhauling too — a
reorientation in its literature — a clean sweep of all its puri-
tanical, Pharisaic, Sabbatarian, kirkified, douce, commonsense
views of life. But I am waxing lyrical — if I can influence
you, Willie, to take a hand in the business, I'll become still
more lyrical and with more reason.

Next morning, a postscript was added.

> It came into my mind this morning to ask you how you stood
> in relation to Burns — what degree of appreciation you have
> for him? To me, he is the greatest master of the 'direct
> utterance' that ever lived; the greatest lyric poet in all
> literature and soon to be the recognised greatest Communist
> poet in the world. Looking back over a lifetime of poetry
> reading, I believe his is the only reputation that has increased
> in my estimation the more I have studied his work.
>
> You can discount anything and everything Christopher Grieve
> has to say on this subject, as I myself have done long, long
> years ago — as a matter of fact, I never paid any attention to
> what he had to say about Burns — he just can't understand
> him — they are a pair of incompatibles. I have, however, no
> doubt about Burns being the true line for any Scottish poet
> to take and that Chris will in retrospect appear more or less
> like a deviation, however interesting.
>
> Burns is by far the more complete poet — in psychology, in
> a sense of the dramatic (one of Christopher's weakest points)
> and in a realisation of living as distinguished from thinking.
> I have pointed out to Chris scores of times Burns's sense of
> the comedy of manners, but so far with no resultant effect
> . . . You will readily understand how scathing I have been
> to our Communists about his and the Auden-Spender attempts
> to put the 'Manifesto' into verse; about the writing of any-
> thing like poetry for the people — aye, even the Scottish
> people. He and they just can't do anything about it. I don't
> know of a single poem that would convert even a working
> man into a Communist let alone one that would shame a local
> banker. Outside Burns, what is there? — and yet both Marx
> and Lenin were able to hail Burns as a true poet of the
> people.
>
> I had this line of thought at the back of my mind when I was
> writing my letter to you. You have the words, you have the
> skill to handle them and above all you have the *character* to
> give the requisite driving force to what you say. 'Mair the
> heart wad say' — for God's sake, why don't you say it!

It is curious to find Scott harping on so much about the
theme of workers' art. He himself had apparently planned some
'workers' songs' during the 'Thirties, but all that has survived
is one thoroughly commonplace sketch made in 1940 to verses
by Soutar. It is as if he had discovered the impossibility of

producing music for the multitude that is not 'written down',
yet failed to appreciate that the same problem is applicable to
literature.[5] In any case it is odd that he should have expected
a crippled and long bed-ridden poet to reflect a 'gutsie' quality
of life that had eluded even his deeply committed turbulently
life-involved friend, MacDiarmid.

Soutar accepted Scott's criticism, coupling it with comment
on the criticism of another sort from his friend the Reverend
James Finlayson in the entry in his Diaries for 8th September.[6]

DICHT AND DINNA BE DAMNED

(Impromptu on the G string)

Jim Finnel ca's me Pilate
(And maybe he's no far wrang),
F. G. Scott takes my bairns by the throat
And strangles maist o' their sang.

There's douceness in a douncome;
And sin friends wud work ye well,
I take the lot frae Finnel and Scott —
And hae guid hope to grow hale.

Sae let the hert by canty
Whether it flochter or fa';
And at ilka clout come up wi' a stot
Mair bouncy nor a ba'.

Souter explained in a footnote that: "In his letter today,
J.F. proclaimed that I had washed my hands, like Pilate, over
the truth that confronted me in the Pict Party Programme:
Scott's analysis of my verse has a great deal of truth in it".

That analysis, Scott had told Soutar on 2nd June, 1940,
was based on "a microscopic examination of your work, (I
always said to Christopher that I knew his poetry better than he
did himself) in the process of thinking the poems into musical
terms".

Soutar — by now to Scott "My Dear Willie" — sent the
composer *But the Earth Abideth,* on its publication in 1943,
and Scott, newly back in Glasgow from holidaying in Taynuilt,
acknowledged the gift on 2nd September, 1943.

"You won't thank me for putting on record a bunch of
felicitous phrases about my 'keen enjoyment', 'my lively interest'

H

etc., in the new work: you wouldn't expect that of me. So I'm paying you homage by giving you my reactions in detail."

Scott marked the sections of the poem of which he approved, and those of which he did not, adding: "A final query must be your adoption of the ballad stanza. I definitely think you were wrong to do so. The ballad stanza is so closely associated with narrative — its tripping metre and fragment rhythms hurry on the reading of the story, but I feel impose an unnecessary handicap on the expression of ideas. I should have preferred 'blank verse' as more suiting the argument . . . However, the batsman will have to play the ball, and I'll be mighty glad to see him perform."

Once again, it was to Soutar that Scott gave his by now rather grimly-held religious philosophy. After quoting Wordsworth's:

> The stars at midnight shall be dear
> To her and she shall lean her ear
> In many a secret place
> And beauty born of murmuring sound
> Shall pass into her face —

which Scott calls "one of the greatest verses in the language", he considers Soutar's sense of oneness with nature as expounded in *But the Earth Abideth*.

> I can see the inorganic world as God, the Father; the living moral world as Jesus Christ and the future spiritual world as the Holy Spirit; or as Saurat's 'Three Conventions' — the physical, the moral and the metaphysical, but I'm not quite sure even yet . . . how you have got there if not by a purely materialistic pathway. I am not rejecting a materialistic reading, but if the life of man is just a beginning with dust and an ending with dust, it's a mighty poor show, don't you think?, and pointless into the bargain. From the conflict of opposing forces (the dialectual) it is quite conceivable that all kinds of changes are possible in the future, but I find great difficulty in explaining to myself the 'whys and wherefores' of the changes without bringing 'purpose' into the mechanism. There is certainly little enough evidence that man is progressing (except in a 'backward' sense) from what is taking place all over the world today where there are none 'noble and wise' — Section 72 of Soutar's poem — and 'the brotherhood of men' is the fancy description for the cockpit. In other words, I accept the war and the slain in battle not as a moral conse-

quence but as an economic, and am tempted to conclude that God must certainly exist if only to get us out of the mess we have made of living. You will see from this that I'm both realist and idealist, master Facing-both-Ways in fact.

Soutar duly replied, defending himself with gay insouciance. Scott's last letter, dated 13th October, 1943, tells Soutar that "while I was doing my afternoon fire-watching in College" he came upon Soutar's poem 'Corbie' in a magazine, and "turned it into music in about ten minutes — a very successful song I think I've made of it". Apparently Scott did not continue to think so, for the song has remained unpublished (wrongly, in my view) even though at the time it seemed to the composer "unusually apt to my muse". What he wanted, he told the dying poet, was "something just odd, rather sinister, uncommon, with dramatic point to it that allows me to become vivid and adventurous . . . The only other thing of yours I've never been satisfied with is my setting of 'The Gowk', but surely you must have lots of domestic vignettes that would keep my head engaged and my imagination too?" To this Soutar could not reply. Two days later he was dead.

In that year, 1943, I had come upon *A Drunk Man Looks at the Thistle,* had been thrilled and captivated by it, and was reminded of Scott's existence by the poet's eccentric dedication to him. Eagerly I obtained the five volumes of *Scottish Lyrics,* which proved to be as much of a musical revelation as the discovery of MacDiarmid's masterpiece had been a poetic one. As an apprentice Staff Officer stationed in East Anglia, I had begun broadcasting occasionally in Alec Robertson's BBC programme on Sunday mornings — 'Forces Music Magazine'. After a spell at Camberley, I went to the War Office in London, where I remained until I was demobilised in March, 1946, spending the first eighteen months of that time in the musical ménage at St. John's Wood run by the BBC's then senior accompanist, John Wills, where Alec Robertson was also a resident. The reactions of these two, and of the Scottish soprano Noel Eadie, another resident (but then on the verge of retirement), to Scott's songs was sufficiently enthusiastic to convince me that my views on the value of the music had not been misplaced.

Eric Blom, then editor of the publication *Music and Letters,* accepted an article from me about Scott's songs. It appeared in

January 1945. Six months later, just before the re-introduction of
the Scottish Home Service after the end of the European war,
I presented an extended illustrated item in the London-
broadcast 'Music Magazine' for June 22nd, an exposure to a
mainly English audience against which the newly appointed
Scottish Programme Controller, Andrew Stewart, protested, on
the grounds that such Scottish material would in due course
be broadcast from Scotland when the Scottish Home Service
was re-opened. His objection, incredulously received, was
ignored.

Several months before, seeking help with both these projects,
I had written to the composer. On 18th May, 1944 he replied,
welcoming my intentions, but revealing his by now well-
developed feelings of mistrust and frustration.

> I think you ought to know something about the feuds that
> lie behind the musical life of London. Sorabji is of course
> at war with most of the coteries and especially the Willie
> Walton, Constant Lambert, Cecil Gray, Michael Ayrton gang
> . . .

Scott had enthusiastically praised Walton's String Quartet
when he heard it in Salzburg in 1923, and had received an
adulatory letter from the youthful Ayrton some time before.
Gray, an expatriate Scot, had apparently half promised to do
something about Scott's work, suggesting getting "singers who
could sing"; but nothing happened. Scott concludes:

> I mention this merely for your own guidance by way of
> showing that there is a considerable number of folk in London
> quite aware of my existence who for reasons of their own
> have preferred to keep quiet and say nought.

> And this to me is a very good reason why I am delighted and
> thankful that you are doing the review, that you are outside
> the petty animosities of the various sets in London and not
> interested in anything besides the music being discussed . . .
> it's just on 3 a.m.

When next on leave in Glasgow, I rang to ask if I could
call on him, and there followed an experience that was often
to be repeated over the next twelve or so years. From that first
meeting I was enormously drawn to him, not so much for his
views on music as for his sheer impact as a person and his

astonishing powers as a literary critic; powers, incidentally, not at all evident in his own early verses, and which he would sometimes wickedly misapply when talking about a poet whose work was for him 'unsettable'. He deplored the way in which poetry, thanks to Eliot, had become casual, without drama, much of it about everyday things. Yet confronted with a set of new verses, his comments were invariably penetrating. I soon got into the way of showing him all my own work, then couched in Lallans which for about five years seemed to me (wrongly, as I now think) an essential ingredient of any continuing Scottish Renaissance. Very little of what I showed to Scott in those days has found its way into my *Collected Poems*. Indeed, even the one poem of mine he set, 'Luve of Alba', has not. Towards the end of the period when I was seeing him fairly frequently, he expressed interest in my "Bairnsangs", but by then he was composing very little, and it was in fact Thea Musgrave who successfully set them.

There was an enthusiasm, intensity and integrity about Scott's criticism that made the harshest strictures acceptable. He did, however, have an inability to understand the position of the poet in the modern world aware of the fragmentation of traditional values and conscious of the need to reflect this aspect of the human dilemma. He was thus insensitive to the work of such writers as Eliot, and even to some extent to that of his nephew by marriage, George Bruce.

Scott's judgments on other composers seemed less detached and therefore less interesting than his views on poets, although I shared his sense of unease about aspects of Britten's emotional alignment, and indeed have never altered my partially mistrustful view. While Scott had no words warm enough for a passage he wanted to illustrate by Mozart or Schubert — "marvellous", he would exclaim: "the man can do anything" — I disagreed with his complete dismissal of Vaughan Williams, his mockery of Walton, and his contempt for the "shapelessness" of Bax's music. However, when he wanted to demonstrate a new song of his own, he would magnetize you over the piano. By then his playing was only barely adequate and his voice weak; but in a kind of half-croon he somehow managed to convey the essential imaginative quality of what he had just set down on paper. When he first played and 'soughed' his way through his setting of the ballad 'Edward', composed in 1943 but the subject of alterations and amendments for another year. I ventured to suggest that the long piano coda of twenty-two bars after the singer's last despairing cry was something of an emotional letdown. I received a lecture on the proportions of Greek tragedy and the psychological need for so powerful a climax to be gently unwound. Whenever this song has been performed in public, either in the original version or in its orchestrated form made soon afterwards at the request of the tenor John Tainsh, this unsatisfactory coda has attracted adversely the attention of critics.

Another new friend of the early 'Forties was the sculptor Benno Schotz, who first encountered Scott at a Glasgow poetry reading. He was to model the composer's head three times. Later, he described his subject as having ". . . a leonine head. A big full head, sweeping backwards, and surrounded with a halo of white, magnetised hair, I would say that he has a sharp, sensitive nose, full but firm mouth, a round chin, not too large; but above all one is struck by his eyes. They are fierce and full of fire, and at the same time they have a great intensity. They have a fanatical fervour yet they have a great intensity. They have a fanatical power, yet they are kindly and smiling — even, you might say, mischievous eyes".

That mischievousness was soon to lead Scott into a controversy not without value in the outcome, but in which he overplayed his hand.

On 16th August, 1943, Dr Henry G. Farmer, who earned his living conducting the Empire Variety Theatre Orchestra in Glasgow but was also the learned author of a number of books and pamphlets, including a *History of Scottish Music* (strong in matters of fact but decidedly weak on value judgment), published a letter in the *Glasgow Herald* complaining about what he considered to be bad programme-building at a recent BBC Scottish Orchestra concert in Glasgow Art Galleries. He asked:

> Why cannot the BBC Scottish Orchestra steer clear of ground already well covered . . . and seek fresh pastures? There is still the field of Scottish music, which is already well sown and needs only sympathetic cultivation.

> When did one last hear the works of W. V. Wallace, the composer of 'Maritana'? Look at the whole series of the

works by that later William Wallace, which have been heard only in London. How many of the little-known compositions of Mackenzie are still awaiting audition? Why cannot we have an occasional item by the rarely heard Thomas A. Erskine, the sixth Earl of Kellie? Could not room be found, just once in a while, for a work by Hamish MacCunn, Learmont Drysdale, McEwen, or Charles Macpherson?

What makes the neglect all the more palpable is that the chief reason for the establishment of the BBC Scottish Orchestra was to remedy this acknowledged neglect of Scottish composers. I can say this with some authority, since I was the prime mover in its formation.

Writing from his holiday address at Taynuilt, Scott leant his support to Farmer, but widened the area of conflict.

At the present time . . . it is almost impossible for any Scottish composer to hear a single performance of any of his orchestral works. Dr Farmer's letters refers to only one programme of the BBC Scottish Orchestra. I wonder what he would say about fifteen programmes published in three issues of the *Radio Times* (August 1-21) . . . These embrace 58 orchestral items; not one of them is by a living Scotsman; one item is by MacCunn (conductor, Guy Warrack) and another by Mackenzie (conductor, Clarence Raybould) . . .

If it be thought unfair to select evidence from only three issues of the *Radio Times* I would ask anyone sufficiently interested to examine the files of that journal not only for three weeks but for three months — or for three years — and tell me if in his opinion the BBC Scottish Orchestra has fulfilled the chief reason for its establishment — i.e. 'to remedy the acknowledged neglect of Scottish composers'.

Scott ended by enquiring: "Who is responsible for the programmes?".

Other correspondents joined in, some hostile, some irrelevant. Kenneth G. Finlay (3rd September) added:

A perusal of the BBC Year Book for 1943 is instructive (and, for a Scots musician, depressing). In the section entitled 'Wales' first place is given to an account of the visit of Sir Adrian Boult and the BBC Symphony Orchestra.

At one concert a number of works by Welsh composers was played, the reception was enthusiastic, and in the mining area, especially Aberdare and Treorchy, was almost overwhelming

. . . Under the heading 'Scotland', apart from an allusion to pipe bands and to 'martial music', the only music-makings recorded are those of the BBC Scottish Orchestra.

On 21st September, Dr W. B. Moonie joined in:

Many of the most precious things in life would be utterly ignored by the public if they were not carefully and sedulously pointed out by those whose duty it is to instruct them in matters of which it is to their advantage to be cognisant.

It appears to me that the BBC is placed in just such a position of responsibility — that of instructing the public in things they ought to know about. And one of the things the Scottish public should get a chance of knowing about is surely the work of their own native composers. It is just a trifle fantastic that Scotland should possess a BBC Orchestra which plays not more than one original Scottish work a year, if it even does as much as that . . .

On 9th October, Scott wrote to the head of the BBC in Scotland, Melville Dinwiddie, drawing attention to the more important published letters in the controversy and at the same time, by way of protest, declining to "accept an engagement . . . for a performance due on Monday 11th October as set forth in the *Radio Times*".

Dinwiddie replied on 21st October:

Our policy is still to broadcast new works of merit. The BBC submits all new work to a Panel for its judgement. The members of this Panel are not on the BBC Staff, and have no contact with staff programme planners. Our choice of new works — by Scots as well as other composers — is therefore governed by a desire to represent living composers, and is subject to the findings of the Music Panel, as to the merit of the composition. I am glad to say that since the war began, works by Scottish composers have continued to find a place in our programmes.

This admission that a 'Panel' had been constituted, although the pre-war Music Advisory Committee had been disbanded, and Dinwiddie's rather naive attempt to defuse the issue by confusing old and new works, provoked Scott to further attack on 3rd November:

When was the Panel instituted? Who are its members? Is

there a Scotsman on it? How often has it met? . . . After examining copies of the *Radio Times* between 18th July and 30th October, I believe that I am right in saying that the only contemporary Scottish contributions to orchestral programmes between the dates were made by members of the BBC Staff in Scotland . . . Your Musical Director has for years past made so many contributions to Scottish programmes that he is not likely to suffer unduly whatever the findings of the Panel may be about the new compositions.

It was, indeed, the case that Ian Whyte, in the double position of being in charge both of BBC Music in Scotland and conductor of the BBC Scottish Orchestra, was the most frequently performed of Scottish composers. Shortly after the end of the war the two posts were separated, Whyte retaining control of the Orchestra.

Dinwiddie and Whyte convened a meeting of the composers, led by Scott, at Broadcasting House. According to one of those present, Scott became angry and alienated some of his own colleagues by the ferocity with which he pursued personalities. Nevertheless, the outcome was a gradual increase in the number of performances by Scottish composers thereafter, even if to this day historical perspective is still rather neglected. The energy with which Scott threw himself into the struggle undoubtedly served to remind the BBC of its unfulfilled responsibilities.

While this row was being brought to the boil, Scott launched another project. Writing from Taynuilt on 8th August, he proposed to MacDiarmid a private edition in collaboration with Johnstone and himself; "a three-pronged volume of poetry, painting and music" which would contain six to ten of Mac-Diarmid's lyrics.

There was, however, one awkwardness to be overcome. "The question of whether your lyrics would be new ones or old is a most ticklish point to settle — it being problematical whether either you or I could produce to order either 10 or even 6 items to rival our very best." Nothing came of the project, no doubt partly because of war-time difficulties in securing fine printing.

Public performances of Scott's own music were curtailed because of the conditions of war. A London concert had been organised by Saurat in 1942, at which Scott first met Michael

Ayrton. Ayrton, then 21, next day wrote enthusiastically to
Scott.

> In spite of my discomfort being thick with the cold last
> evening, I was very greatly excited by your songs, and I want
> to write this note to thank you for the experience. Even with
> clotted cheek-bones and bubble eyes, conditions none too good
> for hearing music except perhaps by young English composers,
> I felt keenly the vital quality which you so rightly compare
> with the songs of Moussorgsky.
>
> I returned home, slab and fubsy, mumbling Hum-di-hi-dri-
> ho-dri through the mucus.
>
> You have certainly given me something to think about. I
> am at the moment looking through the score of 'Pierrot
> Lunaire'. Schönberg seems to me, in a somewhat moribund
> way, to have got something of quantitive setting in parts like
> 'Die Heiligen Kreutzen'. But then I am most ignorant of the
> business and may be barking up the wrong tree. Anyway
> again, thanks, and I greatly hope that we shall soon meet
> again.

At the top of the page he squeezed in a postscript:

> Aside from some of the intellectual patter I seem to have
> written below, I thought the songs like the one about Finlay
> and Minni (I do not remember the exact titles) very good
> stuff, causing laughter from the belly — not like our young
> English sterile ingenuity (quotations from Rossini, etc.) and
> orchestral witticisms.

Ayrton and Scott did meet again, when Ayrton called at
44 Munro Road. By this time, however, Scott had come to pin
his hopes on anyone who responded to his own enthusiasms,
believing that they would "do something" to further knowledge
of his songs. Ayrton apparently did nothing, which presumably
led to his being classed with Cecil Gray as part of the despised
"London clique" in the Autobiographical Letter.

On 19th June, 1949, at the Institut Français du Royaume
Uni in South Kensington, London, Saurat arranged another
recital, a "Concert Spécial Franco-Ecossais", at which Helen
Sandeman and William G. Noble, accompanied by Noble's sister,
Agnes, performed twenty-four songs — ten Burns settings, four
of the Dunbar songs, three of the MacDiarmid settings and

three to words by Amy Sylvel among them. The composer travelled to London to introduce his own music. The anonymous critic of the *Daily Telegraph* wrote:

> I was much impressed by the attractive music Mr Scott had given to all these songs. He has an unfailing sense of the fitness of the music for the words . . . How is it that we hear so little of this gifted composer? It is odd, too, that it should be the French Institute, mainly through Professor Saurat, who should be the first to introduce him to London.

A recital in Glasgow's Stevenson Hall in December, 1944, also received warm reviews, although R. E. Anderson in the *Evening Times* strongly objected to the long concluding piano ritornello at the end of 'Edward', then receiving its first public performance in the city.

Scott's continuing interest in Gaelic had led him to begin a correspondence course in the language with the Sgoil Eolais na h-Alba, a course interrupted by the outbreak of the war. He resumed his studies in October, 1944, and carried through twenty-four lessons until July, 1945. His tutor was the Reverend John MacKechnie, and Scott's working papers are preserved in his archive in the Mitchell Library, Glasgow.

Scott also seems to have given several public lectures about this time. In the Autumn of 1944, at the British Council's Czech House in Edinburgh, the Warden of which was then Edwin Muir; and at Glasgow and Edinburgh Universities, where he lectured on 'France and Britain: Parallels and Contrasts' on 7th and 8th December of that year. This lecture reflects the low ebb to which the reputation of Elgar had then temporarily sunk. Scott comparing the "self-taught" Englishman unfavourably with the learned and sophisticated Fauré.

The supporters of Czech House heard Scott talk about 'The Music of Words'. One of his arguments reinforces the views of those who defend the singing of opera in the original language:

> Speech pattern related to music pattern implies that different languages will give rise to different kinds of music.

His knowledge of poetry was also much in evidence:

> We have all heard or read about poets, quite considerable ones

too, who had no ear for music, and of others, like Swinburne, who wrote so musical a language that it was just bad poetry.

Again, on the impact of speech as opposed to the written word, he said of 'pen-friends':

> Why do we know more about them after five minutes of conversation than after five years of letter-writing? If the poet said — 'Speech was given us to conceal our thoughts', he must surely have been confusing it with language as written and used. Isn't every letter we write more or less an evasion? And what a crowd of misunderstandings even a straightforward letter can bring about. But when a person speaks it is with difficulty that he conceals his meaning, for the slightest shade of tone can betray him. 'It wasn't so much *what* she said as the *way* she said it'.

Scott then went on to illustrate his point with a story he was fond of telling, about "the French Lady of fashion who, when her daughter's education had finished, began preparing her for entering into high Society by teaching her the use of two words, 'Oui, Monsieur'. With the correct inflection of these words, the young lady was told, she would be able to meet with assurance any and every situation likely to arise. When you have worked out the possible number of inflections the young lady had to learn," Scott told his audience, "you'll know more about the subject than I do! In the light of this, it is no wonder that Frenchwomen are generally regarded as amongst the most intelligent in the world."

When Scott was in the process of forming his style during and after the 1914/18 war, he often quoted Manuel de Falla[7]:

> Moussorgsky was the true initiator of the new era in music; and thanks to him, Rimsky-Korsakov, Balakiref and Borodin, the melodic forms and ancient scales that, despised by composers, had taken refuge in the church and the people, were restored to musical art . . . It is a widespread error, the belief that modernity in music depends on a prodigality of harmonic dissonances. This is to such an extent untrue that I make bold to declare that the modern spirit in music can subsist in a work in which only consonant chords are used, and what is more in music consisting only of an undulating melodic line . . .

Lecturing on 'The Melodic Art of Scotland', also during the 'Forties, Scott said:

> The Scots are essentially a melodic people that have never quite succumbed to the rule of harmony and have remained outwith the great harmonic evolution that has taken place in Italy, Germany, France, England and elsewhere during the last three centuries . . . We are not only a melodic people, but we are the greatest melodic people that have existed, for with us the melodic tradition has persisted longer and in a purer form than anywhere else in Europe. The basis of all Scottish melody, whether in the north or the south, is the pentatonic scale of five notes, represented by the five black notes on the piano. It is the most ancient of scales . . . One might almost call it the ur-motiv of the world's music.

Scott's *Seven Songs for Baritone Voice* was published in 1946 by Bayley and Ferguson. Two of the songs are of a light nature, the decidedly banal setting of Burns's poem 'Macpherson's Farewell' and 'The Cameronian Cat', a somewhat laboured joke (complete with Wagnerian quotation) to a set of psalm-tune nonsense-words devised when it was thought profane for choirs to rehearse scriptural words. These songs seem to represent an attempt to secure a wider popularity than the serious songs had up until then achieved.

There are two Hay songs in the collection, both master-pieces of simplicity and effectiveness. 'The Old Fisherman' is set strophically to the simplest of slow airs, the accompaniment supporting it with arpeggiated chords suggesting the sweep of the clarsach. Incidentally, the beautiful image 'My dancing days for fishing are over' is an echo of a similar phrase to be found in Hay's father's novel, *Gilespie*. The other Hay song, 'The Kerry Shore', is a happy example of Scott at his melodic best; a spontaneous vocal gem evocative of the scene the words describe.

As in the Hay songs, MacDiarmid's 'Reid E'en' — according to tradition, the one night in the year, in November, when harts and hinds mate — is a folk-like melody distinguished by the clarity of its accompaniment. The Burns setting 'Gane is the Day', though not one of Scott's most inventive, might easily be mistaken for a straightforward folk-tune were it not for the composer's accompaniment. The remaining song, a 1940 setting of Soutar's poem 'In time of Tumult', is a pictorial mood-miniature, matching the evocative purpose of the words.

The appearance of *Seven Songs for Baritone Voice* coincided with the year of Scott's retirement from Jordanhill College.

"I have sometimes wondered", he said in a farewell address to his colleagues, "why 'teaching' should be singled out as a 'calling', a 'vocation', and instinctively feel there must be a catch somewhere when we use the term. I might, for example, have chosen to have become a Doctor or a Minister without necessarily acquiring a special birth-certificate. Personally, I am convinced I was really never born at all, but was 'untimely ripped' into the teaching profession when I signed a document called an indenture.

Like the aged French comtesse, the really pleasant memories I have of the distant past are those of my youthful indiscretions."

He then recalled his rows with 'Moses' Patterson when a student at Moray house — the threatened expulsion, and the docking of part of his salary for failing to attend the voluntary Friday class.

> Such are a few of my training college memories. For the succeeding twenty years I'd have been ready to wager I would never again see the inside of such a place. Yet here I am today with over twenty years of Jordanhill College behind me. So far I haven't heard a word about expulsion — I have been retained for a year and a half beyond my date of retiral. I can now claim to have been 'never absent' when I should have been present, and instead of forfeiting money by abstaining from voluntary Friday morning meetings, I am actually being given *money* on taking my departure.

> Today therefore I want to thank . . . all of you for making my second experience of a training college such a happy one. I have enjoyed myself here and although I nowadays sometimes think 60 years of education about ten times too much of the same kind of thing, I must be honest with myself and admit 'je n'ai pas de regrets', which is just the same as saying 'I'm as happy today as ever I was'.

Now at last he was a free man, able to devote as much of his time he wanted to composition, though in his sixty-seventh year. Recitals and broadcasts within Scotland were multiplying, and the old carping had disappeared from the reviews of the new gerenation of Scottish critics. Ian Whyte at the BBC had to some extent given way after the wartime onslaught, conducting the first public performance of *The Seven Deidly Sins* on 6th June, 1946. It was to receive a second performance in 1954 under the young conducter Alexander Gibson.

Other encouragement followed. Scott was represented at the 1948 and 1949 Edinburgh Festivals, and critics from London gave his songs high praise. After the 1948 concert, even the *Glasgow Herald* opined that: "The songs of Francis George Scott made a deep impression. Some of them are more familiar to concert goers, but this was their first full-dress hearing." And there was special praise for the soprano, Joan Alexander. Along with Margaret Sandeman, William G. Noble and John Tainsh she had proved one of the composer's most loyal and musically gifted advocates over the years.

She was also to be the singer at a Sunday night concert organised by the *Scottish Daily Mail,* unofficially marking the end of the 1951 Festival. Scott's songs drew the attention of the *Mail's* London critic, Ralph Hill, a somewhat pugilistic writer who had dismissed *The Seven Deidly Sins* as "not worth a moment" of his attention, but thought the songs of major importance. Scott Goddard, the more sophisticated critic of *The News Chronicle* wrote:

> A relatively small item, but the most significant, consisted of some songs by George Scott, admirably sung by Joan Alexander, they had an authentic note of more character than anything I heard during the evening.

> For a moment Scottish emotion and European culture were linked together, and the way seemed free for larger development of the music of this northern country.

Many of the recitals of Scott's music in Scotland were presented by the Saltire Society, a body that came into being in 1936 with the avowed aim of furthering the interests of Scotland's culture. For the next quarter of a century or so it achieved outstanding success in drawing attention to the qualities of traditional architecture and the merits of the best of the new; in providing texts through selected editions of older Scottish poetry and prose at a time when these were not available on the open market; publicly advocating the teaching of Scottish literature in schools and universities; and by encouraging Scottish composers and music. A measure of the success of its pioneering efforts in the early days is the vastly improved state of all these concerns half a century later.

In 1946 I became associated with the publishing activities of the Society, and at once set about organising the appearance of a major selection of Scott's hitherto unpublished songs, for the first time not at the composer's expense. A generous grant was secured from the Cross Trust, and in 1949 *Songs: Thirty-Five Scottish Lyrics and Other Poems* by Francis George Scott came out. The Scottish Arts Council, not then supporters of publishing ventures, sponsored recitals of all the songs in the collection in Glasgow, Edinburgh, Ayr and other centres. Press notices were highly favourable. At last Scott seemed to be coming into his own.

But while the negotiations for the publication for this new collection were being conducted — Scott was invited to include all the unpublished songs he wished preserved — his hopes were to be raised and dashed in what must have seemed potentially the most important break-through of his career.

In 1947 the Sadlers Wells Ballet (now the Royal Ballet) at Covent Garden were invited to prepare a Scottish ballet for the second Edinburgh International Festival. Leonide Massine was to be the choreographer. Scott was approached with a view to his providing a score using traditional Scots airs. In December 1947 he went to London to examine the project in detail with Massine.

Two pencil-written letter-cards to his wife chronicled the progress of the negotiations, the first headed 'Wednesday at 4 p.m."

> I have received the *Seven Deidly Sins* full-score and this morning the orchestral parts. About mid-day I sent off a wire for the *synopsis of the ballet* (which I think will be found inside the other full-score). . . The reason for all this 'to-do' about the *Seven Deidly Sins* is that the Committee of Covent Garden, which includes the two Principal Conductors there, want to see if I am a suitable person to write music for the Massine Ballet (Gaelic in story) for the Edinburgh Festival. Massine is very friendly with me and I'm sure he would support my claim. Tonight I am meeting him at 8 o'clock at the Sadlers Wells School of Dancing, W.14, where he is going to practice the various Highland Steps. Tomorrow I am to meet him at 2.30 (his secretary phoned up today) and he'll run me up to Oxford Street to continue our hunt for the best

Highland records. She said I could go any night to Covent Garden. Ella (Saurat) was there with me on Monday — Box B in the Grand Tier — looking right into the stage and orchestra pit: a staff box which Massine said I should use at any time. He suggested having the orchestra to play the 7 Sinnis but that's going to be difficult for timing. I'm going to propose to him to forget about his own Gaelic idea and stage the 7 Deidly Sinnis. He'll get a shock!

'Thursday night at midnight' is the heading on the second letter-card.

I have spent all the afternoon at Duncan Morrison's house with Massine listening to the tunes (all Gaelic) which are being selected for the Edinburgh Festival Ballet. Morrison has picked out a large number to select from and appropriate choice was made for the story to form the basis of the ballet. The situation at the moment is that SCOTT is to weld all this material into a unity like de Falla's *3-Cornered Hat* and I am doing the ballet *if* the Covent Garden Committee give the word. To help them come to a decision in the matter I'm taking in 7 Sins score to Covent Garden tomorrow at 11 a.m. to meet the conductor of the orchestra David Webster,[8] and there may even be a try-over with the orchestra, but this will be difficult as the band is playing for opera and ballet on alternate nights, all requiring rehearsal, so the final decision must wait.

I'm visiting Sorabji for tea at 3 o'clock, also tomorrow. Meeting again at Morrison's home on Saturday. Taking Ella or Cecile[9] to the ballet either afternoon matinee or at night, and returning I hope on Sunday (maybe). I'm naturally very familiar with Massine by now, having driven about in his car all over the place and discussed his Stravinsky, Brahms symphonic ballet (choreartium) etc., etc., and how he and de Falla made the 3-Cornered Hat in Spain. I think we understand each other and I've even discussed with him the possibilities of my 7 Sins. *Rejoice* but remember the decision isn't with him.

Unfortunately, it was not. The Committee apparently took a decision against the project, although no reference to it was recorded in the minutes. The project was shelved, and the first Scottish ballet to be produced at Covent Garden in modern times became Ian Whyte's *Donald o' the Burthens* (1951), which at one point introduced bag-pipes to the orchestral score.

It might reasonably be wondered if a composer who had

I

only ever made one tiny arrangement[10] during his whole career and was not at his ease in handling an orchestra, would in fact have been the right person to realise Massine's idea. Nevertheless, Scott's disappointment was understandably considerable, though he managed to put a brave face on it before younger friends like myself.

There were still to be some consolations. The London publisher Max Hinrichsen, who had subscribed to the Saltire volume, at once wrote to Scott enquiring if he had any other songs available for publication. Scott's reply has not survived, but Hinrichsen's answer to it has. Dated 25th February, 1948, Hinrichsen said:

> I am very pleased to hear that, if not a regular publisher, at least the Saltire Society is taking some interest in your work. The date of the subscription leaflet shows that I 'woke up' about a year too late.
>
> From all I have heard and read about you — the last was the article by Ralph Hill and the first was from Dr Farmer — I came to the conclusion that you are a composer. This profession seems to be almost extinct today. Of course there are lots of people who write music, and who get their music published, but that does not mean that they are composers.
>
> My father was the publisher of contemporaneous composers: Greig, Hugo Wolf, Sinding and Moskowski. I have at present one composer, Inglis Gundry, in my catalogue and so there is some scope for another. But how can that be achieved that will bring us together? According to your very frank letter — I am most grateful for your frankness — your very best songs are included in the Saltire Society volume. I don't know anything of the other songs which you published at your own expense. Could you enlighten me as to what was published, how many copies were printed, how many sold, and whether there were any performances or broadcasts, and what are the names of the musicians (and others who have shown and who are showing interest in you)?
>
> And further, I would be glad if you would advise me what other compositions you have written. From the leaflet I learned about works for orchestra, etc.
>
> Of course you don't need to answer all these questions, but that I put them to you will show you that I am enquiring not just for the sake of curiosity but because I am really

interested in the work of a composer. It is too bad that I did not meet you when I was in Glasgow last month. We could have settled so many questions in an hour.

Dr Farmer probably has spoken to you about my qualifications. In short: Managing Director (and part owner) of Peters Edition from 1927-1937; removed to England 1937; started Hinrichsen Edition 1st March, 1938; war-work with London Regional Committee for Education among H.M. Forces; Naturalised early this year. In case you can envisage collaboration between us, I would be pleased if you would let me have some more particulars and perhaps also those works which you think would be the best to publish first.

The offer of a London publisher came too late, for Scott was by then bound by contract to Bayley and Ferguson and to the Saltire Society.

Another consolation must have been the letter he received, dated 8th May, 1948, from Carmen Weingartner-Studer. She had spent an evening in London with the Johnston's, and they had shown her some of Scott's songs. From the Hotel Rembrandt, she wrote:

I heard about your compositions and I was able to glance roughly at some of your songs which I found very interesting. I am myself a conductor and the widow and pupil of the conductor, Felix Weingartner, whose name may be familiar to you, and so you will understand that I take the liberty of writing to you. I am looking forward to my return to London in the autumn to see more of your compositions.

Almost at the same time another female musician, Isobel V. I. Dunlop, a kindly, cultured lady of independent means who did much to help young Scottish musicians and was herself an amateur composer, sent Scott some of her work for criticism. Evidently he wrote in a gentle way, for she acknowledged his advice on 16th May, thanking him "so very warmly for your kind and encouraging letter. Your appreciation really does give me fresh courage to go on from 'here' — I do feel very aware of my lack of technique, but that can be learned . . . I value your letter above all others".

Scott must have derived great enjoyment from the acquaintanship struck up with the witty and many-talented Professor Sir Alexander Gray, whose re-creations in Scots of German and other folk-songs could well have stimulated Scott's musical enthusiasms had he discovered them earlier. As it was, he indicated to the poet that he wanted to set 'The Deil o' Bogie'. Gray immediately agreed. Some discussion followed as to the stress-value of two of the words, and in response to Scott's queries, Gray sent him a typically erudite and witty reply. Like all Sir Alexander's communications, when it came through Scott's letter box on the last day of October, 1948, it was contained in a re-used old envelope addressed on the reverse side, an economy the poet habitually practised. Wrote Gray:

> If this letter sounds brief and snappy, like the replies to an enquiry from the Income Tax authorities, it is because I should like to get it into the pillar-box as soon as possible so that you may get it tomorrow morning.

> (1) 'oure' or 'ower' has set me thinking! Throwing my mind back, and listening in imagination to my mother and my multitude of aunts, it is more a disyllable than a monosyllable. But in truth, it is rather a syllable and a half, if such a monstrosity is permissable. It approximates to a semi-quartered dipthong. And thinking round this, there are quite a number of words which may (in Scots) be printed as monosyllables, but which, in fact, almost require to be regarded as two-syllabled . . . In the 'Deil' 'ower' certainly is longer than one syllable.

> (2) You are quite right about 'By God'! The emphasis is all on 'God', and the 'by' is cut down almost to the point of extinction. Indeed I am inclined to think that my villagers usually omitted the 'by' altogether. What they said was 'God' with a very long 'o'. It occurs to me — I have never thought of it before — that possibly 'God' had a somewhat different pronounciation in the Church from what it had as a swear word! The parsons and the elders (in their official capacities) said something like 'Gawd'. The man at Dunnichen (a blatant outsider) said something like 'the Lurd Gud'. But in the public bar and mucking out the byre, they said God, with a very pronounced Greek Omega, not an Omicron. Memories of the Greek classroom 50 years ago!

> (3) Yes, certainly 'Alexander Gray' is good enough. It is what one naturally puts in the title-page of a book; and when one is privileged to mix with the world's elect, the poets and the musicians, these excresences are as well left outside.

He added a postscript:

> My regards to the 'Deil', and congratulations to him for having got so far.

The song, marked 'nicht schleppen!', was soon completed. It was to be the last really outstanding song the composer wrote, and it carried into music the traditional Scots good-humoured familiarity with the Devil. The tune swaggers along confidently, while the changing emotional states of the young man with matrimonial troubles are matched by the accompaniment — a suggestion of churchiness at the reference to the prayer to the Devil; the clip-clop of the yoked mare harnessed to the dung cart; triplet agitation as the man remembers how his first wife plagued him; and the more elaborate variation used to depict the 'lound'rin' so soon meted out to him by his new second wife. When Gray first heard it at an Edinburgh Saltire Society Recital, he wrote on 27th January, 1950:

> I congratulate you on your 70th birthday and (contrary to the usual practice whereby birthday celebrations receive rather than give) the excellent entertainmnt which the maker of music gave to those who attended from afar. I greatly enjoyed the whole of the song recital; though perhaps, quite naturally I was especially interested in my step-son, the De'il o' Bogie. I was very proud indeed to be connected with the programme, even if in a minor capacity.

The Saltire volume contains many of Scott's finest songs, the earliest dated 1916, the latest 1948. Of the seven MacDiarmid settings 'Hungry Waters' was written in 1925 and belongs, with 'Country Life', — also in the volume — to Scott's 'bi-planal' settings. 'The Innumerable Christ', with its use of a C pedal point and its restless chromaticism, matches the poet's extra-terrestial vision. Here, too, is that vigorous song 'The Sauchs in the Reuch Heuch Hauch'. Scott was particularly fond of playing over this song, about the toughness of the dockens in a well known Hawick spot. He would then tell his listeners that he once had "a grandfather who was a miller in the Reuch Heuch Hauch".

'Edward' is in the collection, complete with the postlude that seemed such an error of judgment to many critics, but which the composer resolutely refused to alter. There are groups of French and German songs, demonstrating the ability of the composer to match the mood of a poet without sacrificing his own musical identity. Hay's 'Alba' has a robustness not inappropriate to the text, while the composer's setting of some lines of my own, 'Luve of Alba', in which identity with Scotland is compared to the unifying experience of physical love between man and woman, has an accompaniment again suggestive of the clarsach. There are also several infectious folk-like Burns settings — 'Robin Shure in Hairst', rightly a popular song — 'O steer her up' and 'Landlady, Count the Lawin', the last, a remarkable musical evocation of the release brought about by semi-drunkenness, surprising perhaps from one as temperate as Scott in real life.

The great songs, two or three of the MacDiarmid settings apart, are Burns's 'O Wert thou in the Cauld Blast', Soutar's 'The Tryst', Dunbar's 'To a Lady', (already discussed) the ballad, 'The Twa Corbies', and two songs remarkable for their direct lyricism, settings of MacDiarmid's 'First Love' and Thomas Campbell's 'Florine'. There is also a very beautiful setting of the Scots version of Luther's 'Ane Sang of the Birth of Christ' from *The Gude and Godly Ballads,* a kind of domesticated companion-piece to 'Rorate Coeli'.

Scott was impressed by the drama inherent in Burns's lyric 'O, Wert thou in the Cauld Blast', written to Jessy Lewars when she was nursing him on his death bed. In a conversation, preserved by chance by the BBC,[11] while they were preparing to record a performance of the song by John Tainsh, Scott's bursting enthusiasm as he explained his intentions, is evident. He illustrated his points by soughing over phrases of the song.

> By God! I remember what that was about. I remember how I wrote that . . I always thought that the poem was highly dramatic, because it's merely an evasion of the terrible plight Burns was in. It's an evasion on his part in using this, 'O, Wert thou in the Cauld Blast/On Yonder lea, on yonder lea/ My plaidie to the angry blast/I'd shelter thee, I'd shelter thee'. There's not a word about him at all. You see, the man was in such a desperate condition that it was impossible for him to continue living much longer. And that's why I've put it into the form I did. It's the drama behind it.

All of this was interspersed with bouts of singing. Then Scott sang on:

> 'Or did misfortunes storms/Around thee blaw, around thee blaw',/Thy bield should be my bosom,/To share it a', to share it a',/He's giving her that. That's all he has. That's all he

can give her. There's nothing else to give. He's avoiding his
own situation in order to try and explain hers, and say that
he still loves her.

Burns intended his verses to go to a slowed-up version of
the Strathspey tune 'Lennox love to Blantyre' (Ex. 16) Scott's

melody has obvious kinship with it (Ex. 17). The song does,

indeed, rise to an ardent climax when it moves into the major
key, and is throughout animated by a moving pathos.

Soutar's 'The Tryst', one of his finest lyrics, depicts the
embodiment of physical desire and its dream-like departure,
taking with it the bed-ridden poet's 'Simmer days/Like they had
never been'. The imaginary nature of the poet's dream-
substitute for physical love is matched by the melancholy modal
air, and the suggestion of a heart-beat at the climax (Ex. 18).

There is such an inevitability about the rhythm to which
Scott set the words that, intense as they are in themselves, the
music raises them even further above their ballad four-
squareness.

Scott maintained that 'The Twa Corbies' was a dialogue

between a male and a female crow, the female and crueller bird being concerned with eating and lining the nest. The ballad's depiction of the utter indifference of Nature to quarrelsome man is atmospherically caught, and the bleak vision of eternity, with its aimlessly shifting winds, is held throughout the last dozen bars or so, an unforgetable imaginative stroke.

Of the MacDiarmid settings in the volume, 'The Innumerable Christ' and 'Lourd on my Hert', though by no means without interest and worth, do not 'push through' as do Scott's settings of the half-dozen great MacDiarmid lyrics. They are content to reflect literal meanings rather than recreate them in purely musical terms. 'First Love', on the other hand, matches MacDiarmid's rather Hardy-like lyric with unpretentious pictorial skill, the D pedal-point suggesting the poet's stay in the garden 'all the long day', the high register arpeggios catching the falling light from 'the hard green apples', with the wind in the orchard springing up to arpeggiated octaves opening out to triplets, with rising and falling arpeggiated chromatic chords suggesting the 'fog and cold'. To pull apart the ingredients of so delightful and inevitable a song is perhaps rather like Keat's accusation that philosophy 'would clip an angel's wings/ Unweave a rainbow'. The more one examines Scott's characteristic musical reaction to words, however, the clearer it becomes that in his mature songs he always suceeds in matching in an appropriate manner the particular imagery of whatever poem he is setting. He has thus no stock mannerisms, each re-use being individual working of sets of reactions sensitively alive to the situation of his texts.

The decade ended with an increasing number of fairly regular broadcasts of some of Scott's songs and part-songs, and the first broadcast of his 'Lament for Heroes' by the Glasgow String Orchestra under John MacArthur, a gifted violinist well-known to Glaswegians through his John MacArthur Quintet, which played every afternoon in the galleried elegance of Copland and Lye's Sauchiehall Street store. But 1949 also brought sadness, for Scott's old friend from the Langholm days, William Burt, died in May. Writing from Strasburg, Saurat sent his deepest sympathy to Carrie, Burt's widow, on the loss of her husband; "such a deep and beautiful being, gifted with wisdom and tenderness". Scott also wrote to the widow, telling her that he had passed on the "particulars of what had taken place and the tragedy of it all" to Grieve, adding characteristically: "I not only hope, but know, you are keeping a stout heart for 'a stey brae' ".

REFERENCES

1 Letter in Edinburgh University Library.
2 28.8.40 Ibid.
3 5.3.41 Edinburgh University Library.
4 Scott's letters to Macdiarmid are not, at the moment of writing, in a public archive, nor have they been discovered among the poet's papers.
5 As an instance, take MacDiarmid's collection of *Socialist Poems* (1978). It could be said that those which are Socialist are not poems, while those that are poems are not Socialist.
6 *Diaries of a Dying Man* (1954).
7 *MacDiarmid: A Festschrift.*
8 Later Sir David, who, however, was Administrator of Covent Garden, never a Conductor.
9 One of Saurat's daughters.
10 The unpublished 'Fairy Lullaby' for solo soprano and piano, to an air by his son, George.
11 BBC broadcast *Men of Mark.*

Chapter 6

THE FIFTIES

The 'Fifties opened for Scott with another disappointment. I had for some time been endeavouring to persuade one or other of the major London-based recording companies to issue records of Scottish music — or, indeed of any music — by Scottish artists, but had met with little success: a very different situation from that now pertaining, when a rich variety of Scottish recordings of all sorts is commercially available. However, in 1950, I managed to interest the Artistic Manager of Decca in the possibility of issuing a 78 r.p.m. disc of Scott's songs — Long-Play was still a year or two away in Britain — with Joan Alexander and John Tainsh as the artists. The Company got in touch both with Tainsh and with Scott. In due course I received two letters from the composer, the first dated 11th October, 1951. I had recently moved from Glasgow to Loch Lomondside, a change that evidently puzzled Scott.

> You are shifting quarters down to Gartocharn — this is surely a very awkward kind of place if you continue your newspaper critiques and concert-going and your many other activities . . .
>
> Your news about the Decca record is most encouraging. I like the bit about the American market — where's your 'Lallans Scots' now? I'd an American girl visiting me last week — she thought the Cecil Day Lewis 'Hornpipe', being in English, was the most *fetching* song I played. Have I to cut out all the MacDiarmid items to make a partial hit in the U.S.A.? The Yanks just won't take the trouble to translate 'Lallans' into appreciation . . . I'm now just about to write brief notes to Joan Alexander and Tainsh regarding the Decca proposition — and I'll mention the 'American Market' slant on their choice of songs.

The letter added: "I've written quite another dozen or so songs since I have returned from France" — where he had been on holiday — "so you must break your journey and pay 44 a visit soon".

A week later, on 17th October, the proposition had begun

to assume shape. I was instructed to find out from Decca whether the disc was to be ten inch or twelve inch. Tainsh had decided to sing 'O were my love yon lilac fair', 'Phillis' and 'O wert thou in the cauld blast', while Joan Alexander was being urged by the composer to choose songs which would give a wider conception of the variety of his songs.

Unfortunately, the company official with whom I had been negotiating suddenly died, and his successor had no interest whatever in this, or any other Scottish project.

I duly visited 44 and heard the new songs, none of which surpassed what had gone before, although George Bruce and I broadcast a selection of them in the BBC radio programme 'Scottish Life and Letters', shortly after the composer's death.

The publisher William Maclellan had run the somewhat shadowy Dunedin Society since the early years of the war, mainly to advance interest in the music of Erik Chisholm. On 6th June, 1952, it was instrumental in organizing another London recital at the London Institute of Contemporary Arts, in collaboration with the London Contemporary Music Club.

Against my urging, Maclellan invited MacDiarmid[1] to act as 'chairman'.

Four days before the event MacDiarmid wrote to Scott saying that he would be a purely formal Chairman, and that his introductory remarks would be brief. The occasion, he felt, was an important one. A bevy of leading critics — "especially highbrow ones like Edward Sackville West" — would be there. There would, of course, be no opportunity, even if he wished it, for him to be political on this occasion.

I had been invited in my capacity as music critic of *The Bulletin,* and had promised Maclellan that I would do my best to secure the presence of the two most important music critics of the day, Ernest Newman and Eric Blom. Both were invited. Newman accepted, but did not appear. Contrary to the report in *The Scotsman* the following day — its critic arrived late, if I remember correctly — Blom did turn up. *The Scotsman* regretted the length of what its critic described as "an extended introduction by Hugh MacDiarmid", and further commented: "A scarlet chair suspended from the ceiling at an interesting angle near the piano offered a sardonic commentary on the special pleading inherent in much of the speechmaking".

In my professional capacity as music critic, I was rather more direct in my comments on what proved to be an organisational fiasco. Headed 'Odd Display of Scots Culture', my notice in *The Bulletin* ran:

> Musical Londoners must have got rather an odd impression of Scottish culture from the recital of music by Francis George Scott and Erik Chisholm given last night at the Institute of Contemporary Arts.
>
> There was nothing the matter with the music itself. On the contrary, Miss Joan Alexander, accompanied by Miss Ailie Cullen, sang eighteen of Scott's songs, and Miss Agnes Walker played half-a-dozen pleasant little pieces by Chisholm. If these artists were not altogether on top of their form, I would certainly be the last to blame them: for before Miss Alexander could sing a note we had to listen to a discourse (lasting fifty minutes) by Mr C. M. Grieve (Hugh MacDiarmid), and further diatribes amounting to another twenty minutes-worth. The purpose of these remarks was to introduce the evening's music, but Mr Grieve's speech did not suggest that this was a very suitable assignment for him.
>
> Responsibility for this lamentable display apparently lies with the Dunedin Society, the constitution and membership of which cannot be ascertained . . . In spite of the interminable nonsense talked about them last night, both Scott and Chisholm have something to offer, which can and should be judged on musical grounds alone.

Twenty minutes after MacDiarmid had launched upon his arguably irrelevant ranting, Eric Blom got to his feet and left, followed at steady intervals by other members of the very small audience.

There was no doubt about the artistic possibilities of the recital. As *The Scotsman* put it: "Whereas Chisholm's pieces were in a sense experimental and with only a local appeal, Scott, with his wonderful synthesis of voice and verse, had evolved an international art-form out of purely natural ingredients". By driving away Blom, and perhaps other unrecognised critics in the general exodus from verbal boredom, MacDiarmid had once again done his old friend and collaborator a major disservice.

Such are the facts. They led to a period of estrangement between MacDiarmid and myself, clouding briefly an otherwise

enjoyable friendship extending over thirty-five years. Mac-
Diarmid, who always intensely disliked any sort of criticism
of himself, took his 'revenge' with a personal attack upon me
in a book about the National Bard, *Burns Today and Tomorrow.*
The vindictive side of MacDiarmid's nature has never been easy
to excuse, even though genius must be allowed its dark side.
Perhaps it is best simply to reflect upon the wisdom of Edwin
Muir's remark, made 'very sadly' to Helen Cruickshank in
an Edinburgh hotel: "I never can make up my mind just how
much of Christopher is genius and how much charlatan".[2]

During 1943, Scott had begun a series of simple little piano
pieces that he called 'Intuitions'. Over the next ten years he
was to write down, in all, about fifty-seven of these short pieces,
some of them little more than melodic fragments, none of them
harmonically adventurous. Many of them are 'Gaelic' in character, and one or two are piano versions of imagined pibroch
urlars. Most of them were composed during night-hours of
insomnia. They have titles like 'Border Riding-rhythm', 'Old
Irish', Deil's Dance', 'An Seanachaidh', 'National Song', and
'Gaelic National Anthem'. There is a touching setting of the
Latin hymn 'Salutis hostia' that some enterprising religionist
might usefully rediscover and press into service as a hymn tune.
The last bars Scott ever wrote, dated 8th July, 1943, form a
piece actually titled 'Hymn Tune' (Ex. 19). In the autumn of

1952, Scott set these pieces in order, prefixing them with an
epigram from Paul Valery's Socratic dialogue *Eupalinos*: "Tu
sais bien les puissances de l'âme procèdent étrangement de la
nuit . . . Les voici, toutes chargées de clarté et d'erreur? 'O
malheureux, lui dis-je, que veux-tu faire pendant un éclair! "[3]

In the middle of this activity, Scott suffered an annoying

illness which confined him to bed for a week or so. It resulted in an eruption of boils which affected, amongst other areas of his body, his scrotum. "By God", he roared when I called on him and found him in bed: "I've had plenty of fun from the damned thing all my days. Now it's getting its own back"!

When I next visited Scott in June 1953 he played over many of these 'Intuitions'. By then his mind was beginning to cloud, and he had difficulty in focussing his memory. His last song, a setting of the first Alexander Scott's poem 'There is not ane Wench' is dated September, 1952. At about this time Scott received a visit from Frederick Rimmer (later Professor of Music at Glasgow University) bearing a commission from the University Court under the terms of the McEwen bequest. Scott was to be invited to produce a new work for the following year's annual McEwen Memorial Concert. Scott suggested that he might submit some of his existing songs. With considerable tact Rimmer explained that the University Court would feel "much more honoured" if a new composition could be produced. The commission was never taken up, for by then the fire had gone out and the anvil was cold. A year later, it became all too obvious that he was gradually lapsing into a state of senility.

It seems to have been towards the end of 1953 that MacDiarmid saw Scott for the last time. He tells the sad story in *The Company I've Kept.*

> Scott became increasingly reactionary in the last decade of his life. One day I took Jankel Adler, the painter, to see him, and Scott immediately expressed himself of the most violent anti-semitic opinions. I signalled to Adler and we rose and left. I did not see much of Scott after that. I published a pamphlet about him, as a tribute on his seventy-fifth birthday, and members of his family told me afterwards that he was enormously pleased with it — but he never acknowledged the copies I sent him. I wired him my congratulations when Glasgow University gave him an honorary LL.D. but he did not acknowledge this either, nor did he send me any congratulatory message when Edinburgh University did me a like honour. The rift between us was complete. I have said we had, for many years, a deep community of insight, and that I never knew a man for whom I had a greater respect. Were both these merely aspects of the 'illusion of friendship'? Was I wrong all along? Various friends of mine thought so. I do not know. But I fancy that one of the hidden reasons

was that Scott was partly of Jewish blood, one of his grand-mothers having been a Greenvelt, of a family who, coming to Scotland from Yorkshire, did a good deal to build up the Border textile industry. But I was not wrong about the incomparable quality of his song settings or the fact that he was the only Scottish composer who succeeded in doing what all of them should have at least tried to do.

Proverbially, there are three sides to every story; A's, B's and the truth. One would at least have liked to hear B's side over this happening. There appears to be no truth whatsoever in MacDiarmid's astonishing assertion of Jewishness in Scott's ancestry. Indeed, had it been the case, it would never have occurred to Scott to conceal it. Certainly, expert searches in both the Hawick and Rochdale records reveal absolutely nothing to substantiate MacDiarmid's claim.

One of MacDiarmid's last letters to Scott apologises for not coming to see him and lists by way of excuse his heavy programme of lectures. He gives news of an impending visit to China made on behalf of the Communist Party and a long list of proposed literary effusions. Edinburgh University, he explained, had offered him an LL.D. which he intended to accept, although he did not believe in Honorary Degrees, and despised most of the people who got them. He hated to be "bracketed with them in any connection", but nevertheless, felt "obliged" to accept to be in a stronger position to fight for the cause he had at heart.

MacDiarmid enclosed a brochure on Janacek, sent by the daughter in Czechoslovakia of an Edinburgh friend, H. A. Scott, who, being a great admirer of F.G's songs, asked that it be forwarded to the composer. By then, Scott was too far withdrawn into his own declining world to be particularly concerned.

But many of his old friends did keep up their contacts. With George Bruce, I prepared and presented a programme to mark the composer's seventy-fifth birthday. Muir, now Warden of Newbattle Abbey, wrote to Scott on January 24th:

This is to wish you a very happy and distinguished birthday and many happy years for yourself and Burges. I think many people must be paying homage to you now, and honouring themselves in doing it. I listened to Maurice Lindsay last

> Sunday, and I hope that the BBC will remember this time and
> do honour to you. Whatever they do they are moving now to
> make up for their shortcomings. You have had to wait a long
> time for recognition, and the recognition is far less than it
> should be, but it is growing. May it grow in this unhappy
> country.
>
> I have often regretted that I have seen you so seldom in the
> last two years. George Bruce told me that you were keeping
> very well. Recently I have been bedevilled by a pain in the
> chest; I get it whenever I make any unusual effort or worry
> . . . The work with the students I enjoy thoroughly, but the
> committee is beginning to get me down, and if that involved
> the continuance of the chest pains, I suppose it would be
> wiser of me to give the college up. But as it is I have had to
> cancel lecture engagements, and journeys as well, otherwise
> I would have come over long before this to see you . . .

There was one further honour to come. On the promotion
of the Professor of French, Alan M. Boase, Glasgow University
announced that it would confer an honorary degree on the
composer. John Tonge at once wrote from Edinburgh: "So
Glasgow University is going to honour itself! I was most glad
indeed to read the news half an hour ago: it will be welcomed
by all those friends who are so much in your debt and can
never express what your example and achievement have meant".

Muir wrote from his last home in Swaffham Priory, Cambridge:

> I have heard of the Doctorate which Glasgow University is
> giving you, and I am writing to congratulate you on the
> mark of honour, and Willa sends her congratulations too.
> The recognition of your work from official and academic
> sources has been shamefully long delayed, and I am glad
> that this has come along at last. I hope there are others to
> follow.
>
> It gives me as well a chance to write to you again. I'm afraid
> we are both bad correspondents. And I have been in America
> for a year; you can never tell where to find Willa and me;
> we have stravaiged about so much. But now we have had the
> sense at last to settle down, and we have settled in a little
> house here in a village 8 miles from Cambridge, where we
> hope to end our days. (I was 70 last week). We are very quiet
> here; we see very few people; but we are very glad of that
> — we saw so many in America. I mustn't write about
> America, or I would never stop; but we found that the

Americans are at least a very kind and generous people: endless in their kindness, and not only because they are so much richer than we are: though the prosperity there is fantastic compared with ours in Britain, and widely spread too. But I would need a volume about America. One of the things that struck us in New England (where we were most of the time) was the devotion to the Royal Family! They are very proud of having come three centuries ago from England, or later on from Scotland. There is quite a cult of the bag-pipes.

I often think of those wonderful days when you and Saurat and I met each week and discussed everything under the sun. It meant a great deal to me at the time. I think that was when I began to have some understanding of music, a little, and it is nothing more than a very little still. But it has given me immense enjoyment, which I would not have missed. I never see or hear from Saurat now, but he was more your friend than mine.

At any rate, here's to friendship and the old times, and our good wishes for you and your music, and love to Burges and Lilias.

Willa added a postscript:

Here's a hooray from Willa. I don't know how I shall survive knowing so many doctors! (Dr Grieve, Dr Scottt, Dr Muir — did you know when you were all carrying on around Montrose that you would all end up as doctors?) I am very glad indeed about it: almost as gratified as if I were a doctor myself: it makes me think a little better of Scotland.

MacDiarmid wired his congratulations, and reinforced them by letter from Chungking, South China.

The Degree ceremony took place on 19th June, 1957, and the citation read:

The 25th January has in days past been more conscientiously celebrated in Scotland and by Scots the world over than the 25th of December itself. The same date was also chosen by Francis George Scott when seventy-seven years ago he first saw the light of Hawick, where the traditional gallantry of the weavers at Flodden is still remembered, and the Cornet still conducts the Common Riding. Nothing could be more fitting, since the musical genius of Scott has been as essentially Scottish as the poetic genius of Burns — with whom he has not infrequently indulged in a posthumous collaboration. Yet

K

such a comparison may be positively misleading without recalling to mind the pattern of a lifetime spent in teaching
literature and music, during which the proverbial family
pugnacity and brio has mingled with a fair dose of our national
caution. Despite Saintsbury's spell Scott was at 20 too
immersed in his music to stay the course at Edinburgh. If Durham gave him later her Bachelorship of Music, a quarter of
a century was to elapse before he became Director of Music
at Jordanhill Training College, the years between filled by
teaching in Falkirk, Langholm, Dunoon and Glasgow.
Against that bleak official record we must write in the real
evolution of an intense, boisterous and sometimes wayward
personality. As the original moving spirit of that group which
produced between the wars a genuine Scottish Renaissance
in the Arts he has been gratefully recognised by his co-
conspirators, Edwin and Willa Muir, Neil Gunn, Denis
Saurat, and youngest but not least, his old Langholm pupil,
Christopher Grieve. 'As good as anything Strauss himself had
done', this overheard comment at a concert after the performance of one of his early songs was the critical moment when
he fully realised his true role — the elaboration of a Scottish
musical idiom based less on modal flavouring than on the
speech-rhythms and inflections of Scots poetry, old and
new, — a role fulfilled with genius in the six volumes of
Scottish Lyrics. The couthie vigour of 'I'll Gar our Gudeman
Trow', the drama of the setting of a ballad of his own Borders
such as 'Edward', the beauty of Dunbar's 'Rorate Coeli
Desuper', or the fruits of his collaboration with C. M. Grieve
(alias Hugh MacDiarmid) whether the eerie 'Watergaw', the
mysterious 'Milk-wort and Bog-cotton', or 'Crowdieknowe',
that macabre and sarcastic vision of the last judgment — to
have heard these is to recognise Scott as a great master of
the Lied. As such he has had to wait for his singers, for
talented accompanists, as well as for a public to listen.

Face to face with the intensity, the humour and the
exacting fastidiousness which have characterised Francis
George Scott, the old phrase *Perfervidum ingenium* takes on
a new meaning. We ask you, Mr Chancellor, to show our
belated recognition of a great man by conferring on him the
degree of Doctor of Laws.

It was, indeed, belated recognition. Many of those present
doubted if Scott even realised what was going on round about
him. The ceremony was followed by a lunch, at which it was
suddenly noted with concern that the composer was no longer
present.

About the time the guests were taking their place at the

University's top table, Betty Anderson and her sister happened to be travelling along Great Western Road on the top of a Corporation bus. Looking out of the window, she was astonished to see the gowned figure of Francis George Scott striding along the pavement, his scarlet robe and his white hair streaming in the wind. She got off the bus and intercepted him. "Aren't you supposed to be at the University Lunch?" she asked. "I got bored, so I decided to walk home," said Scott. She persuaded him to allow himself to be escorted. Waiting at the Kirklee bus stop was a crowd of small Kelvinside Academy school boys, some of them carrying violin cases. Surveying them from his fantasy world, Scott stopped, looked at them and growled: "Damned amateurs": a sad and a ridiculous comment suggesting, perhaps, that his subconscious desire to have been a 'full-time composer' which the practical facts of life had forced him as a young man to abandon, had even then not quite been sublimated.

George Bruce and I again came together to present a feature in the 'Men of Mark' radio series, broadcast on 17th July, 1957, to commemorate the Honorary Degree. In that programme Muir spoke of: "The similarity between Scott's problem and that of Burns. Burns was doing something new in Scottish poetry. He was a very great artist. Scott was doing something new with Scottish Music. He was, I think, a very great artist. He is like Burns in the extraordinary variety of his songs, in the tenderness, also in the rumbustious and milder humour, which is also a part of Burns and, I think, probably part of the Scottish genius."

Another poet remembered earlier images: behind the conventional façade of Scott, the teacher of English, those of the future composer were already maturing. As a child, George Bruce had caught a glimpse of an image of the man that was to be:

I think that I was six or seven. I remember my chin was not far above the height of the keyboard. I was looking along the keyboard and two large, very strong hands were at the piano. They were making melodious and beautiful sounds, which swelled into my ears like the very sound of the ocean itself. Above this was the sound of a voice singing, the voice of Francis George Scott. I didn't know what it was all about,

but it was something very important. Quite suddenly, the
voice stopped, and the piano stopped. He was interrupted,
apparently by some other voice. Something important had
happened. Years later my father explained to me that Francis
George Scott had suggested that he might do certain things
to Gaelic melodies, and my father didn't approve.

Saurat[4] had this to say of the reawakening of Scottish
consciousness after the First World War and Scott's part in it:

> I think it could be called the fore-runner of the Scottish
> Renaissance movement, because in those years, 1920 to 1925,
> began certainly a sort of furious spiritual awakening among
> some people in Scotland and they looked to Scott as their
> master. The fact that he didn't write, but that he went only
> for music, gave him a greater authority. He wasn't a com-
> petitor with any of them. They weren't jealous of him, but
> they respected him so much that what he said went. It could
> be said that it was he who educated Hugh MacDiarmid into
> real culture. He had a great influence over Edwin Muir at
> the beginning.

The most direct musical assessment came from Cedric
Thorpe Davie, who spoke, quite simply, of Scott's genius:

> That genius seems to me to lie in the capacity shared by few
> composers to illuminate and enhance poetry. Really great
> songs are almost all partnerships between a poet and a
> musician. They fuse into one masterpiece, which is greater
> than the sum of its parts.
>
> In his finest songs, F. G. Scott has shown that he shares
> with composers like Fauré, Hugo Wolf or Schumann this
> elusive capacity to take a lyric poem and put it into the
> setting which will enhance it and show of its beauty to the
> best advantage, as a master craftsman may do with a precious
> jewel. And it's one of the things that we lesser composers may
> emulate, but it isn't likely that any of us will succeed as
> F.G. has done.

Even his former sparring-partner at the BBC, Ian Whyte,
observed, somewhat grudgingly, that he held "in very deep
respect, any man who can write one gem of a song".

A song-writer necessarily depends on singers, particularly
on the singers who give his first performances. John Tainsh
had many such experiences with F.G.:

> I was singing at a lunch-hour concert in Glasgow, and out

of the blue dashes F.G. He never said a word about the concert, whether or not you sang badly or well, or anything about it. He just said to me and my accompanist, Johnnie McGrogan: 'Come on, I've got a sang for ye'. Then he dragged us out to Munro Road. We sat down and he sang us 'Edward'. Now this was something! Anyway, I studied it and worked on it with him. The funniest thing of all were his instructions. One of these was 'Allegro naked — Move like Hell'. I have it in my music to this day — 'Move like Hell!'.

Finally, the distinguished English critic A. K. Holland gave his verdict:

Surely the quality that distinguishes the songs lies in his discovery of a perfectly natural and fluent declamation, so natural that it seems inevitable. And this applies no less to the songs in strophic form than to those in a freer style. It is the directness, the swift capture of mood and sentiment, the complete finality of these songs that sets them apart from the generality. Above all, they are wonderfully singable. Scott meets his poets on their own ground, with a love of the fine phrase and the subtle rhythm; but chiefly he meets them as a singer-poet. His accompaniments are never over-wrought, but always contribute to the spirit of the poem. And sometimes he achieves sublimity.

Muir's last reference to Scott was an affectionate and characteristically gentle entry in a notebook entitled 'Dreams and Diary Items'. Dated November, 1957, it records a dream of "F.G. my old friend who has lately relapsed into senile decay, though a wonderful creature. I dreamed I met him, and that he was handsome and young, younger than when I first met him, a radiant young man in his twenties. At the same time I thought that my hair had grown quite white and neatly barbered . . .", a dream similar to a slightly earlier one which he was to transform into his poem, 'The Brothers'.

The year 1958 was scarcely as significant for new music as had been 1880, the year of Scott's birth. But in 1958, Benjamin Britten's 'Nocturne', for tenor, seven obligato instruments and strings, Lutoslawski's 'Funeral Music' and Iain Hamilton's 'Concerto for Jazz Trumpet and Orchestra' were given their first performance. Tippett's opera 'King Priam', and Henze's 'Der Prinz von Homberg' were both staged for the first time. The world was introduced to Berio's 'Differences for five instruments and tape', Ligeti's 'Articulation for tape', and Thea

Musgrave's orchestral piece 'Obliques' (based, as it happens, on some early lines by the present writer). In London, the long career of that most English of composers, Ralph Vaughan Williams came to an end. And on 6th November, at his home in Glasgow, Francis George Scott died.

A funeral service was held in Glasgow, attended by the family, MacDiarmid and, as the poet later commented "only by Mr Harold Thomson, the Musical Director of the Scottish BBC and Mr Maurice Lindsay".

It was Scott's wish that he should be buried in his native place. His body was therefore taken to Hawick and interred at a ceremony attended by the family, MacDiarmid,[5] and the Provost of Hawick, 'in an official capacity', in the Wellogate Cemetery, on a hillside overlooking the town. On his tombstone is the epitaph he himself had chosen, a line by Walter Savage Landor:

"Nature I loved and next to Nature, Art."

REFERENCES

1 Letter of 2/6/52, Edinburgh University Library.
2 *Octobiography* by Helen B. Cruickshank.
3 "You well know that the soul's power is born of the night . . . Behold it, taken with certainty and doubt."
4 In 1948 Saurat, whose health never fully recovered from the bombing, became a Fellow of King's College, Cambridge. In 1950 he retired to Nice, as Director of the Centre International d'Etudes Françaises. He died there in the same year as Scott's death.
5 MacDiarmid survived until 9th September, 1978. His last years were cheered by well-deserved honours from various quarters. He was buried at Langholm, the town that consistently refused to honour its most famous son when the giving of the Freedom of the Burgh lay within its power.

Chapter 7

CODA

On the centenary of Scott's birth, and almost a quarter of a
century after his death, it should be possible to measure his
achievement objectively. Both Denis Saurat and James Whyte
regarded Scott rather than MacDiarmid as the real founder of
the Scottish Renaissance. The point is of little practical conse-
quence now, except perhaps to enable us note in passing that
Scott certainly made the earlier contribution. Yet his position
as a Scottish Renaissance 'father-figure' drew forth absurd
propaganda, and inspired inflated comparisons not of his own
making. Inevitably, these strident claims prejudiced his reputation in the eyes of the musical public. Even as shrewd a literary
critic as Edwin Muir eventually fell into the ritual of overpraise
where Scott was concerned, and his correction by Helen Cruickshank as long ago as 1942 was entirely justified. She relates:

> I occasionally went straight from my office to some lecture
> arranged by Edwin. At the Polish House, one evening, I found
> he had brought the composer Francis George Scott from
> Glasgow, to speak with musical illustrations of his own song
> compositions. Edwin introduced him as 'the greatest song
> writer in Europe'.
>
> Meeting Edwin, accidentally on top of a tram next day,
> during my lunch hour, I told him he had been exaggerating.
>
> For some years I had been incensed at the way 'C. M. Grieve
> & Co.' (which included the 'Modern Scot' clique) had plugged
> Scott's work in season and out of season, belabouring their
> reading public with contumely because they did not recognise
> Scott's genius. 'Blast you! Take that for being an ignorant
> nitwit' was their slogan. And down would come the
> word club on the head again.
>
> I had myself told Scott that his partisan friends were doing him
> more harm than good by their wrong psychological propaganda
> on his behalf and he seemed a little alarmed at this reading
> of the situation.
>
> So when the same extravagant praise was voiced by Edwin,

who seemed to me the soul of integrity as a critic, I had to
express my disapproval. My criticism was not of the composer,
many of whose song settings I greatly admired, and indeed I
had many special journeys to Glasgow to hear them.

To come back to the top of that tram, Edwin confessed that
Scott had 'been so undervalued in Scotland that I felt I had
to give him a special boost'. At this point I had to get off
the tram, having reached my destination. I left some fellow-
passengers sadly disappointed at the cessation of what had
promised to be a 'rare good flyting-match'.

Scott always made it plain that he did not believe a Renaissance could come about through propaganda. All that ultimately
matters therefore is his creative achievement.

He was no Schubert, no Schumann, no Moussorgsky, not
even a Wolf. He never once at any time in his long life gave
any encouragement to ridiculous comparisons of the sort put
about by some of his friends. But he was a distinguished
miniaturist with a voice of his own and the ability to catch
in music some of those indefinable feelings, reactions and
gestures of the mind that go to make up the quality we recognise as Scottishness.

His best work is available for all to perform or hear. But
there remains the question of Scott's unpublished songs. In the
archives of the Mitchell Library (based on work done by Professor Erik Chisholm in 1962, who caused Scott's entire archive
to be photostated) there are listed 86 unpublished solo songs
and 15 unpublished part-songs. I have already indicated the
desirability of the publication of the Dunbar choral setting of
'Welcome to Scotland', a most attractive part-song.

The position with regard to the large number of unpublished
solo songs is a different one. Many of the songs are 'prentice
work', and it would do no service to Scott to have them brought
before the public. On the other hand, there are three kinds of
song in which the public might reasonably be interested. The
most important category consists of songs which add to our
knowledge and appreciation of Scott's understanding and musical
treatment of the Scottish character. Nothing that is unpublished
at the time of writing is actually better than what has already
been published. On the other hand, there are several attractive
songs that would broaden, rather than deepen, our view of
Scott's achievement.

One group of three songs is from the 1920's, and includes 'As I came o'er the cairney mount', a Burns lyric, melodically strophic but with plenty of harmonic interest in the accompaniment. It is a spirited 6/8 swagger of a song in which a woman tells of her pride in her Highland laddie. It dates from about 1925. From possibly a year or two earlier, comes another Burns setting. 'Beware o' bonnie Ann', once again a song of sexual swagger, but this time from the male view-point. 'Come rede me, Dame', and 'Bessie at her spinning wheel', both by Burns and both from about 1929, give us, in the former case, another piece of genuine Scott rumbustiousness and in the latter, a rather greater musical probing than what at first sight seems to be simply another spinning song. There is an exultant setting of a bawdy song from *The Merry Muses of Caledonia*, 'Madgie cam to my bed stock', written in 1930, and even in these liberated days not likely to achieve public performance. There is also the Burns-like 'My Daddie is a cankert carl', an extended character song for female voice, written, in 1940, and that 'Corbie Sang' to words by Soutar, written as Scott himself related, while fire-watching on a night in 1943. In this song, the openness depicting the fancied sweetness of nature of the mavis and the merle is contrasted with the crow's chromaticism, as he gloatingly describes his nastier predatory habits.

In the last years of his life, Scott turned back to the Makars, setting Alexander Scott's 'To luv unluvit', the modal melody of which has a decided ring of the fifteenth century; the satirical and very funny song 'Of the false fire of Purgatorie'; Scott's 'There is not ane wench' (1952); and his last song of all, to words by an anonymous contemporary of Alexander Scott, 'The wife wha would a wanton be'. No country with respect for its heritage would allow songs of this quality to remain indefinitely unpublished.

The second group is more problematical. Scott turned to German texts in the mid-'Thirties, and three German songs — 'Brüder' to words by Heinrich Lersch (of which Soutar was later to make an English version, though in ignorance of Scott's musical setting); 'Begrüssung' by Stefan George and, from 1936, 'Weltende', to words by Elsa Lasker-Schüler — all show some degree of harmonic adventurousness and an awareness of the national colouring of the text. In 1949 Scott set C. Day Lewis's

'Hornpipe', which has delighted more than the American visitor referred to in one of his letters.[2] There are also two MacDiarmid settings that should be added to the group of songs based on the work of this poet, even if they are not among the best, 'An Unco Sang', dating from about 1940, and 'Sabine', composed in 1924 but re-written in 1945. Two settings of poems by George Campbell Hay are worth the attention of singers: 'The Two Neighbours', a pibroch-like extended song hampered by the fact that the poem itself fails to 'push through'; and, more importantly, a beautiful setting of 'A Misty Morning', dating from 1951.

There is a final category about which I cannot make up my mind. It consists of competent, even effective songs, which do not reflect the composer's mature personality. In 1922 Scott set 'When I am dead, my dearest' by Christina Rossetti. It is a song that would hold its own in any recital of contemporary songs of the period, and has the potential of winning a wider popularity. So, too, has his setting of Hood's 'I remember, I remember/The house where I was born', dated 18th July, 1943. Underneath the score is a note to his daughter, which begins, "Dear Lovey, I didn't remember! — you did! — that I sang 'impromptu' this tune to Hood's poem two years ago when we were in Taynuilt. When I heard you singing it some days ago I thought it one of your own, but you assure me that *I* wrote it, so I have written it out in a form you can play and or sing, so it is your very own after all . . ." Together with a song from 1950, 'In Normandy', to words by that same daughter, these two songs, and the Rosetti one, seem to me also to have the potential of securing a wider popularity that would in no way be connected with the nature of Scott's real and individual achievement. Since he already enjoys popularity of this sort with his boyish 'Our Bonnie Border Toun', at least in Hawick (which otherwise appears not to want to know that he ever existed), perhaps there is also a case for issuing these songs, although not in the context of his finest work.

Of his works for small instrumental groups, a 'Ballet-Prelude' for strings and piano to George Reston Malloch's play *Thomas the Rhymer* exists in manuscript. His *Lament for Heroes* for string orchestra is worthy of occasional revival. His only wholly successful orchestral piece is the Overture *Renaissance*, which should certainly not be allowed to disappear from the public ken. Doubtless the orchestral version of his setting of the ballad 'Edward' will be revived from time to time, as well as at least some of the movements from his ballet suit *The Seven Deidly Sinnis*. The final Reel, for instance, could well stand on its own.

It is thus with forty or so of his finest songs that he has made his permanent contribution to our heritage, a contribution the neglect of which would be to our serious loss. Measured by any musical standards known to me, ten of these songs are as imaginative as any written this century by anyone. A further thirty or so fully measure up musically in their own way to the songs of, say, England's Warlock or Finzi, and in addition enshrine aspects of our Scottishness in much the same way that the operas of Sémetana, on an altogether larger scale, enshrine the indefinable quality that makes up "Czechness". Coming as Scott did at the receding end of the tidal wave of European nationalism, no other composer has achieved so much for Scotland. In speaking of Scott, though we are dealing with a miniaturist, a minor composer, we are without doubt also speaking of a composer of subtle native imaginative distinction.

There is one unarguable difficulty that stands in the way of his songs being widely sung furth of Scotland. As A .T. Cunningham remarked: "They are Scottish songs, and few people say with T. S. Eliot 'While Lallans is a language I read with difficulty, I can nevertheless enjoy it, and I am convinced that many things can be said, in poetry, in that language that cannot be expressed at all in English' ". Regrettably, not only Hugh MacDiarmid's 'synthetic' Scots, but even Burns's Scots, once widely spoken, frightens off foreign singers. Yet there is no real reason why it should. Many singers who perform in German, French or Italian, do not really know these languages. Certainly they may sing them, secure in the knowledge that the majority of their listeners are even more ignorant. It could be, however, that it is, indeed, on the awareness and good taste of Scots singers that Scott's living future must rest.

For the moment, music's fashionable accent is once again an international one, as it was in the first half of the eighteenth century, when uniformly respectable Concerti Grossi could be turned out on demand by *immigré* Italians, and pupils drawn from the land of their teacher's adoption. At the same time, the gulf between the music *avant garde* and the public, whose patronage must ultimately pay all the pipers, is now so hopelessly wide that one is tempted to suggest the coining of a new word for the currently fashionable manipulation of electronic synthesisters, mathematical serialism, street noises-off, or whatever: 'soundage', perhaps, rather than music, since its construction, where such a formal procedure is even attempted, is often a mere inhuman mathematical formula.

But music, like all great art that exists in its own right outwith our world of daily time, is about people, whom ultimately it must delight or move, and their feelings, which it must satisfy. Small though his output may be and limited in what it attempts and achieves, Scott's best songs seem to me likely to meet both these criteria, not only in tomorrow's Scotland, but wherever music that reaches out to the heart continues to be valued.

APPENDIX A

BIBLIOGRAPHICAL NOTES

The checklist which follows covers Francis George Scott's published music: first, the collections of songs, then the songs and other pieces that were published separately.

For MS material the major collection is in the Mitchell Library, Glasgow. There the originals have been copied and the copies bound in nineteen volumes. These include 'Published Songs', 'Part Songs' (two volumes containing more than a hundred 'Unpublished Songs', among them some that are quite well known, such as the setting of William Soutar's bairnrhyme, 'Corbie Sang'), a volume entitled 'Songs and Drafts' (70 songs, all of which have been published except four), a further two volumes of 'Drafts', the dance suite for orchestra, 'The Dance of the Sevin Deidly Sinnis', in four volumes (full score, string parts, orchestral parts, and drafts), a volume of 'Various Works' (including 'The Ballad of Kynd Kittok', for baritone solo and orchestra, the ballet-prelude to George Reston Malloch's one-act play, Thomas the Rhymer, *the ballad 'Edward', for baritone solo and orchestra, and the 'Lament for the Heroes', for string orchestra), a volume of piano and other pieces (including the 'Intuitions'), and six volumes of lectures, notes and miscellaneous memoranda.*

There are other smaller collections elsewhere. The National Library of Scotland contains eighteen songs in manuscript, some notes on musical matters, and the short score of his overture, 'Renaissance'. In Edinburgh University Library there are a number of settings of poems by Burns and MacDiarmid, a setting of a sonnet by Edwin Muir, ten sheets of drafts for other lyrics, a number of letters to MacDiarmid about these settings, and Scott's unpublished lecture on pibroch.

COLLECTIONS

The eight collections of songs are here listed chronologically by their dates of publication or copyright. The date of publication of a collection is, of course, no indication of the dates of composition of the individual songs in the collection. In some cases Scott dates the song, and others can sometimes be dated by reference to the MSS. It is to be noted that different principles are used in arranging the sequence of songs in different collections: in Scottish Lyrics, Book 3, *for example, where eleven of the twelve songs are individually dated, it is clear that the arrangement is chronological by date of composition, but in the Saltire collection of thirty-five songs, of which twenty-seven are individually dated, and cover a period of thirty-two years, from 1916 to 1948, the arrangement is not chronological and may be best described (paraphrasing Palgrave's words) as the most 'musically-effective' order.*

A number of the songs published in collections were published previously elsewhere: thus, the twenty-five songs in Books 3 and 4 of the Scottish Lyrics *were all printed in the* Modern Scot *between April 1932 and January 1936, and four of them were reprinted in* Towards a New Scotland, *J. H. Whyte's selection from that quarterly, published in 1935.*

Three short songs. No. 1 Medium voice. No. 2 High voice.

    London: Enoch & Sons, © 1920. 13p.

    Contents: All night under the moon (Wilfrid Wilson Gibson)
              Tremulous grey of dusk (Seumas O'Sullivan)
              The laverock (Walter Wingate)

Scottish lyrics set to music. 5 books.

    London and Glasgow: Bayley & Ferguson, © 1922-39.

    Book 1, for female voice. © 1922. 39p.

    Contents: The carles of Dysart (Burns)
              We'll hap and row (William Creech)
              I'll gar our gudeman trow (Anon.)
              Ay waukin, O (Burns)
              Last May a braw wooer (Burns)
              The wren's nest (Burns)
              The lovely lass o' Inverness (Burns)
              Hey, the dusty miller (Burns)

    Book 2, for male voice. © 1922. 42p.

    Contents: Wha will buy my troggin? (Burns)
              Weel I lo'e Mary (John Imlah)
              My wife shall ha'e her will (Anon.)
              O merry hae I been teething a heckle (Burns)
              Mary Morison (Burns)
              The weary pund o' tow (Burns)
              Crowdie (Burns)
              O were my love yon lilac fair (Burns)
              Gruel (Allan Cunningham)

    Book 3. © 1934. [4], 46p.

    Contents: Twist ye, twine ye (Scott)
              The auld man's mear's dead (Patrick Birnie)
              Rorate caeli desuper (Dunbar)
              Wheesht, wheesht (MacDiarmid)
              The eemis stane (MacDiarmid)
              Crowdieknowe (MacDiarmid)
              Moonstruck (MacDiarmid)
              St. Brendan's graveyard: Isle of Barra (Jean Lang)
              Love (MacDiarmid)
              Cupid and Venus (Mark Alexander Boyd)
              Milkwort and bog-cotton (MacDiarmid)
              An apprentice angel (MacDiarmid)

Book 4 (Baritone). © 1936. [2], 39p.

Contents: The tailor fell thro' the bed (Burns)
       Of a' the airts the wind can blaw (Burns)
       My wife's a wanton wee thing (Burns)
       O, were I on Parnassus' hill (Burns)
       The twa kimmers (Dunbar)
       Phillis (William Drummond)
       When I think on the happy days (Anon.)
       O dear minny, what shall I do? (Burns)
       Fare ye weel, my auld wife (Anon.)
       Of ane blackamoor (Dunbar)
       Scroggam (Burns)
       My luve is like a red, red rose (Burns)
       Amang the trees (Burns)

Book 5 (Low voice). © 1939. [4], 38p.

Contents: I hae laid a herring in saut (James Tytler)
       Since all thy vows, false maid (Anon.)
       Wee Willie Gray (Burns)
       The discreet hint (Burns)
       O, wha my babie-clouts will buy? (Burns)
       Wha is that at my bower-door? (Burns)
       Rattlin', roarin' Willie (Burns)
       To a Loch Fyne fisherman (George Campbell Hay)
       The love-sick lass (MacDiarmid)
       Empty vessel (MacDiarmid)
       The watergaw (MacDiarmid)
       Ane his ain enemy (Dunbar)
       'Scots, wha hae' (Burns)

Seven songs for baritone voice.

London and Glasgow: Bayley & Ferguson, [1946]. 23p.

Contents: The old fisherman (George Campbell Hay)
       Gane is the day (Burns)
       Reid-e'en (MacDiarmid)
       In time of tumult (Soutar)
       The Kerry Shore, Loch Fyne (George Campbell Hay)
       The Cameronian cat (Anon.)
       Macpherson's farewell (Burns)

Songs: thirty-five Scottish lyrics and other poems set to music.

Glasgow: Bayley & Ferguson for the Saltire Society, 1949. [4], 151p.

Contents: The sauchs in the Reuch Heuch Hauch (MacDiarmid)
       Lourd on my hert (MacDiarmid)
       To a lady (Dunbar)
       The wee man (Willa Muir)
       On receiving news of the death of Charles I (Marquis of
         Montrose)
       Hungry waters (MacDiarmid)

Whistle, whistle, auld wife (Anon.)
Edward (Anon.)
The twa corbies (Anon.)
First love (MacDiarmid)
An admonition to young lassies (Alexander Montgomerie)
I wha aince in Heaven's heicht (MacDiarmid)
The sea hounds (Dora Sigerson)
The tryst (Soutar)
O, wert thou in the cauld blast (Burns)
Sunny gale (MacDiarmid)
Robin shure in hairst (Burns)
O steer her up (Burns)
Glances (Pittendrigh Macgillivray)
There's news, lasses, news (Burns)
The man in the moon (MacDiarmid)
Ane sang of the birth of Christ (Anon.)
The innumerable Christ (MacDiarmid)
Landlady, count the lawin' (Burns)
Alba (Scotland) (George Campbell Hay)
Country life (MacDiarmid)
Love of Alba (Maurice Lindsay)
Florine (Thomas Campbell)
The deil o' Bogie (Alexander Gray)
Im Tiroler Wirtshaus (Georg Britting)
Verlasst mich hier (Goethe)
Dein Gedenken (Will Vesper)
La belle est au jardin d'amour (Anon.)
Je descendis dans mon jardin (Amy Sylvel)
Au miroir de ma mère (Amy Sylvel)

Songs of Francis George Scott: Centenary Album
   Wendover, Bucks: Roberton, 1980. 148p.

Contents: Milkwort and bog-cotton (MacDiarmid)
            The tryst (Soutar)
            To a lady (Dunbar)
            My luve is like a red, red rose (Burns)
            First love (MacDiarmid)
            Empty vessel (MacDiarmid)
            The love-sick lass (MacDiarmid)
            Wheesht, wheesht (MacDiarmid)
            Cupid and Venus (Mark Alexander Boyd)
            Phillis (William Drummond)
            Ay waukin, O (Burns)
            O were my love yon lilac fair (Burns)
            Mary Morison (Burns)
            Reid-e'en (MacDiarmid)
            Since all thy vows, false maid (Anon.)
            Florine (Thomas Campbell)
            The twa corbies (Anon.)

The deil o' Bogie (Alexander Gray)
The eemis stane (MacDiarmid)
Moonstruck (MacDiarmid)
Country life (MacDiarmid)
The watergaw (MacDiarmid)
Crowdieknowe (MacDiarmid)
An apprentice angel (MacDiarmid)
The twa kimmers (Dunbar)
Of ane blackmore (Dunbar)
Scroggam (Burns)
Wee Willie Gray (Burns)
The discreet hint (Burns)
Wha is that at my bower-door? (Burns)
Rattlin', roarin' Willie (Burns)
The wee man (Willa Muir)
St. Brendan's graveyard: Isle of Barra (Jean Lang)
The old fisherman (Hay)
The Kerry Shore, Loch Fyne (Hay)
To a Loch Fyne fisherman (Hay)
Rorate caeli desuper (Dunbar)
Ane sang of the birth of Christ (Anon.)
The seuchs in the Reuch Heuch Hauch (MacDiarmid)
Lourd on my hert (MacDiarmid)
'Scots, wha hae' (Burns)

SEPARATELY PUBLISHED SONGS AND MUSIC

The songs and part-songs published separately are here listed chronologically by their dates of publication or copyright. Two instrumental pieces follow. Scott's orchestral music, including his overture 'Renaissance', remains unpublished.

Oor bonnie Border toon (Robert Hunter)
Hawick: W. & J. Kennedy, [1902].
This song was first sung at the Hawick Common Riding festivities in 1902. It is reprinted in *The Hawick Songs: a complete collection,* arranged by Adam L. Ingles, sponsored by the Hawick Callants' Club, Hawick, 1957, and published by Mozart Allan, Glasgow.

Aye she kaimed her yellow hair (Henry Johnston) [for SATBB]
Bayley & Ferguson, © 1919. *Scottish part songs,* no. 181.

Lullaby (Richard Middleton)
Bayley & Ferguson, © 1919. *Songs in unison,* no. 48.

A child's night song (Richard Middleton)
Bayley & Ferguson, © 1919. *Songs in unison,* no. 49.

Dream song (Richard Middleton)
Bayley & Ferguson, © 1919. *Songs in unison,* no. 50.

L

The warning (F. W. Anderson)
Bayley & Ferguson, © 1920.

Whistle, whistle, auld wife (Anon.)
Curwen, © 1922. *Curwen ed.* 2244.

O Jesu parvule (The bairnie Christ) (MacDiarmid) [for SATB]
Bayley & Ferguson, © 1924. *Scottish part songs,* no. 202.

There was a lad was born in Kyle (Burns) [for mixed voices]
Bayley & Ferguson, © 1924. *Scottish part songs,* no. 203.

Hie away (Scott)
Stainer & Bell, © 1925. *Part songs,* no. 147.

The blossom (Blake)
Stainer & Bell, © 1927. *Unison songs,* no. 64.

Hungry waters (MacDiarmid)
Curwen, © 1927. *Curwen ed.* 2412.

There grows an elm-tree (Arthur Waley) [for SATB]
[Three poems from the Chinese, no. 1]
Bayley & Ferguson, © 1932. *Choral album,* no. 1492.

New corn (Arthur Waley) [for SATB]
[Three poems from the Chinese, no. 2]
Bayley & Ferguson, © 1932. *Choral album,* no. 1493.

Plucking the rushes (Arthur Waley) [for SATB]
[Three poems from the Chinese, no. 3]
Bayley & Ferguson, © 1932. *Choral album,* no. 1494.

Sea buckthorn (Helen B. Cruickshank) [Trio for female voices]
Bayley & Ferguson, © 1932. *Collegiate choir,* no. 441.

A fairy lullaby (An coineachan) (Anon.) [Arranged for female voices]
Bayley & Ferguson, © 1932. *Collegiate choir,* no. 442.

Where dewdrops glisten (William Jeffrey) [Two-part song for treble voices]
Bayley & Ferguson, © 1932. *Collegiate choir,* no. 443.

The deuk's dang o'er my daddie, O (Burns) [for SATB]
Bayley & Ferguson, © 1932. *Scottish part songs,* no. 212.

The three fishes (MacDiarmid) [for male voice choir]
Bayley & Ferguson, © 1932. *Scottish part songs,* no. 213.

The plumes of time (Lewis Spence) [Three-part song]
Bayley & Ferguson, © 1933. *Collegiate choir,* no. 448.

Pretty Nell (E. Picken) [for TTBB]
Bayley & Ferguson, © 1933. *Scottish part songs,* no. 217.

Spring (Blake)
Stainer & Bell, © 1934. *Unison songs,* no. 138.

Ode to the cuckoo (Michael Bruce)
Michael Bruce Memorial Trustees, [1940].

Wee Willie Gray (Burns)
Saltire Society, [1950].
Reprinted from *Scottish lyrics,* Book 5 (1939).

Ane sang of the birth of Christ: Luther's Christmas carol (Anon.)
Saltire Society, [1950].
Reprinted from *Songs* (1949).

The skylark (Hogg) [for two voices]
Bayley & Ferguson, © 1952.

The gowk (Soutar) Unison song
Boosey & Hawkes, © 1952. *Boosey's Modern festival series,* no. 86.

A bairnie's sang (James A. Sidey) [solo with two-part chorus]
Bayley & Ferguson, [1953].

Cumha (A Gaelic lament) [for the organ]
London: Weeks & Co., © 1912.

Oran Mor MhicLeoid by Ruairidh Morrison, 'An Clarsair Dall' (The
Blind Harper), arranged for clarsach accompaniment.
Comunn na Clàrsaich, © 1933.

ABOUT FRANCIS GEORGE SCOTT

Lindsay, Maurice. The Scottish songs of Francis George Scott. *Music &
Letters,* 26(1) January 1945, p. 1-10.
Sorabji, Kaikhosru Shapurji. The songs of Francis George Scott. *Mi contra
fa: the immoralisings of a Machiavellian musician.* London: Porcupine
Press, 1947, p. 217-23.
(See also *Scottish Art and Letters,* no. 1 (1944), p. 22-3).
Lindsay, Maurice. Francis George Scott. *Grove's Dictionary of music and
musicians.* 5th ed., edited by Eric Blom. London: Macmillan, 1954.
Vol. 7, p. 669-70.
MacDiarmid, Hugh. *Francis George Scott: an essay on the occasion of
his seventy-fifth birthday, 25th January 1955.* Edinburgh: M. Mac-
donald, 1955. 42p.
Young, Percy M. *A history of British music.* London: Benn, 1967. p. 567.

Stevenson, Ronald. *Western music: an introduction.* London: Kahn & Averill, 1971. p. 178.
Elliot, Kenneth, and Rimmer, Frederick. *A history of Scottish music.* London: BBC, 1973. p. 73-4.

There are frequent references to Scott throughout Hugh MacDiarmid's autobiography, Lucky Poet *(1943), and in his 'essays in autobiography',* The company I've Kept *(1966), Scott shares chapter 3 with Patrick Geddes and William Johnstone. Scott is also mentioned in a number of the books concerned with literary and artistic matters in Scotland in the period from about 1920 — in, for example, the reminiscences of such figures as William Power* (Should Auld Acquaintance . . .) *(1937), Edwin Muir* (An Autobiography) *(1954) and William Soutar* (Diaries of a Dying Man) *(1954).*

W. R. AITKEN

APPENDIX B

EDWIN MUIR AND FRANCIS GEORGE SCOTT: A CONVERSATION

from

FREEMAN VIII (19th December, 1923) (U.S.A.)

SCOTT

After the concert last night I was still not quite sure about that song-cycle of Schönberg's. It is perfect in what it attempts; and it is all sustained on one key, and that is not an easy thing to accomplish. A greater man would have found it impossible to remain for such a long time on the same key. He could have done it theoretically, for his power would have been sufficient. But he could not have done it in reality, because common sense, or the lyrical impulse, or whatever you call it, would have broken in and would have varied the mood. He would have asked himself, Why am I doing this, this in particular and nothing else? and he would have widened the basis of his cycle.

MUIR

I believe you are right, F.G., though you must acknowledge that what you say goes against your preference for French literature. The French have poisoned us all with the itch for unity. I must confess — though it is shocking — that I have always found myself a little unconsciously ironical in reading "Madame Bovary," marvellous work as it is and much as I admire it. I always feel that at any moment what you call common sense may break in and raise "Madame Bovary" to the first rank in literature, and disturb the inexorable tenor of the story, and destroy its unity of mood. What a relief that would be! as great a relief as seeing a rare vase splintered to pieces after years of anxiety lest it should be splintered to pieces. I have a gross suspicion, F.G., about both you and myself. The thing which makes you not take Schönberg seriously, and what makes me not take "Madame Bovary" seriously, is a fundamental lack of reverence for art; for these are art, art distilled and concentrated, as it were, until there is nothing else left. We have an essential lack of reverence for art — a very rare quality in this age.

SCOTT

You have more reverence for art than you think, Muir. Why, you admire the Germans, who have always put reverence between them and art. You object to my liking for the French, but there is a very good reason why the French should be liked. They know what's what; and they know it not, like other races, in flashes but habitually. They are aware that art is one thing and life another, and they do not try to crush into art *das Ganze, das Geheimnis, die Seele, der Zeitgeist,* and on top of all that a *Weltanschauung.* They are too much in earnest to be reverential. You said last evening that you thought French writers must work far harder at their craft than English or German ones, seeing that their form is so much more inevitable and finished. But that is not it. They do not work harder than we do; they think more closely. They always know what they are doing, and in art that is an uncommon thing. Flaubert's problem in "Madam Bovary" was to get a certain effect, and he took good care that he obtained it. He obtained other effects in "Salammbô" and "Bouvard et Pécuchet." It was a matter purely of seeing his end concretely and using the best means for attaining it. When an artist reaches that stage he sees the whole problem too clearly to be capable of reverence; for it is impossible for a man to stand in awe of the effects he gets when he knows exactly how he produced them. French artists are behind the scenes the whole time — exactly where they should be; and they are more like actors than the artists of other nations. They know that art is *artificiel,* a word that in French, and quite rightly, has a far more respectable meaning than our "artificial". They know what to do to produce the phenomenon people call beauty, while they live among the means, which are themselves no more beautiful than the stage-properties seen from behind. They know this, simply because it is their business. It seems to me that French art is the most fundamentally irreverent art there is.

MUIR

Yes, F.G., I acknowledge that French art is irreverent, but it is not irreverent towards art. I can imagine a French poet regarding a really beautiful verse he has manufactured and smiling ironically, as Wordsworth could not have done, or Goethe either. But afterwards he will take art with enormous seriousness. He will acknowledge that it is a convention, but about this convention he will be more solemn than the most solemn German poet. German poetry has become much more serious since Stephen George began to Frenchify it; quite that solemnity it never had before. And then how much in earnest the French have taken the matter of form! They narrowed and conventionalised their whole literature for two centuries, and ours for one, by their deadly seriousness about form. They are doing so still, not in France only, but all over Europe. You can see the influence of France in Schönberg's adherence to one emotional key in his song-cycle. You can see it everywhere: in the conventionalisation of the novel in England, in the conventionalisation of the forms of unconventional verse, in the general blossoming of schools, which exist only for the sake of settling a form before it is practised and made alive. Is it not so? Well, all this I call taking art with intense and disproportionate seriousness. Our people, the artless Scots, thank God, could do nothing of the kind. Is it conceivable that any audience in London, in Dublin, or in Edinburgh, would stop a dramatic performance because the corresponding English word for *mouchoir* was used instead of the corresponding English word for *tissu?* No; our race, praise be to God, are not cursed with a sense of literary style. But, seriously, in all this inviolable respect for unity, propriety and so forth, what becomes of your common sense, and the man who shows his greatness by letting it break through?

SCOTT

Oh, there is a great deal to be said on both sides. After all, even if art is limited, that is not reason why it should not be taken seriously. If you have a concern for art, it must be a serious concern; and if you are an artist, that is all the French require of you. You desire a beauty as perfect and accomplished as possible, they say. Very well, then; you must take with deadly seriousness the rules of your art; and when you have done your utmost — and this you must do — when you have fulfilled the most exacting demands of your art, you must not imagine that you have worked a miracle; no, at the best, you have only accomplished a work of art. You have not put all life into this work. It is not a scripture — a religion, philosophy and life, rolled into one. No, it is a literary work; and if you feel inclined you are perfectly at liberty to smile ironically at it. But take the Germans! They want art to be everything; they want it to be mystical, a three-in-one of religion, philosophy and art; but if it is to be everything why should it exist at all, seeing that everything exists already? They assert that art is a function of life, and of everybody's life; not knowing that it is something to be learned, and so difficult that we call genius the capacity to learn it. No, art is not a function of everybody's life, nor a necessary category — I am sick of such phrases — for people could get along quite well if Shakespeare and Beethoven had never been born. There is no doubt of it, Muir, We do have an obsession for art — and I do not wish to lose it — "imagine" lots of things. We habitually think it has a far wider significance than it has really; and because it has become necessary to us we imagine that other people suffer because they are bereft; but that is all German-English hallucination. Keep a strict notion of art, as the French do; think of it always concretely, the totality of the works of art which have been produced; and you will be saved from such gross errors against proportion and fact.

MUIR

Certainly the Germans have written a lot of nonsense about art, and, when it comes to that, about everything. But why? Because they have tried to find answers to questions which the French, and the classical peoples generally, have never been much concerned with. I mean such questions as, Why should a man wish to create a work of art at all? Why, if it is merely a personal satisfaction for him, should it give pleasure to other people? What is beauty, an affirmation or a denial of life? On such themes, seeing that they are ultimate, as much nonsense was bound to be written as there has been written about metaphysics. Yet you do not escape from these questions by saying that art, on the one hand, is the totality of works of art, and that mankind, on the other, can live perfectly well without them; for you establish no connexion between these two raw facts, and we know that there is a connexion. I do not deny that this may be roughly the French attitude to the problem; but it seems to me to be founded on a particularly hard and unsatisfying dogma.

SCOTT

Leave it at that then. All our attitudes are founded on unsatisfying dogmas. Even the German attitude is founded on a dogma, although it is one which they have not discovered yet. What does that mean? It means that the German dogma is wasteful and uncertain, while the French dogma is economical and sure.

MUIR

No, F.G. It means that the French are easily satisfied, and that the Germans are not. The French do not ask the questions I mentioned: because they know they are unanswerable, you may say: but who are they that they should know? At any rate, answerable or unanswerable, it is a sign of vitality that these questions should be asked. What is wastefulness here? An effusion of the spirit, a sign that there is a superfluity of spirit to be exercised. But, when I regard it more closely, I deny that there is waste at all in such things; for if a man is of mean intellect he writes meanly on any subject at all, whatever it may be, even economics; and if he is a great spirit, then he writes profitably even if it is on a subject so apparently impossible as the meaning of art. But we are getting away from the point that interested me most, your notion that people can get along quite well without art. In what sense precisely did you mean it?

SCOTT

Oh, I had in mind the most ordinary idea! Common people live their lives; are born, breathe, see people being born and dying around them; have now and then pain, joy, thoughts of death and of what is beyond it for them; know all the passions; are visited with remorse; have intuitions just as a poet has. Well, that is life; that is all of it. Ordinary people who live their lives just as life is given to them bear the full burden of the mystery in common with all of us. We pity them, or we despise them a little; but what we always forget is that they live.

MUIR

They do not live much, F.G. Just consider what I have seen with my own eyes on my way here to Salzburg. There were two Americans and an Englishman in the next carriage, and they were talking so loud that the whole corridor could hear them. What were they talking about, do you think? The different regulations under which a man can be hanged or otherwise put out of the way legally in America and in England. They were patriotic, I can assure you; they each claimed for his own country a precedence in the matter of hanging. The honour of two Great Powers was at stake, and they felt it keenly. But though they quarrelled excitedly, they were agreed in one thing; in their detestation of the criminal, and in their wish that there should be more executions. Well, accept the problem even on a level as low as that! What did these people comprehend when they used terms such as hanging? Hardly anything at all. They were quite incapable of imagining the agony of a man shut up in his cell counting the dwindling hours until he is taken out, blind-folded and — it disgusts me too much to proceed. It is the same with the other experiences which you say they have like the rest of us.

They are incapable of comprehending the suffering of the world, and they are unable to partake in its joy, except in that kind which is physical. I say so confidently, for art is the rarest common fund of joy in which man can learn to partake; it is the spiritual principle and expression of joy; and if a man passes his life entirely oblivious of it, then we should pity him, as we pity a man who can not run. But I have turned back to art inadvertently. You say rightly that men see birth and death around them, that they feel pain, passion and remorse, and have intuitions. So they do; but all the same their life is an attempt to hide these things away, and not to see them, not to acknowledge intuitions — for intuitions are as disturbing as a conviction of sin. What is the final end of this? That birth, death, pain and guilt become mere names to these people, artificial as the phraseology of fashion; and they have no concrete image, no experience, for they feverishly forgot their experiences, to set against these things. These are names only, and so people can light-heartedly talk of hanging, and can tolerate and approve a thousand evils which, had they imagination — that is, were they capable of the high kind of enjoyment to be found in art — they could neither tolerate nor approve. No, F.G.; the important thing is not that we should have life — though that is essential — but that we should have it abundantly. Life is a frightfully common thing; everybody has it — a fact, as you say, generally forgotten. It is the other that is important, and therefore to us, constituted as we are, valuable.

SCOTT

Did I not say, Muir, that you had far more reverence for art than you thought? Here you are, setting up art, whether you know it or not, as a sort of religious principle, a kind of enjoyment which is not of this life; taking life, in your own words, to be a very common thing, as no doubt it is. But you are wrong. To me art is a thing to be enjoyed like everything else; like a street-scene, a conversation such as this, a finely proportioned tree, or a glimpse of these mountains seen from the train between here and Innsbruck. To tell you the truth, I think perfectly ordinary people enjoy these things too. They observe more habitually than we do who live in a cloud of ideas; they see landscapes and incidents very clearly, and enjoy them all the more because they do not stop to note their feelings. It may be that to them birth, death, pain and remorse are only names, but, seriously, does that matter so very much? Birth and death are, after all, things which do not concern us vitally; at least, our own birth and our own death do not; and why should we be more troubled by the fate of other people than by our own? These are not the real business of life, but only its beginning and its end; and every-thing lies between them. Absolutely everything! It is natural, too, of course, to forget pain and remorse; and not only that, but it is the best course if we are to live with fortitude. The poet remembers them, but that is because he can do nothing else. Every artist groans under a curse, and art is the blessing that is vouchsafed him to make it tolerable. But ordinary people do not suffer under the disease, so why should they be in need of the remedy? And, as I say, outside these categories in which we think and feel far too much, there is a great deal left to them: there is everything, I often think, except the categories. Sometimes I am made sad by the thought of how much happiness there is in the world, and there quite inevitably and naturally, so that you can do nothing with it, and neither fight against it nor advance it, any more than you can fight for or against the procession of the seasons.

MUIR

Yet, F.G., you would not have this sense of the richness of ordinary life if you were what you call an ordinary man. You would not write your music, and it would not be so soundly and magnificently Scottish, for this attitude of yours I am convinced is characteristically Scottish. I doubt if you exchange your vision of the unconscious and beautiful happiness of ordinary people for the thing itself, which would necessarily exclude the vision. That brings me to the point which it seems to me you have avoided: that art infinitely widens our field of experience, making us live not merely within our skins, like your unconscious happy man, but in mankind, sharing their sorrows and joys vicariously in a way beyond the reach of moralists and reformers. This widening of experience is made possible partly by the use of the categories you speak of, that is, such concepts as birth, death, pain, guilt, and so forth; but these are only the means, and as little beautiful as means generally are, and the emotional experience is a thing totally unlike them, and as pure and beautiful as the joys which you attribute to the natural life of men. But they are also more spacious and more impersonal; they can be communicated on a large scale; and they are capable of humanising mankind more than any personal joy growing in its place. All happiness, I admit, whatever kind it may be, humanises us, even the happiness of rascals and tyrants; and a happy man has an influence on every one he meets which can not be computed, though Browning has spoiled the idea for us. But that is a thing which we can not argue about, for we have nothing but our feelings to refer to. But we can recognise the difference in range between a feeling of joy expressed in a work of art — "joy in widest commonality spread" — and the modest happiness of a man living in a private world. And art does disseminate joy, and in doing so humanises us; and when I speak of art doing that I do not mean art in the sense in which you, and according to you the French, speak of it. I mean art as it is felt in the works of the very greatest men, whom all the world would acknowledge to be kin, such as Shakespeare, Molière, Goethe and our own Burns. I mean especially the art where common sense or the lyrical impulse breaks through, for that is what humanises art, as it is what aestheticises humanity in the rough. That brings me back to your first remark, which interested me most of all, that a greater artist disturbs the tenor of a work by breaking in with common sense; for that showed me exactly where my reverence lies. My reverence is not for art in itself, nor for your artless life as it is, but for the significant point where they meet and as it were interpenetrate each other.

SCOTT

Well, thank God, we can agree about something at last. I acknowledge that your point is the solution of the riddle, for that gives art a meaning, which is what we have been seeking for; and art, too, in its turn, though in a secondary degree, gives meaning back to life — though life, it seems to me, does not need it very much. But that, I imagine, is where we shall never agree, so let us leave it over. What I meant by common sense was, I fancy, more exactly a sense of proportion, the feeling of the artist, having a certain mood of life prominence, he must bring the others in also. He must get as much into art as possible, and make it as sound as life. Now Leopardi, for instance, whom you admire, had a marvellous mind; he hardly ever set down an observation which does not strike one as true; yet I can not read him at any time without feeling that his constant observation of life from one point of view makes him just a little ridiculous. There were a thousand other ways of looking at existence, and he stuck persistently to one. A work of art, the more perfect it is, the more it is divorced from life, tends to give one more and more a vision of life from one single point of view, like Leopardi's; sticking to that point of view, even although it is the most difficult thing in the world, for the sake of preserving artistic unity; and not recognising that this artistic unity is humanly sometimes a little ridiculous. That is what makes me take Leopardi not quite seriously, although I know he was in deadly earnest; and it is what, I fancy, makes your appreciation of "Madame Bovary" not quite unconditional. But all this does not mean that a man, supposing himself inspired, is at liberty to set down anything that comes into his head, on the chance that it may be true or beautiful, but really not knowing anything about it. So I still like the French for knowing what they mean, and, as artists, for knowing what they do. They are right; but so, on the other hand, is the man who breaks up a conversation, or the unity of a book, from a sense of proportion, and to get in more life. There is nothing that can be said against him then, for when he does that he is like a force of nature, and it would be as idle to condemn as it would be to condemn the lightning for falling here after a fortnight's uninterrupted sunshine. But that is common sense and nothing more; and you will not persuade me that there is any mystical German theory needed to explain it.

MUIR

I shall not attempt it, for I am content with what you say. Shakespeare showed his greatness in the thing for which he has been condemned so often, his introduction of comic relief into his tragedies, and in his most exalted scenes knew how and where to sink, his sense of proportion never failing him. Perhaps he did this inevitably and without thinking about it; but Goethe, who had theorised much about art, did it deliberately in "Faust", introducing the Cellar Scene to lower and enrich the severe opening of his tragedy. These are the two writers who in modern times have shown the greatest command of life. But as I listened to you it seemed that an explanation of all the great blossoming times of European literature had nearly flown into my hands. I can not explain it clearly at the moment, for it always seems to be fluttering just outside my reach, but it is something like this. All the great literatures of Europe have been written by Northern races when they have encountered in one form or another the shock of the South. The fair-haired Greeks were obviously Northern people, and they saw the beginning of European literature, for the Bible is not a European book, and no one has felt it to be so, or has treated it as we treat Shakespeare or Homer. The Renaissance in Italy was the belated outcome of the successive invasions of barbarians which swept away the Roman Empire. France is a sort of synthesis of North and South, but most of its great writers have come from the north, or from some part not distinctly Southern. England and Germany are almost purely Northern; but they did not begin to blossom into literature until in one way or another they came into the atmosphere of Southern culture, and the German *Sehnsucht* for the South is the sign of a racial need. The North can not do without the South in some form; but nevertheless it is the Northern people who have been the productive agents in all these literatures; the Southern races have been the passive element; they have merely given the condition of productivity, that is, a profound and deeply sunk-in culture. But that is not all; for the Northern peoples correspond to your man who lets common sense break through; they are the inartistic race who produce art; while the Southern peoples are instinctive artists concerned with form and with artistic unity, but producing very little. If you examine the history of Europe, you will be at a loss to find any great body of literature whose creative body came from the South. It is almost all the work of the Northern peoples. So there, very roughly, for I have not scrutinised it yet myself, you have your upsetting, common sense principle revealed as the agent behind every great blossoming of literature. Probably it is a question of race in the end. What do you think of it?

SCOTT

I really do not know. Your theory requires a great deal of evidence, and we have none. Perhaps there is something in it.

EDWIN MUIR.

APPENDIX C

'PIBROCH' LECTURE TO THE SALTIRE SOCIETY IN EDINBURGH

23rd November, 1946

Music in my opinion is a kind of language using sounds instead of words and is able to express just as speech can, the most subtle of all meanings by variations of tone — or inflection. Unlike speech, however, it does not stoop to naming things, actions and ideas, it can rely entirely on sound to express what it means.

From this point of view it is an easy step to the conclusion that just as different races have different languages so too will they have different kinds of music — the French and the Germans differ radically in both speech and music while on the other hand Italian music and French music are not so dissimilar. One need not labour the point — even the dialects of different parts of Scotland produce characteristic differences in musical expression.

So at the outset I wish to make a confession — I have neither skill at the Gaelic nor at the 'pipering'.

Born within walking distance of the Cheviots, I had the good luck as a lad to spend part of my leisure with a working tailor from the Highlands who never tired of singing songs in the Gaelic language. The music of these songs I still retain in memory but the words I found were merely cause of merriment to college students from the north-east. With regard to 'pipering', I have never even blown into a full set of pipes and this I maintain proves that I am at any rate an unbiased student of the art.

So now to *the* bagpipes — or *a* bagpipes — or *the bagpipe*, for you must all have noticed that it, the bag, has no fewer than five pipes fitted into it — the three pipes over the shoulders are the drones — droning away on one pitch all the time: a 4th pipe to the player's mouth carrying breath to the bag and a 5th the chanter pipe on which the player's fingers manipulate the notes of the music.

It is to this chanter pipe that I must first of all turn my attention, because the construction of it, the bore of it and the position of the 8 holes on it are responsible for the kind of sounds that go to make up the music. The number of sounds which this chanter can produce is a humble *nine* and on the piano starting with the lowest note they are G A B C sharp D E F sharp G and A — the very limited compass of an octave and one note. Just 9 different sounds, without mechanism of any kind such as all orchestral wind instruments have for altering the pitch of the notes or increasing their number. Out of these 9 sounds all bagpipe music is fashioned — may I remind you that a piano has 84 keys!

Now the first thing to notice about this series of 9 notes is that it never reproduces the 8 notes of the scale with which we are most familiar — that of d r m f s l t d'. It just can't do it! If I begin on G and play G A B C sharp D E F sharp G — the lower half G A B C sharp doesn't sound d r m f because C sharp is too high. The D E F sharp is quite correct and sounds s l t d'.

Again, if I commence on A — playing A B C sharp D E F sharp G A I am disappointed, as E F sharp G A do not sound s l t d'. This is all very easy of course to everyone who has practised a few piano scales, for the scale of G requires only *one* sharp — not *two* and the scale of A requires three sharps — not two.

Without troubling you too much about this piper's predicament, I ought to explain that mankind, at any rate since history began, has been making music in hundreds of different scales. The Greeks, to instance only one race, made use of seven different scales — that is to say they could go from a note to its octave (low doh to high doh) in seven different ways: thus —

C	(1)	d	r	m	f	s	l	t	d'			
B flat	(2)		r	m	f	s	l	t	d'	r'		
A flat	(3)			m	f	s	l	t	d'	r'	m'		
G	(4)				f	s	l	t	d'	r'	m'	f'	
F	(5)					s	l	t	d'	r'	m'	f'	s'
E flat	(6)						l	t	d'	r'	m'	f'	s'	l'
D flat	(7)							t	d'	r'	m'	f'	s'	l'	t'

These Greek scales or modes as they were called, took their names from neighbouring countries where the *MODE* or kind of music had a character of its own, and so we have the Ionian mode; the Lydian mode, the Phrygian mode, etc. It would take too long to deal satisfactorily with this matter, and moreover, your late Professor Sir Donald Tovey assured me there was no satisfactory account of the Greek musical system — So I confine my remarks to pointing out that the 4th scale I played (the Lydian mode) sounding f s l t d r m f is the bagpipe scale beginning on G, and the 5th scale (the Mixolydian mode) sounding s l t d r m f s is the bagpipe scale beginning on A.

Now I am not committing myself to the statement that Celtic music derives from the Greek modes. That would be rash on anyone's part, for nobody knows — not even Sir Donald Tovey, so we must be content to leave the subject and try some other line of enquiry.

Some of the world's earliest music requires only five notes instead of seven to cover the distance from d to d' (by which I mean, of course, the interval of an octave). The five notes may be set down as d r m s l d', the high Doh not counting as a new note. This 5-note or pentatonic scale

is said to be a 'gapped' scale because it has a leap in it from m to s and
another from l to d'. It can easily be remembered as it corresponds to
the black notes on the piano — the group of 3 black notes sounding
d r m and the group of 2 giving us the s and l. If we try to fit these
5 notes into the 9 notes of the bagpipe scale we discover that we can do
so in two ways and make use of the whole vocabulary of the chanter,
thus —

	G	A	B	C sharp	D	E	F sharp	G	A
	d	r	m		s	l		d'	
and									
	d	r		m		s		l	d'

which gives us two pentatonic scales, one on G, the other on A.

We can go further, for it is not necessary to begin a pentatonal scale
always with the note doh. We are only using another form of the scale
when we begin with ray, or with me, or soh or lah just as the Greeks
did with their modes, so let us see how some of these fit into the nine-
note series.

	G	A	B	C sharp	D	E	F sharp	G	A
		r	m		s	l		d'	r'
		s	l		d	r		m	s'
			l		d	r		m	s'

Which gives us another 3 pentatonic scales = 2 on A and 1 on B.

If we add the two complete 7-note scales — the one on G and the
other on A to our list we can only marvel that such a primitive instrument
as the bagpipe, is so constructed that it is able to produce 7 different
modes or, as I said, kinds of music. And this isn't theory — it is an
induction from the whole range of bagpipe music whether in the form of
March, Strathspey, Reel or Pibroch, and it is at the same time a key
to the understanding of Highland folk-song and all that is best in the
music of the Lowlands.

So in future if pipe music sounds peculiar or unfamiliar to you,
perhaps you will treat with some consideration the genius of the Celt
which long ago extracted no fewer than 7 scales out of 9 notes. His
language is a difficult one to acquire and the language of his music is
almost as difficult.

A recent analysis of 50 pibrochs gave the following results —

Pentatonic Scale with G as Doh = 9 pibrochs
Pentatonic Scale with A as Doh = 13 pibrochs
Pentatonic Scale with A as Soh = 11 pibrochs
Pentatonic Scale with A as Ray = 3 pibrochs

a total of 36 out of 50

The remaining 14 pibrochs had 6 note scales — not a single pibroch making use of the 7 note scale.

Before I invite you to listen to a pibroch, there is yet another aspect of music I must deal with, namely, Rhythm. As everyone knows, when God created this and the other Worlds, what he really said, was "Let there be Rhythm" and there *was* rhythm everywhere — in day and night; the ebb and flow of the tides, the unfolding of plants, the pulsation of the blood, the development of our instincts and the recurrence of our moods. "I've got rhythm", croons the crooner, though surely he need not make a boast of it. I suspect that what he means is, that he has more of it than other people — or more of it than he ought to have.

It is not surprising then that the Gaels, living as they do so close to nature, base both their folk-songs and their instrumental music on a very definite sense of the importance of rhythm, and give priority to it over the melodic principle. Their melodies in other words grow on, and out of, a pattern of rhythm. Thus, taking at random such a pattern as this and using it four times, we have a rhythm-scheme on which a melody can be built.

1. Let us have it reversed in the order of Bar 4, 3, 2 and 1.

2. If we add notes to this from one of the pentatonic groups we could get.

3. The notes of the tune don't matter so very much. The mere repetition of the rhythm carries the notes along with it.

But maybe I'm giving too much away — is this the explanation of the 'lilt' in Gaelic music and the cause of so much stamping of feet?

[per contra. play through the English 'Drink to me only with thine eyes']

As further Gaelic examples:
My bonny Mary and/or 'Fear a bhata'

With these principles in mind we can proceed to a very simple description of Pibroch — the 'ceol mor' or great music of the Gael. Let us take for example "MacCrimmon's Sweetheart". The theme, called the 'Urlar', meaning foundation or ground, is announced first of all, and is generally in slow, deliberate tempo, broken up occasionally by what to an uninitiated listener may sound very like interruptions to the flow of the music. It is from the principal notes of this Urlar that all subsequent variations are derived — the variations being of the rhythm, not of the melody.

VAR. I (in the pibroch Mr Calum Johnston is about to play) is almost identical with the theme or urlar, the only difference being that a high A (doh) is substituted for the lah of the theme, and as the high A is played by the thumb, this kind of variation is usually styled a "thumb variation".

VAR. I   Thumb Var.

VAR. II is an extraordinary development of Var. I. The persistent repetition of one phrase, which at the end of the line becomes

m r m s r d

makes it a very remarkable bit of musical daring — and (at least to one hearer) humour

Var: II

M

VAR. III is built on a very simple rhythm-unit which our school children know as 'taafe'. The long note is generally doh and the short one a melody note.

d m d l d s m m r m d l d s r r   etc.

Siubhal

VAR. IV is called a doubling of Var. III — the word 'doubling' signifying that you hear the preceding variation this time without any halts in the playing of it.

Siubhal Doubling

VAR. V. This is known as a Taobhludh variation. In this pibroch it is really derived from Var. III but with a triple repeat of the doh — the effect being

d d d m d d d l d d d s   etc.

Taobhludh Fosgailte Singling

VAR. VI is a doubling of Var. V — that is without halts or pauses in the performance of it.

Taobhludh Fosgailte Doubling

VAR. VII is known as the Creanludh Variation, the rhythm patterns of which is too complicated for any verbal description.

Creanludh Fosgailte Singling

VAR. VIII is the same as Var. VII — a doubling, without halts in the music.

Creanludh Fosgailte Doubling

VAR IX is a Creanludh-a-mach Variation — one of the most complicated and beautiful rhythm patterns to be found in pibroch. I can only say — it must be heard to be believed.

Creanludh Fosgailte a mach

EX. 30

WAR OR PEACE. (Very old).

Ground

EX. 31

Ground. LAMENT FOR THE CHILDREN. (Probably about 1650).

It should now be clear that etch Variation has a rhythmic pattern of its own and that this pattern continues throughout the Variation.

This pibroch is described as being in 6 4 4 structure that is, the first line of it has 6 bars, the second line 6 bars and the 3rd line 4 bars. The scale of the music is a doh-pentatonic on A: i.e. A sounds doh and the only other melody notes are r, m, s and lah. It may be a help if I indicate the 2 outstanding notes in each bar of it

line 1   d l s m d l s m r l s r

line 2   d l s m r l r l r l s r

line 3   d l s m   r l s r

The first 2 bars of each line are the same and the last 2 bars of each line are the same.

The name of the piece is "MacCrimmon's Sweetheart".

The general effect produced by the playing of a pibroch, is of something gathering momentum as it moves from one position to another. This of course is brought about by the fact that each rhythm-pattern in turn is followed by a more intricate rhythm-pattern, and the tension and sense of urgency which this brings about, provides at the close a powerful climax to all that has gone before.

Calum Johnston plays 'MacCrimmons Sweetheart'.

PART 2

I had the exasperating experience about a year ago of listening to a well-known Scottish author describe pibroch as 'nothing but a great big tune!' He undoubtedly imagined he was putting the whole matter in a nut-shell, giving his audience quite a satisfactory explanation of the 'great music' and saying something that nobody else had ever had the wit to put into words. I propose therefore to discuss briefly the question — "Is pibroch just a big tune?".

From what I have already said, what you have heard Mr Johnston play, you may have come to the conclusion that not even a pibroch urlar has much tune in it. Your judgement in this matter will largely depend on your idea of what constitutes a tune. I can only say here that good tunes don't necessarily make good pibroch themes, any more than good tunes make good fugues. In painting we know that the colours must be mixed with brains, and in music the same commodity is essential to the making of any great work. Enthusiasm, which is often mistaken for inspiration, may provide an idea for a work of art, but intelligence is necessary if the idea is ever to find adequate expression; and it is this intelligence — this musical intelligence of the Gael as shown in pibroch — that I am anxious to commend in tonight's lecture.

Pibroch is not 'Ceol Beag'. It would, on the contrary, be better to think of it as the only musical form Scotland has given to the world; as an aristocratic art in classical shape and as keeping its distance away from the common and popular. I doubt if it ever was popular, even in the Highlands.

So let us choose another sample and examine it — "War and Peace" in the version of the urlar given by G. F. Ross. It begins (see Ex. 30 on page 180) which you will probably recognise as another example of gapped structure.

The first line begins with a phrase which sets the pattern for both melody and rhythm — | m m m r r r | d d d s - d | — and this is repeated at once, which is then followed by the same pattern in sequence beginning a note higher but actually ending a note lower:

| f f f m m m | r r r f - ta |

The 2nd line begins like the 1st line with m m m   r r r d d d s - d and is followed by the variation of one note | f f f   f f f | f f f   f f f | and concludes with 1st phrase again but ending with f - ta instead of s - d.

The 3rd line takes all its material from the first line

| m m m   r r r | d d d s-d | f f f   m m m |
r r r f-ta |

Now in my opinion it is no use setting this before an audience and telling them it is a 'big tune'. It is nothing of the kind — no, not even a 'little tune'. It is a remarkably subtle piece of musical construction, analogous to the Knotwork and spirals of Celtic art and is found no-where but in the north-west of this country. We saw what the ingenuity of the Celt could find in a quote scale and here again the same ingenuity is applied to the construction of musical phrases strong enough to support the weight of the 15 variations that follow.

When we turn to the same theme of the "Lament for the Children" I agree at once that we have a tune and a very great one. The inspiration of the melody in no way hindered Patrick Mor MacCrimmon from doing some curious things to knit his phrases together (see Ex. 31 on page 180).

The full scheme of the melody, giving each new bar a number, runs as follows:

1st line	1	2	3	4	5	6	7	8	
2nd line	1	2	3	4	5	6	7	8	viz repeat of 1st line
3rd line	3	6	9	2	10	2	11	6	
4th line	5	6	7	8	12	13	5	4	

The handling of the rhythm of the tune is thoroughly Gaelic, for out of 24 bars no fewer than 18 of them have exactly the same pattern. The Gaelic composer maintains his rhythmic unit and prefers to secure variety by occasional subtle alterations in pitch.

There remains only one other area I would like to refer to — that of "Colin Roy Mackenzie's Lament". This pibroch has had something of a dubious past under the title of "Lord Kintail's Lament" and been in some kind of relationship with "Craigelachie" — the only pibroch I'm told that comes from the eastern Highlands.

To give you one short peep into the kind of controversy that goes on about everything connected with 'Ceol Mor', this Colin Roy Mackenzie's Lament' is said by the Piobaireached Society to be made up of 6 bars plus 10 bars plus 8 bars and therefore "peculiar".

General Thomason, who evidently spent his whole life examining pibrochs, says the tune should be in 4 lines of 6 bars each viz 6 bars plus 6 bars plus 6 bars plus 6 bars.

Another authority (I must just whisper this) told me he thought the urlar was really in 4 lines of 8 bars with the second line missing! — but I hadn't the heart to ask him where it had gone. The Piobaireachd Society's Editorial note concludes with these words: "Thus the tune, as now presented, is really a *fragment* put into shape comparatively recently by Angus Mackay." The result, however, is a pleasing production which seems well worthy of preservation.

Francis George Scott then played "the kind of 'fragment' *Colin Roy Mackenzie's Lament* is" on the piano, and the lecture concluded with Calum Johnston playing 'The Bells of Perth', called by Scott "certainly one of the greatest among great pibrochs . . . The scale is again a pentatonic one, but doh r m s l is now on G instead of on A. This is a much darker mode and quite unlike the tune in the A mode. The whole music is, of course, a full tone lower, and the clash of the music in Key G against the drone of the med. pipes in A will, I fancy, be a new experience to everyone who hears it now for the first time. I hope you will be able to hear the bells".

APPENDIX D

F. G. SCOTT TO C. M. GRIEVE (HUGH MACDIARMID):

A SURVEY OF THE LETTERS

After his death in September 1978, Dr C. M. Grieve's papers were bought by a manuscript and antique bookdealer, and subsequently sold to Edinburgh University Library. This book, however, was already page-proofed by the time these letters reached the public domain, and were in due course catalogued. Obviously it was not possible to indulge in substantial re-writing of the main part of the book at so late a stage; yet the character of Scott's letters to MacDiarmid is of unique value, both for the light they throw on the composer himself and on the relationship between two distinguished Scottish artists. The publisher readily agreed with my suggestion that these letters should form the subject of an extended Appendix; a survey that is, in effect, a major additional chapter. To allow time for the writing of this extra material, the original publication date of the book — designed to coincide with the centenary celebrations on 25th January, 1980 — had to be be put back by several months. No other course would have been possible, since a study of Scott taking no cognisance of his letters to his closest friend and most inspiring collaborator, would have been of of limited value.

Much of the earlier part of the correspondence is taken up with Scott's detailed comments on new poems sent to him by MacDiarmid. Because most of Scott's criticism of MacDiarmid's first four books appears to have been made verbally, the earliest written comment in these letters relates to the *First Hymn to Lenin*. Indeed, there is only one letter from the nineteen-twenties in the collection. Dated Sunday 11th December, 1927, and written from 103 Woodville Gardens, Langside, it thanks the poet for his congratulations on the birth of Scott's second son and fourth child: "I hope you observe how well, even in procreation, I am maintaining a perfectly classical balance", Scott jokes: "two and two — and you can have my assurance, here and now, that I am not disturbing it — no, never!"

From what then follows, it becomes clear that his 'Forties quarrel with the BBC had long-established roots:

"The Missus last Monday had a communication from the BBC about giving a recital of my songs (composer at the piano) on 13th January — first of a series on 'Living Scottish Composers'. We turned it down . . . They can damned well whistle for all eternity as far as I'm concerned — not even first of a series is good enough for me these days!"

The long series of letters written throughout the Thirties alter in character as the decade progresses. From 1930 to 1934, Scott was willing to devote a great deal of time to the manuscript verses that arrived in bundles from MacDiarmid. At first, the poet paid careful attention to

Scott's suggestions many of which appear to have been incorporated the final versions of some of the poems making up *Scots Unbound* and *Stony Limits.* Thereafter, Scott's increasing impatience with what he regarded as the frittering away of his friend's talents on futile political, indeed megalomanic gesturing, made the contribution of such detailed criticism pointless. The letters from the later 'Thirties deal almost entirely with family and general matters.

On 12th April, 1932, Scott acknowledged his signed copy of the *First Hymn to Lenin and other Poems.*

"The 'Hymn' ''", Scott thought, did not "cut very much ice but some of the things in the latter half of the volume, 'Charisma', 'Water of Life', and the 'Seamless Garment' (especially the last) had the authentic note . . . To the 'Seamless Garment' I have just one objection — that you have my Jamieson[1] and I had to guess (without certainty) . . . The auld Emmle-dugs o' the past are curjate and devauld!

"The poem to me was the best in the book — 'Woven owre close for the point o' a pin, Onywhere to win in!' '' But the political overtones must have worried Scott, for he added: "Just remember however — Lenin didn't write poems and Rilke didn't bring out the Russian Revolution''.

Having thus early in the correspondence expressed his belief that poetry and politics rarely mix, Scott defined the limitations of his own currently fashionable intellectual curiosity about Communism.

"So you're a Communist. Extraordinary! It must be true that good minds think alike for my one study for many a month has been the Leninist-Marxist dialectic, and I've been trying to work out all its possibilities in the artistic sphere . . . I needn't add that I'd find difficulty in accepting 'Communism' and 'Art' in one and the same breath, but I'm intensely interested at the moment in the relation between the two.''

Scott then suggested that they should both try their hand at a new national anthem for Scotland, a proposal that came to nothing, though several times advanced over the years.

By 7th May, the manuscripts of MacDiarmid's poems 'Tarras' and 'Water Music', both eventually to appear in *Scots Unbound,* had reached Scott.

"The *Tarras* is all right. Viewing the poem as a whole perhaps the sex-imagery (an illustration, after all, and not the principal theme of the poem) gets the upper hand in places and leaves the reader wondering whether Tarras is not merely an excuse. You have precedent for this, of course, in Rozanov[2] who wrote his stuff with his hand on his penis, but the results are good material for the Freudians of the future, so it really doesn't matter much. I'd have said more on this theme if I hadn't got the 'Water Music' yesterday. It assured me that you are retaining some few notions of objectivity and the concrete in art. Before, however, leaving the final impression the poem gives, I would like to warn you in your own words not to revolve too much round yourself —

> 'And O! I canna thole
>   Aye yabblin o' my soul   } 'Drunk Man'
> And *fain I wad be free*
>   O' my eternal me.'

(Don't you see you're not *free* as an artist while yet you're in bondage to the flesh! — St. Paul).

Copulation's a fairly common form of amusement and not much remains to be said on that head! Besides, I've a vague notion that in the long run the *impersonal* in art becomes the most *personal*".

Detailed comments on several of the poems followed, in the case of 'Tarras' difficult now to check in detail, because Scott's comments seem to have resulted in a complete re-writing of the poem, his further comments on the revised version being made on 15th May. In this letter, too, he was provoked by the sight of the draft of the 'Second Hymn to Lenin' to a sustained bout of self-revelation:

"The 2nd Hymn really makes me *serious* and compels me to drop matters of diction altogether and think hard on the nature of poetry and art in general. Not only does it make me *serious* — it makes me *suspicious,* and I find myself grubbing amongst lots of queer notions about yourself and Eliot and the Criterion. What in hell's name does Eliot want to do with this in the Criterion, for instance? Is he adding you to his collection of freak writers, letting the young lions roar while he stands pontifically aside and faintly smiles? . . . I really don't believe you've gone right down to the roots of the Communism business at all for ultimately it leads to a denial of your own gift and is certainly not 'art as communication' . . .

'Are my poems spoken in the factories and field.
In the streets of the Toon?' — you ask?

Why, of course not! I can't at the moment think of anything of yours that will become as familiar as lots of poor, uneducated Rabbie Burns who knew from the beginning by the light of Heaven (just as *I* have always known) what you are only glimpsing at in your new phase. I'll bet you a thousand pounds that Russia doesn't disown Burns at this moment. But no amount of

Organic constructional work,
Practicality and work by degrees;
First things first; and poetry in turn
'll be built by these . . .

will matter a hoot. It remains jargon, and not even the arrival of the Socialist Federation of the Whole Cosmos will ever make it anything else.

"I'm particularly 'humpy' on this point, as you will see. And I'm particularly sure of myself too, for I have made a fairly thorough investigation of the problem as it affects creative work of all kinds. I am just as anxious as you are to find a way out of the present impasse, but My God it's going to be a hellish business. For instance, Russia at the moment is little more than Co-operative Stores and educational propaganda: things we're quite familiar with at our own doors. 'Freein' oor pooe'rs for greater things' — what greater things? Give me just one, s'il vous plaît. Reading Hymns to Lenin — I DON'T THINK!"

On 5th June Scott acknowledged two more poems, 'The Back o' Beyond' and 'Cheville', telling MacDiarmid he is glad to receive them for several reasons: "In the first place I'm glad you can still do such a 'gem' as 'Back o' Beyond', for it assures me that the vein remains traceable throughout your work right from the beginning up till this moment, and

that your hankering after fetiches of any variety is of the moment only
. . . for you know already how finicky I can get on certain artistic details
like this. Don't mistake! It isn't naivete or mere ingenuousness on my part
— not at all! — it's just the very subtlest bit of my brain matter that
gets a laugh at cleverness of all kinds, particularly when the clever ones
are looking on. The tight-rope walker . . . does something unheard of,
and asks the spectator, 'How's that?' You'll then hear a chorus of
knowalls telling you — 'Oh, but that's different!' . . . There's no more
savagely philistine a gang anywhere than these same knowing-ones, who
just don't know an inch beyond their own smartness. You've gone through
your experimental stage by now, you've blustered and hectored in resound-
ing neologisms with the best of them, embraced Dadaism, Pragmatism,
Socialism, Freudism and, latest of all, Bolshevism, and you're still C.M.G.
and hardly a sennachie the better for it all. A younger generation is
already at your heels, eager and able to howl down all your -isms into
the dustbin (for we can be certain their new fangles won't be what *ours*
have been) and you've thought of Bolshevism as the hobby-horse of the
future; as big a favourite, in fact, as last Wednesday's 'Orwell'. And I'm
telling you it doesn't matter a damn. You can write pages and pages of
Leninism without a glimmer of fundamental brain or creative energy
and have it praised as oracular, colossal or the like, and all the time
you know as well as I do that 'The Back o' Beyond' is just the tight-rope
performer's inexplicable magic and mystery, and that it is worth all the
rest put together. Most folk for a long time to come will fail to realise
that it has happened. That's its inevitable badge of merit. No applause,
thank you — just silence!"

On June 28th, Scott told MacDiarmid he had received a copy of
Muir's *Six Poems*. It had made him favourably revise his opinion of
Muir's poetic faculty. Scott explained:

"I refer to Muir here because of an interesting comparison I worked
out between the two of you — interesting to me at any rate as placing
you both in something like philosophical categories — the one as a poet
concerned with 'being', the other concerned with 'becoming'. And in the
process of explaining all this, I seemed to realise clearer than before that
most of the wisecracks I've been serving up to you have just been in the
nature of advice to deal oftener with 'permancies' on which (it may be)
all art is built up and give the 'transiencies' a rest. D'ye think there's
anything in it? Take your last efforts. 'Dytiscus' passes the test: 'Antenora',
whatever the hell that is, almost does the same . . . the 'Filament Factory'
just misses being McGonagall [sic]. Now the only thing that matters for
every one of us as individuals is, are we doing the thing we're best fitted
to do? I don't speak like an oracle, I hope, but it may be that your muse
is a purely lyrical wench (I fancy my *own* is) and fails at the 'higher
flights' and the 'mighty mouthed harmonies'. One could lead evidence,
e.g. your versatility and its many disguises as newfangledness, etc., in
support of what I'm putting forward, but in any case going by results
so far, while you've proved yourself time and time again in the lyric I
don't think you'd be able to justify yourself in either epic or long poem.
The lyrical and the epic are, it would seem, two differing types of mentality
and exclude each other. At anyrate I'm far from convinced by either the

Hymns to Lenin or The Filament Factory that you are really doing in these work that matters either to yourself, or to the world at large.

How's that for the first turn of the 'screwing up' you advise me to adopt with reference to your output?''

On 8th July, Scott is replying to a letter accompanying another bundle of manuscripts. As usual, he immediately picked out the clear winner, exclaiming of 'Milkwort and Bog-cotton':

"You should write several books of this — it's a masterpiece that has a flaw hidden somewhere inside it." The 'flaw' was in the last line of the first stanza, which Scott suggested should be: "Owre milkwort een or milkwhite cotton hair", a suggestion the poet greatly improved upon. But the 'flaw' was trifling. Said Scott:

"I'll stand you another drink on the strength of these two stanzas and I'll find music for them, sure. They are in the very benmaist spirit o' pibroch."

The poem 'Lynch Pin' sounded to Scott "like a Donne or Shakespeare sonnet, and b'gad not far behind one." The first draft of 'Parley o' Beasts', however, failed to gain approval: "The thought is not new to you and in any case not true enough to stand water. It gives it an air of sentimentality which is increased by the looseness of the writing and the occasional rhyming. A good many stanzas have particularly weak last lines which give the reader the impression that you are filling up blank coupons and doing as many of them as you can." Heed was evidently paid to these observations, for the final version of the poem has only four taut stanzas.

Scott reacted fiercely to his friend's increasing habit of verse-cataloguing — a traditional Scots literary trait — which was soon to exercise a disastrous influence on MacDiarmid's later work, although the poet did use it successfully in 'Water Music', if rather less so in the title poem of *Scots Unbound:*

"I thought on reading the earlier pages today that I was listening to a Scots philologist frae Aberdeen giving a broadcast talk on 'Scots and the Senses'. Most folk would conclude 'Quite interesting' — the latest form of 'damning with faint praise'. Watch out for this word 'interesting'. I've heard it applied to some of my music and it's being used all over Europe to indicate a particular brand of modernity.

Of the 14 pages then of 'Scots Unbound', the first five read like a broadcast talk and are just interesting. At the bottom of page five you butt in with a particularly obnoxious couple o' lines — the personal touch once more —

   'As deep to deep speaks source and sea
   Sae I'd hae my verse and vocabulary be
   My land and me.'   (Hee - hee!)

After that bit of foolishness you are fit for anything: and go off with an orgasm that 'les hommes de bons sens' (if nobody else) will thoroughly enjoy watching. I am not (speaking for myself) condemning it any more than I would think of condemning the climax of one of Sorabji's movements, but I warn you the dividing line between the intentionally sublime and the patently ridiculous vanishes, and you become dependent on charity. The charitable and a good many nit-wits and myself will say it's carried through with spirit, and feel that you meant well — the uncharitable will just think it's damned funny and characteristic. The *posture* is in any case not a very dignified one . . ."

Judging by the lines then quoted in Scott's detailed critique, 'Scots Unbound' must have been substantially altered; but at least this draft inspired Scott to set down his views on the difference between doing the thing and just talking about it. Some of MacDiarmid's earthbound bird imagery had provoked Scott's wrath: "It is decidedly bad taste (to me) to refer to 'the techniques that make a Tarras'. I think it's just foolishly egotistical, coming especially as it does after the exhibition of flying you've just given. And then 'THOCHT' itself fails you and you curse thocht itself as only the instrument to cry down our real ends as faulty — and infra dig! There can't be much left after that but your own ego in very big letters with 'my soaring sang'. At this point, if not before, those of us whose scepticism (contrary to what you think) is even more profound than your own, just become charitable or say nowt. You've certainly unbounded belief in some directions at anyrate.

To me all this sort of thing is just bluff and bravado and I either know or think I know what brings it about. It is 1000 times easier to talk about a thing in art than to do it (ars longa, vita brevis) and very, very few poems in any age get beyond the stage of being promisory notes. They talk a lot about flying i.e. they flap a lot but you never catch them above hedge height and making a hellish ado about even that. Personally I'm not long in concluding that they are birds that simply *can't* fly (poets, musicians, etc. that can't sing). Let me refer you for an example to the Sibelius concert last Thursday night in London — London has, since the publication of Cecil Gray's book on him, discovered that he *can* sing and *does,* and I tell you the stock of every other composer in Europe has suddenly flopped 100 per cent. The London critics are now talking about him in the same breath as Beethoven, as a symphonist, and it is just possible that he is one of the big men and outside the Zeitgeist altogether. So not so much, please, about 'yourself' and this monstrosity called the 'modern consciousness'!"

Of the poems Scott reacted to on 19th July, only 'Depth and the Chthonian Image' won his approval: "Almost a 'seamless garment' and very good indeed. You seem in this to have risen to your high theme. There's a lot I could say (and will some day) about the discrepancy between your matter and manner, but for the nonce 'There! a manner for every matter.' Just say that three times and repeat it every morning and night for the rest of your life. Here you seem to have got the *manner* for the *matter* . . . It's a poem. I'd cut out the references to Douglas[3]. He isn't in the *manner.*"

In the same letter the poet is reminded that you "can't glorify the spirit within you and at the same time find humanity so despicable. The antithesis is much too violent and startling to live by, and I conclude my homily with a phrase of your own:

'The peak o' things
That canna whummle!'

and the peak o' things, whether in thought, or art or morality, has a pretty broad BOTTOM. When you come to realise more truly that *all* the spirits and brains of the past have put you and me here at this peak of time, well, you have had your first lesson in humility and thank God for your privileged position. So please don't try to stand the mountain on its head! It will fall and bury you."

On 28th July, a poem called 'Coming Home' drew from Scott: "You should know by this time that your appeal to authorities in psychology is the very worst testimonial you can give yourself for having any savour of your own. It's all too obviously in the modern style, like Willie Johnstone's physog of you, and it's time you were both growing up. You should leave this sort of thing to undergrads at Universities and Art Colleges — it's generally all they ever manage to do."

For the magazine *The Free Man* — to which MacDiarmid was a regular contributor — Scott sent the poet a draft introductory note to accompany the publication of his new setting of 'Scots Wha' Hae" He claimed that his tune laid stress "on the 'doing' rather than the 'deeing'," and that a "new impulse, a new orientation, demands a new song, a new form of Address to all who are prepared to fight for the National cause." A postscript, written before the letter itself but mislaid and tacked on to the second letter, referred to 'Coming Home'.

"You're running out of 'thought'. You really should go off on a new line of thinking altogether. You're in danger of growing stale and most readers will be able to place you without bothering to read you. Practically everybody is thinking just what you're thinking, but your friends . . . are looking for solutions, not further conundrums . . . Who in Hell's name is all this poetry meant for — what audience are you addressing? D'ye ever think of *that*? . . . You're behind, man — away in the rear among the romantic decadents still worrying about your soul and religious ecstasies."

On 2nd January, 1933, Scott was repeating his question: "What about a half-dozen things like 'Milk-wort' for 1933?", adding of his newly-finished settings: "I've freely embraced the quintessence, I assure you, and am ready to begin on another as soon as you turn it up." In this song, as in 'St. Brendan's Graveyard' — about the floating loveliness of which, incidentally, I have changed my mind since hearing it beautifully sung by Isobel Buchanan and Fiona Milne, both associated in different ways with the Scott Centenary celebrations — Scott felt he had achieved musical 'transcendentalism'.

He tells the poet on 4th January that their friend Burt had had an emergency stomach operation in Edinburgh Royal Infirmary — he never thereafter enjoyed robust health — and the poet is urged to call and leave a card. Scott adds: "I've finished — yesterday — a decidedly smart setting of 'Lourd on my Hert'. One day is perhaps overdoing it, but I keep asking myself, why not one a week?"

Scott's prickly nature in dealing with musicians he considered less gifted than himself came to the surface on 26th January, when he withdrew from an Edinburgh concert organised by Stewart Dees. There were difficulties, too, with the Active Society concert in Glasgow's Stevenson Hall, described in his letter of 5th February. Some of his songs had been dropped at rehearsal to make way for the piece by Sir Alexander McKenzie that so pleased Percy Gordon (see page 85). Scott, though feeling that the public had got 'an inkling' of what he was doing, confessed to being "pretty near the stage of not caring a damn whether the things are sung or not." It was probably simply frustration that caused him to seem to some musicians so "difficult" a colleague.

After discussing several MacDiarmid poems that do not appear to have survived, Scott gives his definition of the "quintessential of Scottishness: (a) bawdiness; (b) Glasgow filthiness; (c) heather and moor; (d) herring and fishing; (e) the Kirk etc., etc.; (f) sin; aspects of the Scot with nocht but the smell of him in them — a kind of film panorama of adjectives only."

A devastating but penetrating criticism of MacDiarmid's poem 'A Moorlander Looks Forward to a Bride' occupies much of the letter of 6th March.

"About the poem you sent today — Yes, I'm approving up to a point, though it took some time to convince myself even to that extent. I could give you a nice harangue about it, the burden of which would be on the old matter and manner conflict. For instance, I think that what you meant to say is alright but you've bungled it in all kinds of ways in the presentation. Query No. 1:— Who's speaking? A moorlander or H.MacD.? If the former, then it's far too sophisticated and you haven't seen the character objectively enough. Query No. 2:— Has the poem a beginning, a middle and an end? Answer, the speaker gets fankled in 'heather coves', 'Earth's maist prodigal show', 'Whey-draps in a cheese' and swabs the whole down with the 'bottle o' port'. D'ye get what I mean? The writer loses grip on the personality, the characterisation, by being so taken up in the similarities arising from observation. Compare, for instance, your own 'Wheesht, wheesht!', which is, I fancy, the best thing you ever did in this line, and where every stroke tells. By comparison I think you'll agree that the present poem lacks unity of purpose and intention, and wastes itself in side issues when there is not a minute to lose.

"Query No. 3:— Is it a lyric or just a bit of introspective reasoning? If the former, then it shouldn't read like a bit of blank verse — lines too long — rhymes too far apart, etc. If the latter, then cut the rhymes and get down to introspection. You'll see from this that I've taken it quite seriously. I've quite forgotten my suggestion about the Quintessence, but I am glad you're thinking of it. If I dare at this time o' day try to recall what was in my mind then I believe I'd have begun the present poem something like this:

> Fuck, fart, Glaur,
> Christ, and there ye are
> Wi ye're waggin' bum
> Like a reid-het lum etc. etc.

only of course very much more elliptical, but all the same ever so much more real and objective. You've become far too rational, Chris — the fate of all Scots evidently that indulge themselves in disputation — Scott can't write music for it — McCance can't paint for it and Grieve can't poetize for it! It's the curse of everything Scottish to begin as an inspiration (of sorts), develop into a bloody wrangle and peter out in a trickle of petty information. And it's the measure of our size as artists."

By June, Scott is telling his "Dear Chris" of his delight at the information that the Shetland sojourn has given the poet "a new world to look at", as reflected in the first poem to come down from Whalsay. Nevertheless, Scott wrote: "You are still preaching Nihilism, and I don't think *that* will carry any of us very far, since we must accept something or else go off the map."

Insomnia had begun to trouble Scott. On 9th July, he announced that he had spent a weekend in St Andrews with James Whyte, the owner and editor of *The Modern Scot*, "really in hopes of getting for a time some change of scene from this hellish insomnia that keeps recurring. This last week I'd three nights running of hot-bath, hot toddy and lumenal — such preparation in itself being enough to put me clean off altogether unless taken in stiff doses."

MacDiarmid had become fascinated by Charles Doughty's *Arabia Deserta,* and Scott confessed also to being impressed by the quality of Doughty's "mental fit-up", though he thought "the book itself was very mediocre". This leads Scott, apparently forgetting his already expressed opinion that MacDiarmid's muse was a purely lyrical one, to make a suggestion. The poet should write "a modern saga about Shetland — something absolutely stark and realistic . . . That seems to me, Chris, what you're most in need of at the moment — a big theme you could treat objectively — some dramatis personae that would exteriorise your own predicaments in more than life size. If Doughty could find such a theme in Arabia — why not you in Shetland? And apart from the theme as theme, I really do believe you won't do much in your present frame of mind. God knows why *I* should be obliged to speak to you about responsibility (having so little sense of it myself) but will you not misunderstand me if I say that your reaction to circumstances at present is a lyrical, casual one rather than an epical and serious one. It seems to me that you *will not* accept the burden of your own life *seriously* and face the discipline of living and thinking out a solution of your own destiny, in a poetry adequate and commensurate with it. These lyrical things" — MacDiarmid's Shetland lyrics — "are all very well as hints as to what's going on in your napper, but they are obviously too scrappy — like the stuff written on a holiday in Shetland — and the ground swell can only be guessed at. I call therefore for an objective theme — something out and beyond yourself altogether — Prometheus — Prisoners of Chillon — and you pour into this third person the silences of Arabia without sentiment and without fuss.

Don't think I haven't seen signs in some of your last poems that you are putting out feelers in that direction. The two poems 'In Memoriam' to Rilke and Doughty — 'On a Raised Beach' — 'The Breaking Wave' — have each of them something of the quality I'm thinking of — something monumental — sculptural and scriptural. But why explain further — it is just a way of saying

Exegi monumentum aere perennius
regalique situ pyramidum altius,
quod non imberedax non Aquilo impotens
annorum series et fuga temporum

(And now 'tis done; more durable than brass
My monument shall be, and raise its head
All royal pyramids: it shall not dread
Corroding rain or angry Boreas
Nor the long lapse of immemorial time.)
                                    [Horace: Oks]

And it's the *style* as does it! And the *style only!* I've shouted this to you before but you evidently haven't heard it! I tell you it's the *style* and not the *subject matter* that *matters!* (when you *are* a real poet!)"

In the late summer of 1933 Scott went to Ireland and met Oliver St. Gogarty in Dublin. It was to Scott "the best holiday I've had for years", but a touch of Irishry crept into his letter of 9th October: "Gogarty thinks we are a pair of supreme lyric artists with a lyric gift to which Ireland has nothing at all comparable. To Hell with philosophy and economics! Your highest target should be lyrical drama (not ethical) as mine undoubtedly is opera. Cogitate this!" This again was certainly a different assessment of both their abilities from Scott's previous (and correct) assessment of their muses as being primarily lyrical. Evidently he had quite forgotten his dictum that "the lyrical and the epic are two different styles of mentality."

Having in his "sleepless nights" re-read Tolstoy's *What Is Art?*, Scott tells MacDiarmid: "I command you to read it very carefully. It will do you good in all directions. The times are changing." Scott then quotes from a recent issue of an unidentifiable Italian news magazine: "Of late great efforts have been made to re-instate musical values pure and simply by reacting not only against Wagner's theories, but also against Debussy's disintegrating impressionism, programme music, crude soulless aesthetics, and so on . . . The time has come for music to sing untrammelled." From the May issue of the *Zeitschrift für Musik,* Scott quotes: "Modern ways and means are running out . . . Schönberg, after being imitative in sentimentality has become imitative in abstract dialectics. Stravinsky is playacting and grimacing." Along with Hindemith, Scott's translation continues: "the three are at bottom romantics — inhibited romantics, who fear to remain true to themselves because they wish to avoid being imitative."

The important point here is not perhaps so much that fifty years on our assessment may be rather different as that the quotations show Scott's own mind moving back towards increasing lyricism and his old love of commenting creatively on the Scots folk idiom.

Scott's fluent knowledge of German was drawn upon to arm the poet with an understanding of Rilke's *Duiner Elegies* on 5th February 1934. A week later, Scott was thanking MacDiarmid for forcing him to effect "a real introduction to Rilke — a curious half light sort of mental landscape he seems to live in. He seems to me to have been working

N

out a kind of mental geography. I am not altogether convinced that there is much behind it all . . . He made me think of two other fantastics — James Thomson 'City of Dreadful Night' and Hölderlin.''

Early in April Professor Tovey (later Sir Donald Francis Tovey) wired Scott inviting him to come through to Edinburgh and have dinner. "Had enjoyable night of it'', Scott reported on the 5th of the month. "(Tovey) liked the songs immensely but didn't think it advisable to write a preface to the volume. I *now* agree that the book can stand on its own legs and needs no boost from anybody."[4]

The first hint of a completely new departure in Scott's own activities was contained in his letter of 1st October. After explaining that he had "got fankled up with my new radiogram at night and listened to an opera from Prague", he tells MacDiarmid: "I've been hellish busy these last two months, August and September, delving deep into orchestral technique — a perfect furore of intensive study with a view to embarking on orchestral writings, and in the first place writing the orchestral accompaniment to 'Kind Kittock', which composition is finished and is great stuff. For the past fortnight I've been working at the orchestral solo passages and am so stimulated by them that I've fair had a new life given me musically and am seeing visions of a final expression of my ego in symphony and opera. I've really had nothing like such a stimulus for many years and have been so enthusiastic about it that even going to bed for my usual 4 or 5 hours has seemed hardly worth thinking about . . . I'm determined to do the thing in masterly fashion and in no Scottish amateurish style. So you can look out for something hellish and convincing in the shape of Scottish music, with an opera or ballet as a kick-off, after I've finished the score of 'Kind Kittock', which I am hoping to have into shape for Ducasse's opinion about Xmas."

MacDiarmid had recently formalised relations with his second wife, causing Scott to comment: "I was delighted to hear about your marriage for many reasons which can't very well be put on paper, but the chief of which is that it lets you get away from this damned Sex Obsession, or at any rate bothering about it and getting down to business of doing your creative job *as well as* the female. I think you'll understand that. The analogy I am sure is quite perfect — this germination of an idea and its development in darkness for months (if not years) and its final parturition in sweat and travail. And the ladies (God bless them!) don't, let us hope, bring amorphous lumps into existence and take pride in them!''

Following up the notion — probably first put into his head by the irrepressible but unmusical Gogarty — that opera was his real bent, Scott asked MacDiarmid on 24th April, 1935, if he had "'got hope of an opera libretto yet — the world of Glasgow is asking when I am beginning one and the Grand Opera Society has definitely promised to *perform* it![5] So come down with some large-size ideas . . .!''"

It appears that MacDiarmid had some sort of contact with Routledge, the publisher, and had helped to procure Scott his contract to write the book on pibroch in their 'Voice of Scotland' series. As we already know, the book never materialised, though the contract stipulated delvery of the manuscript by November, 1935. Perhaps Scott's new preoccupation with orchestral technique proved to be even more absorbing.

With his growing interest in orchestral music, not dependent on the work of poets, what had been his gradual separation from MacDiarmid as an artistic collaborator was finally confirmed. Not surprisingly, Mac-Diarmid no longer sent him manuscript poems in the old profusion, Scott having by now made it perfectly plain that he thought his poet had "lost the place". Yet in spite of the challenge of the orchestral pre-occupation, a note of reflective sadness increasingly begins to sound through Scott's vigorous epistolary style, notable for the first time in his letter of 31st December 1935.

"I am sitting in my own study, that you know so well, on the afternoon of the Old Year's day, rain and the mist outside over the tennis-courts, making a perfect pall of misery for the departing year, while within, there's a bright fire with FG trying to write this letter with his arse in the armchair and both legs up on another." The "BBC weather-prophet's" frequent gale warnings for Orkney and Shetland make Scott condole with his friend "away up there" and wonder "when some kinder fortune" is to be his lot.

Scott was still struggling with Doughty, and reflecting on the facility of most artistic endeavour. He had convinced himself that "up here in Scotland we're not proportionately pulling our weight at all. I'm speaking in the main about 'musical' efforts, but I'm quite sure that there's enormous talent about in England for stage-craft, light opera and every-thing that might be classed as domestic entertainment. It's made me wonder if we unsociable Scots haven't missed the boat again — I suppose you know that *really modern* has ceased thinking about ART altogether except as a commodity for consumption on the premises, right here and now. The generations that come after us will do the same — the in-artistic will continue to write and read histories of art. At any rate it's along these lines I have been struggling with Doughty — he'll probably go on the shelf as a minor classic but it won't matter a hoot to anybody".

The decision of Whyte to close down *The Modern Scot* — by far the best-looking cultural magazine of its kind to be published in Scotland till then, or since — and return to America was another depressant.

"I spent a very interesting and illuminating night just this past weekend doing a bit of stocktaking (probably brought on with the idea of the 'Modern Scot' ceasing to function and putting full stop to publica-tion of my stuff). I find I have still in hand 50 (Scottish) good enough songs that include quite a lot of your material . . . To play over some of the earliest of these, like Sabine, Blind Man's Luck, The Love-Sick Lass, was quite a shock both from the musical and poetical points of view. It brought very poignantly back that glorious time when you were in Mont-rose and Glasgow wasn't any distance away at all and we were both working like things bewitched with a future overflowing with possibilities. I needn't stress the regret I felt as though for the loss of one's buoyant youth. You'll forgive me on Old Year's day for recalling the idea — has the world so changed or have we?"

By 23rd February 1936, Scott had settled into the style of gossipy reportage that characterised most of his later letters to MacDiarmid.

"I spent a long weekend (mid-term holiday) last week with Whyte in
St Andrews . . . Whyte is very concerned about a love affair he's having
with . . . a teacher in St. Leonard's and is writing a thesis on Proust
— she looks a lesbian — but whatever she is James is trying to effect
something in that quarter and is going to France with her during Easter.
So ——— ——— is playing second fiddle these days, but still he seems to
be playing alright and they have been weekending occasionally. It's a
hellish mess-up, poor James looked almost on the point of tears when he
saw me off on Monday afternoon . . . I've conceived a new approach
to another libretto. Greek drama's the line. A speaker explaining and
the characters singing of their emotions."

On 1st September 1936, newly back from the annual St Andrews
holiday, Scott reported that they had had "Willie Johnstone staying with
them, wife and kiddy", for three days. Willie's full of his new book[6]
which comes out in October from Stanley Nott. I learned quite a bit
about you and London from him. He thinks there's a bit of a 'set' against
you up-by, that you're finished (I'll tone it down to 'in the meantime')
as far as poetry goes but that Butcher thinks your autobiography should
be a best seller both in America and here if you'll put off the prophet's
mantle. For God's sake don't take yourself seriously as Saviour of Mankind, Europe or even Scotland, but do your damndest to view the human
scene with a sense of detachment and a measure of fun. — I am putting
as briefly as possible the gist of what Johnstone said, although he told
me all this confidentially. In the present circumstances I will add that I
think this good advice. It's no use being pig-headed — If the whole affair
is a 'vamp', well then take a hand in it, it's one of the few chances for
'vamping' you'll ever have and you'll be able to fulminate thereafter quite
as effectively as you're doing now on an empty stomach. Whether you
like it or not Hugh MacDiarmid as a world-beater is cutting no ice, not
even here in Scotland. I think myself you should try (if for this occasion
only) a change of clothes and turn gay like the rest of us. It's a chance,
Christopher, and I'd take it. What a grin you could have at your detractors.
A cold £1000 or two or three would rehabilitate you like nothing else."

MacDiarmid, who had more or less simultaneously found himself
expelled from the Scottish National Party for being a Communist and
from the Communist Party for being a Scottish Nationalist, was about
to come up for "trial" by the London Communists. Scott told him:
"From a chance confab, with Mary Litchfield (à deux) on the beach"
— a lady usually referred to by Scott as "the Litchfield bitch" — "I
gathered that she is a very bitter enemy of yours, being also a member of
the C.P., and hoping to God the party will at long last settle your account
when you come up for court martial in November, or whenever you come
South. This hope was on several occasions repeated by the Muirs." Scott's
opinion of the other side of the strange political equation was no better:
"This damned Scottish Nationalist business has been so messed up with
spinsters and dilettante of all kinds that any self-respecting person must
think twice about his appearance in it." When MacDiarmid looked hope-
fully towards the possibility of his acceptance by the Scottish Communist
Party, as distinct from the London HQ, he was told: "I don't see why
you should bother at all about the C.P. Surely to goodness you can't

imagine at your time of life that *any* party in its official capacity can be worth a docken or would be likely to fit you into its ranks."

By this time the friendly scene at St Andrews hade been shattered by the publication earlier in the year of Edwin Muir's *Scott and Scotland*. MacDiarmid personalised the intellectual disagreement the book formalised, but Muir resolutely refused to answer his jibes publicly. A proposed MacDiarmid club, issuing the poet's material from Whalsay, did not materialise, but provoked merriment among the supporters of Muir. Scott, who stuck by MacDiarmid during the quarrel while striving to act as an intermediary, told him that "even Edwin, who can generally be astute, found hilarious laughter in somebody's 'Whalsay front', the MacDiarmid club's weekly, monthly, quarterly and Xmas annual. So you had better mind your step! They are at present finding heaps of amusement to see you wriggling in the net you've set for them. The Whalsay Press working overtime is a good joke to Willa, and Edwin rubs on the salt by adding that he's 'sorry for you, but what else can you expect'."

Scott, however, was determined that matters should not rest there. "Late on Saturday night the Muirs phoned over that they'd like to come over to see us before we left on Monday, and would come later bringing a big bottle of claret (as a peace offering?). I had a long and very exciting talk with the pair of them, told them that I disagreed with everything in the book, proved that in the 'Eemis Stane' you had written a metaphysical poem of the first water, asked Edwin to put anything in English beside it (which he couldn't do), made him confess Burns a *major* poet especially in dialect, pointed out that any stricture on *your* work was equally applicable to *mine* (I suppose I should be writing string quartets for lounge lizards), told him that the book was a justification of himself, that he was only finding out what he was looking for, etc., etc., etc. Willa turned extremely grave and silent, asked timorously if I was prepared to become 'the spiritual father' of Christopher in this conflict. I said I was. My only alternative was to deny myself as a creative artist. Then Whyte and Tonge blew in and tension eased a little."

Scott then warned MacDiarmid of the possible damaging consequences of a circular letter he had sent out attacking Muir, and of the folly of personalising the disagreement, a warning that went totally unheeded. Muir, in the end, won admiration for his dignified public demeanour (whatever he may have said in private) in the face of MacDiarmid's onslaught, and time has largely vindicated Muir's case, even if the argument may have been presented prematurely in 1936.

On 1st March, 1937, Scott was giving MacDiarmid his reasons for applying for the recent professorship of music at Glasgow University: "I'm going in for it with both feet, partly for my own sake and partly for the sake of this benighted race of noodles who can't see where their own interests lie. In the meantime, the inside moves are being held up in an effort to secure funds from the Scottish Education Department to establish the Scottish National Academy as a central institution drawing Government subsidy. I am not sure but this might entail separating the Academy from the professorship of music (it's a joint appointment at present) but at any rate I am advised to do nothing about it till rearrangements have been made and the vacancy is officially advertised."

Another Edinburgh lunch with Tovey had drawn from Scott a promise to write something for the Reid Symphony Orchestra, which Tovey conducted. Both Tovey and the conductor of the Scottish Orchestra, George Szell, had recommended the inclusion of Scott's overture *Renaissance* in the next season of winter concerts.

In the same letter, Scott commented on a cutting about the dispute with Muir that MacDiarmid had urged him read: "I *did* (after a hellish hunt through the files of the 'Bulletin') get hold of the Grieve-Muir fracas. I thought your two articles exceptionally unbiased and to the point and Muir's reply very infantile and waspish. It's perfectly clear to everybody I'm in touch with that the Muirs are a wash-out as far as ideas are concerned and are just cashing in on anything and everything that comes their way. Several folk have spoken to me about Muir's broadcasts on 'Scottish Books' with surprise at the silliness of his comments and the presumptuous air of authority with which he states them. I am afraid he's miscalculating the effect his appearances are having on his hearers — but if people *will* hang themselves we can't and won't prevent them."

Answering three of MacDiarmid's letters on 6th September, Scott tells him:

"You must realise at your time of life that your *own* work is sufficient evil for the day and be content to push aside lots of interests as being outside your immediate range. I have, of course, nothing to say against books you are committed to write, but I myself would reduce as far as possible the number of these and get on with *your own job*. Think for a moment of C.M.G. finishing off as one of yon bespectacled literary cranks that haunt the British Museum and public libraries digging up dead worms of information — dead maggots and dead carcases! I hope the prospect frightens you! To hell with everything that distracts you from the business of writing poetry! If needs must, then write pot boilers that will give you the leisure you require, not these recondite tomes that are taking up so much of your time and energies.

"So that's grouse No. 1 off my chest! No. 2 is about the Autobiography —Who's this Edwin Muir that requires 20 to 30,000 words, the excerpt you refer to? For the love of mike have some sense of proportion. If it's a history of your opinions you're writing, well and good, but even then I'd think Muir could be dismissed in a mere 500 or 50. You wouldn't like to admit that he (Muir) has been so important as all that in your life story? I'm sure he'll feel flattered! It's all rather curious, Christopher — but if you take *my* outlook for a moment you will perhaps see in your attitude a sign of your own nervousness with regard to Muir — which means a want of real confidence in yourself."

Evidently MacDiarmid had complained about Scott's "world-beater" jibes. Scott replied: "My whole point regarding the 'world-beater', taking into account *my* view of things, is that you *think* you are. I pay you a higher tribute than that — I know that you *can* be when you come to terms with yourself and your own destiny, in other words, when you find the confidence in yourself necessary for the accomplishment of your work. You will then stop playing at hide-and-seek with yourself, cut out the arrogance and get on quickly with the job. It's difficult, I know, but it's got to be done."

Scott's difficulties with the pibroch book were meanwhile becoming more explicit. "The 'Ceol Mhor' book is still in the land of maybe. I'd still like to write it but everything pertaining to Gaelic culture is a hellish morass of contradictions and I sometimes feel compelled to leave the Gaels to finish the fight among themselves — the contradictions being in Gaelic and arising out of the language itself. They're quite happy about it all — they have the finest language in the world, the finest poetry, the finest music — and the finest lack of commonsense about everything else under the sun."

MacDiarmid is then given a long lecture on the importance of rhythm: "I say if you're really wanting to be *sung* in the *Communist* sense of 'the people singing' — then you'll have to forswear irregular rhythm and stick to Plain Jane stanza poems with plenty of swing and energy in the rhythm . . . . You and I are both lyricists of no mean order. For some years you have been anxious to appear as a major poet (that is in class B, the philosophical, contemplative, etc.) and you have pushed the irregularity of your rhythm so far that many have described your poetry as *PROSE!* It's inevitable, it's a matter of degree. If there is *no* regularity in the metre (poetic or musical) the thing becomes prose, just prose. I haven't seen enough of the 'Heroic Song', but 'Cencrastus' shows the condition of your muse, large lumps of prose, let's call it for the moment, with swatches of poetry you printed generally in italics. The warning finger points out to you that no matter what the content of your latest stuff may be it will in the end be styled, 'prosy', 'prosaic poetry'. For good or ill, it won't stand as poetry and, worst fate of all, the 'content' you were so proud of will have become stale and outmoded. Like the opinions in yesterday's 'Glasgow Herald', or better, yesterday's 'Daily Worker'."

On 5th December, Scott responded to the news that MacDiarmid was editing for the publisher Macmillan a *Golden Treasury of Scottish Verse*. He thinks this will be a difficult undertaking from Whalsay "without the necessary reference books. It would be a disaster to put out the book . . . and find everybody in Scotland proclaiming your incompetency as an editor of Scottish songs. And that's exactly what they will do — ever ready to find fault and damned slow to see merit in anything. You will see then that I am more than anxious to look through your contents list. This business of ascribing poems to this one and the other is highly difficult and often quite adventitious, but it has got to be finished. I am hoping, at the least, that you have got beside you all the recent Scottish anthologies — they're always something to put the blame on." For several months thereafter, Scott devoted much time and energy to answering MacDiarmid's queries about poems for the anthology, in some cases transcribing copies of texts.

Increasingly, and inevitably, the shades of Hitler, Mussolini and Stalin spread across the correspondence. On 12th June 1938, when the Czechoslovakian crisis was convulsing Europe, MacDiarmid asked Scott for his opinion on his work 'Mature Art'.

"You asked me to give it the once-over, but as a matter of fact

I gave it the *twice-over* and a bit, and even then couldn't feel sure that any opinions I had come by were worthy of putting before you. If I could convince myself that I knew exactly where the world is going at this moment I might be emboldened to tell you straight back that your reading of the situation is a correct or a totally absurd one. But I don't know. . . . . Idiosyncrasy! — that is the word I would like to harp on — but how does that sound in a world swung between Hitlerism and Stalinism? You said in one place, I remember — 'I am a Communist', and had to add a little later that you would have none of it when all the world would accept it.7 So why are you a Communist? Why not say, 'I am an Anarchist'? It would certainly be nearer the truth than the other. Your trouble then comes from how you are going to equate Anarchial Art with dialectical materialism à la Stalin and not find yourself at a Moscow trial . . . So there, Christopher, I have done the best I can for 'Mature Art' . . . . It's probably that I'm hardening in old age — but somehow I don't feel it. I have found myself, on the contrary, more concerned with the future of my own work than with the merit of anything I have done in the past. I believe like you that everything, life, literature, morality and everything else is in the melting pot, that there are no standards of criticism, no rules of composition etc., etc. but maybe I'm more conscious than you of the need to keep swimming, even against the stream. I can't credit, being a real sceptic, that Communism or any other -ism is going to transform life so much that the art of the next hundred years will obliterate all we today know as art, or create life of such a kind that ours will look flat, stale and unprofitable. In my gloomier moments I can foresee a human society that has reached a veritable heaven (or hell) of mediocrity — and uniformity, with bread and circuses, picture houses, wireless, television, aeroplanes, clinics, tractors, wi' nae bother at a', all free, gratis and for nothing, trying to figure out what kind of lunatics the Beethovens and Grieves and Scotts were, who had such fantastic notions about life and who in reality knew so little about how to live. Art will then be purely utilitarian, something to amuse and entertain. It's some notion, this Marxism. I can see whiles that it places value only on the living present — and unfortunately you and I are both getting older and older. Never mind — keep up your pecker — we'll hae munelicht again!"

Referring to MacDiarmid's "spirited response" of 5th July, three weeks later, Scott returns to his belief in the importance of style, and to the sense of inevitability about the greatest art. " 'Our little systems have their day,' our little petty prejudice, our notions, our opinions (political or other) — but just you take any masterpiece you can think of, whether in paint, poetry, sculpture or music and you will find it makes faces at your idiosyncratic, disjointed, over-original or over-personal specimens.

"And I am not thinking only, or at all, of long poems. Isn't your 'Eemis-stane (wonderful poem though it is) just about spoilt with a 'history's hazelraw' bit at the end? Don't you feel a slight effort, as of though something, as they say, dragged in by the hair of the head — something which doesn't *belong* — due to a moment of inattention or lack of technique on the poet's part? And I've been looking at my setting of 'Empty Vessel' quite lately — (wonderful music) that nearly brought the tears to my eyes when I reflected on your Springtide of creative activity, when we ran about from Glasgow to Montrose at weekends and jogged along country roads ready to make a masterpiece at a moment's notice. I ask you, can you do it *now?* For myself, I believe I can answer 'Yes — maybe' — just because I've maintained, (held on to), the certain knowledge that I can't add one inch to my stature, but I am what I am, and that that's enough for the job I've to do. And above all, no hanky-panky with myself, no playing at hide-and-seek with myself, no shooting out my neck, no personalities, as little of myself as possible and *everything for the work in hand.* Which all means that what I call *art* is that *work of art itself* with as little admixture of the person who made it possible (e.g. 'Empty Vessel', 'Perfect'). If this dictum seems to you obscurantist, I can assure you it is a truism in music — in Bach, Handel, Mozart, Beethoven and even in Wagner — in plainsong of course, there is no feeling of authorship at all, just as there's none in Gothic cathedrals, or in Shakespeare, Milton, Spenser, Chaucer, even Doughty. I find that the stupider my students are the more they are ready to think music is what they can make associations with, e.g. Wagner's 'Fire Music'; anything, indeed, they can understand, waterfalls, aeroplanes, power stations, locomotives, that are as far removed from *musical* intelligence as possible. And it's much the same with the personal factor in art — the reader or hearer gets away from the work itself to its accessories, its accompaniments, its experiments, its queer bits, its eccentricities, its oddities — anything but the subject matter in hand . . . Your pre-occupations with linguistics, semantics and quotations of all kinds are in much the same case. You have taken on the job of telling me about Scotland today and its relationship to the rest of the world, in politics, culture and everything else. I read the poem but I'm sorry to say I'd have had difficulty in saying what it was you were really getting at, what exactly was the tenor of your song — not, mark you, what *you* think it's about, but what *I,* as a fairly intelligent reader, think of it. If you imagine that you can put tags of Greek, Gaelic, Russian, Spanish, German etc. into a poem, and then claim you are keeping your eye on the work of art, well, I can only admonish you that you are doing everything but that . . . you're trying to astonish me with your cleverness and it's ten to one that where I can match you with my own specialised information, I can catch you out every time. Whenever you quote, for instance, French or German, I find myself asking 'now what in hell's name has that done for the poem?!' Why in heaven's name have I to be 'fobbed off' with *fehlt-charakeristictischerweise hier, atemberaubend pace,* like a little prig talking about 'jardin' for 'garden'! The point, however, is that when I *can* translate, I think they're silly, and when I *can't* (the Gaelic, Russian, Greek etc.) I pay no attention to them at all! I do *believe* that you can write a first class poem on practically anything you set your hand to — if you rid yourself of all idea of being clever, modern, up-to-date, experimental, omniscient, aye, and anarchist, Communist, and all the rest of it, too. You say America thinks you're the greatest Communistic poet ever — whatever *that* means: the greatest 'evolutionary' poet ever —

try it with any qualification you like — it's just my old reference back
again — the greatest Jew's Harp composer, the greatest composer for
the concertina etc. I tell you for the 1001th time your theories won't
in the long run matter a cuss (for they'll be out of date), and only the
poetic significance, the style, the quality of the poem as poetry, will
survive . . . . So don't frighten me with my declension from experi-
mentalism — or I'll retort that I'm coming to think *experimental art
not art at all,* or at best just *bad* art. The hall-marks of it are that heaps
of explanations are served up along with it, footnotes galore, — all,
just attempts to explain why the thing is poetry, music, etc. *when it isn't
anything of the kind."*

On 14th November, Scott tells MacDiarmid: "The recent CRISIS,
the general debacle that followed from it, have left me with an uneasy
feeling that I'm either the only sane person in Glasgow or else the only
fool in it. If Communism can't do more than *talk* in the present state
of affairs, we're all marked down for the fascist butchers sooner or later—
and such is the hope for the future — another eggshell!"

Looking forward to a forthcoming visit — MacDiarmid was apparently
coming down to Glasgow to broadcast — Scott finishes: "Don't take my
criticisms on 'Mature Art' too much to heart. I don't *praise* you. You
are, shall I say, beyond praise, and I just want you to be beyond blame
too."

On 18th June 1939, Scott returns to the problems that have delayed
his book on Pibroch. According to Scott, Owen Gallacher, one of his
students, had informed him: that "he was a great friend of the poet's
assailant James Barke, the novelist, who was an authority on Pibroch, and
who had convinced him and many others that the original school of
playing wasn't in Skye at all, but was located in Perthshire, and that
the art only trickled out to the Western Islands and was taken up in
Skye by the McCrimmons etc., after all the 'great music' had been
written and a tradition of piping established! This was certainly a new
one on me, and I could only reply that the place of origin was of little
account to me compared with the thing itself."

MacDiarmid seems also to have been interesting himself at this time
in trying to note down Pibroch, for Scott burst out: "How in Heaven's
name you are going to set down in notes variant readings of the same
Pibroch rather amuses me. In the first place, *I* haven't been able to do
it and I've tried often with Kennedy repeating even a single figure over
and over again, but with such Highland subtlety (or stupidity) of difference
in the thing that nothing I could write was just exactly how he played
it . . . The fact is that there is no notation on earth that will transcribe
how pibroch is played. And the reasons why this is so is that each player
plays it as he feels, or thinks he imagines it should be played, just as
a drunk man sings 'Annie Lawrie' to a time and tune of his own, regard-
less of the printed music, and rightly so. I have for some years past
done some occasional research into this business of 'notation', whether
in music or language — viz: the spoken word versus the printed word,
the played notes versus the printed notes. There is obviously no recon-
ciliation between them. Civilisation has come rolling along, has obliged
us to write and print for purposes of communication and set up hornets'

nests of discussion about 'true Gaelic', 'Pure Irish', medieval jargons such as Anglo-Saxon, Old French, etc. etc., and, most obscure and interminable of all — as was to be expected — the true nature of pibroch!" He had come to the conclusion "that like everything prior to the age of printing, pibroch was a happy hunting ground for illiterates of a really primitive mentality — 'throwbacks', that couldn't recognise the eternal spirit here and now, and went searching for it in the rubbish heaps of the long long ago. Therefore, avaunt ye, dead spirits of the past! — the only pibroch that matters, and maybe a better, is the one that wails round 44 Munro Road, just as the Whalsay Edda is the only one you should give a curse for."

On 30th June, Scott was acknowledging a signed copy of MacDiarmid's *The Islands of Scotland.* "I've read every word of it and congratulate you — it's a queer kind of patchwork, and as much about Christopher as the Islands but, this is the point, a very readable document either way." Scott had just set the "Loch Fyne Fishermen" by George Campbell Hay, and was full of enthusiasm for the work of this young Gaelic poet. He was to repeat his high expectations of Hay, in April 1940. "I herewith give warning that George Campbell Hay will be the next star in the Scottish firmament and unite in himself both Gaelic and Scots traditions. I have been in the closest touch with him for the past month and he has spent two different days with me in Glasgow discussing his and other folk's poetry. I am finding something pretty new in his *rhythm* sense (no doubt Gaelic) and in less than a week I had finished music to three of his lyrics — one at any rate as good in its way as 'Callum thonder'. He went back to Edinburgh last Sunday night well posted up (by me!) on what his mission should be, so I'm hopeful we'll all see results that will surprise and delight us. For a lad of 24 he amazes me by the maturity of his judgements of people and literature. I like him immensely as a person and his work, though tentative at times, has a real classical sanity about it, and, as I have said, a rhythm that stirs me right over into music — by which I mean that I *feel* what he is saying and that what he is saying is true. If he continues working with me and develops along the lines we have agreed upon I am certain he'll out-distance any of his immediate contemporaries — yes, Sam McLean included!"

By then, however, the war, from whose crippling shadows Hay the writer never fully emerged, had altered the way of life of many people, the Scott family included. With the Scotts, as with many other city families, those who could be evacuated were sent to country places. Scott told MacDiarmid: "After an amazingly successful time at Taynuilt, we came back to Glasgow on 31st August and sent the boys off again to Taynuilt the following morning. On the Monday after the Chamberlain declaration of war Francise and Lovey went to stay with the Missus's sister in Aberdeen and on the following Wednesday the Missus and myself go up by bus to Selkirk, Willie Johnstone coming up at the weekend with stories of the impregnability of London's defences, and prophecies of what the Germans would do to such benighted and un-guarded spots as Edinburgh and Glasgow. Exactly a week ago, after the first shock was over (people in Munro Road on the War Declaration Sunday were leaving in cars with mattresses and bedding!) we began our trek back to Glasgow to carry out our new plan which is now in operation; the Missus and the two boys are settled permanently in Selkirk and Francise, Lilias and myself are staying on in Glasgow. If the bombs fall, we'll just have to open our mouths and pretend not to hear them."

Scott was much concerned about how his closest friends would make out financially, as well, of course, as about his own future. Writing on Thursday 21st September, he tells MacDiarmid: "Your letter reached me about an hour ago — about a week in transit — and confirms the idea I had already come to, that you'd been having a rough time of late. Nor is that time likely to prove any better for goodness knows how long in the case of any of us. Here's the tale as it affects Willie Johnstone — Camberwell Art School — formerly 1200 pupils and 86 teachers, 8 of whom were part-timers, has now become 30 pupils with 6 full time teachers and all the others sacked. I've had an appeal from Erik Chisholm asking me to try and have him recognised as a teacher of music at the schools: he's lost all his private pupils and is retired with wife and family to Innerleithen. There are stories here of prosperous commercials and others begging for corporation work like clerking at £2 per week, and in tens of thousands of cases men who have served their bosses for over 20 years, like my Italian friend the music lithographer, have been suspended until further notice. In my own case, I fairly got the wind up by a letter calling a staff meeting while I was in Selkirk, proposing that of the men over 41, key men should be retained, and if the others took up national service their salaries would be made up by the Provincial Committee. Cheery prospect for me, taking up national service. What will come of it I don't know; the college is going to continue at Jordanhill, and my good friend Rusk[8] alvises me to sit tight and wait and see."

But all was not gloom. Scott also reported that he had handed over to the printers just before war began the manuscript of the songs for book 5 of *Scottish Lyrics,* and that the book was due out in a week or so.

By June the following year, he was again worried about MacDiarmid's future, writing on the 5th of the month: "I've been worrying about how you're doing in the midst of all this confusion on land and sea and air. I've especially been thinking about your difficulties in finding something to live on and in what direction to look for a solution to these difficulties. It doesn't seem easy even to make a suggestion on the matter. Who's to do the work? You or Valda? I've no idea how things are in the journalist world, but I wouldn't think prospects very bright in that direction unless staffs have been depleted — but here again there is a big hold up in all kinds of printing and the newspapers I see are all scrappy enough . . . What about war work? There must be jobs like the paymaster corps where clerical work is to be had — I know at any rate one chap who seems to be thriving in this line. I hesitate to suggest munition work for Valda, or typing, for instance — the Army is accepting dozens of girls in Glasgow and are even asking at Skerry's,[9] where Francise is at present training, to send along girls. There's certainly plenty of war work to be had in Glasgow at the moment — hundreds of girls are thus employed not so far from Jordanhill. It's difficult to see what can be done in your case — Dollan[10] is Catholic and very definitely 'anti' in his letters to the Glasgow papers — he'd have you rooted out of a job instead of finding one."

At this point a strange prospect opened up for Scott himself. A member of the appropriate committee in Aberdeen had indicated to him in writing that were he to apply for the job of Lecturer in Music at the teacher training college there, he would be made most welcome. He would receive an increased salary, but it would have to be paid in phased stages. With only four or five years to go until he reached the normal retiring age, Scott not unnaturally considered this proposal insulting. Whether or not he ever seriously contemplated going to Aberdeen, up-rooting himself from 44 Munro Road, is, to say the least, doubtful. In spite of the fact that his wife came from that airt, he frequently growled that "nothing good ever came out o' the North East!" However, this bungled 'invitation' gave him the chance of creating what he himself called a "a first-half class row" with the Central Committee in a situation where, quite clearly, he was, for once, entirely in the right. The row, however, swung the balance at Aberdeen against him, and the job went elsewhere.

His creative powers were still in no way diminished. "Evidently the old touch hasn't left me — during the last five or six weeks I've written three to Hay's words; four to Willie Soutar's; one to Muir's; two to yours, and a setting to Michael Bruce's 'Cuckoo'. That's an average of about two a week, and provided I get a constant supply of words I see no reason why I should call a halt."

Scott's references to the causes of the war reflect in some degree not only the continuing bafflement held by many older people during the "phony war" months, but also to a lingering belief in the discredited appeasement policy of the Thirties. "Personally, I am sick of the whole affair and reading about it," he told MacDiarmid; "and would retire to Whalsay or Ettrick Pen or any cannibal island to escape this last exhibition of human stupidity and knavery. My idea of the Russian-German collaboration is that one or other of the contracting parties is mighty insecure on the home front. The way Moscow is putting out night after night the news of this 'glorious red army' led by their Führer, Herr Joseph, doesn't give one confidence they've a nap hand in the game. They *may* have — I hope so! I've just been saying to the girls at the dinner table Chamberlain should *now* ask Hitler, 'Is it peace or war?' I'd give the beggar one last chance (for humanity's sake) and then we'd really know what the war was all about. If Adolph has had a run of luck in the three card trick for a few years and has turned up the wrong 'un this time, I don't wish his stupidity to be the death of millions of innocents (the blockheads in all countries who must have 'leaders' as stupid as themselves) . . . No doubt, like myself, you are more concerned with yourself than with anybody else, with how you are going to fair in the holocaust that awaits the world. If I'm presented with the alternative of national service I'm going to refuse it. I want nothing to do with this stink-pot called politics — like Willie Johnstone, I've come to think of all politicians as frauds — new gospellers with just another opium dose for the noodles that follow them. To hell with them all!" The unreal politics of neutrality, however, appeared to him in a more practical light when writing to MacDiarmid on 14th November 1939; "We have been discussing at the tea table tonight if the rabbit killed in the German air-raid yesterday belonged to you and whether or not they were aiming at your establishment and just missed. It's rather funny to us here that, so far, we have been safer than in Shetland. As for the war, it continues to 'drag its weary length along' and I can see no reason for why it shouldn't continue to do so till we're all bowed with age and glad to exit to some other congenial scene of operations. These last few weeks I've been so pre-occupied with a cold in nose and throat that I've given little time to less urgent matters and the operations of war have taken on rather a shadowy aspect, giant phantoms struggling away in a kind of No-where Land. My 'News and Views' informs me that we are in the middle (or at the beginning) of the Second Imperialist War and that Russia can take no part in it since it isn't a war for the liberation of the working classes etc., etc. All of which isn't very helpful and really smacks of the kind of neutrality he accuses Italy, Holland, Belgium, Finland, Scandinavia, etc. of maintaining. There's a neutrality that waits for some of the booty but prefers not to fight for it."

Copies of Book 5 of *Scottish Lyrics* had by now been sent to various friends. "Muir is warmly appreciative as ever, though it must be nearly two years since we corresponded, and gives me a very kind invitation to come and stay for a few days with them. He would have 'preferred' to write poetry, but since the war has been finishing off his auto-biography — by now completed I should think. I naturally chuckled to read in your last letter about finishing off *your* autobiography, it must have been concurrently with Muir's, and what beautiful contradictions and tangles of cross-purposes will emerge from the reading of the two volumes."

On 20th April 1940, Scott received, through Douglas Young, proof sheets of the introduction to MacDiarmid's *Golden Treasury of Scottish Verse*. Scott was quick to respond.

"I have no fault to find with the ideas expressed in the introd., but . . . you open out on Muir and continue to use his name no fewer than 14 times . . . I think this is a serious mistake. It gives an importance to Muir's opinions on the subject of Scottish poetry which they don't deserve, and what's more important, it gives the reader the feeling that you are carrying into the introd. a personal feud, and even perhaps that Muir's attitude may not be so far mistaken after all, since you think it requires so much criticism to destroy it. Couldn't you state in brief the things Muir is supporting and go on to demolish them one by one without reference back to Muir by name? I know you'll say that this is very necessary to controvert what Muir stands for, but why in Heaven's name give *him* all the credit? A reading of the introd. as it stands makes out Muir to be the diablos in poetica Scotorum, and what-ever his views the constant repetition of his name shows that you attach considerable weight to them . . . I am stressing this point about Muir appearing in a Scottish Golden Treasury, because I feel it is out of place in a book ostensibly 'Golden' — the best that Scotland can do — a book likely to remain for a long time authoritative . . . For somewhat similar reasons I regret your assiduity in notes, footnotes and footnotes to footnotes. You really can't keep anything informative to yourself. But that's a mystery to me — I just can't understand why the whole paraphernalia of cogitations should be dragged out into the sunshine like the old musty carpets and furniture during a Spring cleaning. To continue the analogy, there's more dust than anything else in both operations, and here again I think the introduction to an anthology isn't the place and time for carpet beating any more than a social gathering among friends would be."

Then followed Scott's entirely sane and balanced view of the Muir-MacDiarmid controversy.

"It occurred to me a strange thing that neither you nor Muir had stopped to ask what my opinion of the vernacular versus English controversy was. Much as I'd like to give you my whole 'paraphernalia of cogitation . . .' I'll say just that the language question is nothing to do with poetry — *given a poet,* he can write poetry in any language he's familiar with, but he always writes his *best* poetry in the *speech rhythm* he is *most* familiar with. You and Muir can both chew on this sentence till you understand it. The oracle has spoken! — 'and requires some food', my wife has just added". Later in the same long letter, he returns to "Mature Art", declaring again: "that if poetry isn't musical it's just prose . . . I often wanted to ask you how you came to switch over to your irregular rhythms of recent years. Quite recently I went through 'Sangshaw', 'Pennywheep' and 'The Drunk Man' looking for some explanation, but what came out most clearly was that the success of these books was largely the natural forcefulness of the poetic rhythm they contained. How you came to lose or throw away this sense of rhythm is a mystery to me. You may not think so, but I can assure you not much of your stuff since these books has any musical vitality. A forceful and exaggerated statement is a different thing altogether."

On 21st August 1940, he was telling MacDiarmid about the unsatisfactory outcome of the Aberdeen affair. "A member of the Committee who was present at the meeting wrote: 'The only reason why Mr Scott's appointment was negatived was that his age (60) proved an insuperable barrier, as the college here would have his services for 4 or 5 years at most. There was no other reason.' *This,* after the very grounds on which I appealed for maximum salary were that in view of my 15 years of honourable service and early retiral my appointment was the only decent thing possible. The selected candidate is music master in Glasgow Academy, about 35 years old, was inspected by me and given lots of good advice on how to proceed, and belongs either to Aberdeen or Banffshire. At the age of 35 he begins with £25 a year more than I've had all the time I've been in Jordanhill, and goes to maximum while I stick where I am. It makes me wonder whether any form of totalitarian government would be so inept and unjust. But enough of this: I'm sick to hear more of the 'Granite City' and hope it continues to have the consideration it so richly deserves from the Nazi bombers."

He gives MacDiarmid news of the Saurats, with whom, he says things were in a bad way. Their son, Harold, had been missing with the French army since 2nd June, and their eldest daughter had been "seduced, and abducted by a hack-journalist, a kind of lawyer body of no means, repute or sense of decency." Since the downfall of France, "Saurat has gone 'potty' about Jesus Christ, has been dreaming dreams, seeing visions and having confabs with poltergeists, spirits and God knows what else." Saurat himself, having recovered his practicality, was soon to become heavily involved with the de Gaulle movement in London.

Meanwhile in Glasgow, the publisher William Maclellan had been instrumental, with Erik Chisholm, in setting up the Dunedin Society. An approach had been made about the possibility of publishing a volume of Scott's songs. Scott, however, had the notion (rightly as it turned out) "that Chisholm hopes to push through some symphony of his own, eating up a good £150 of the fund, and is prepared to spend a paltry £50 on me as a blind. He is a real snake in the grass, is Erik, and I get on guard whenever he makes a move in my direction." The Chisholm volume eventually published in piano score was his ballet *The Forsaken Messiah,* and the Dunedin Society had, indeed, no funds thereafter to publish the promised volume of Scott's songs.

As well as the "Scottish Renaissance" side of his publishing activities with which Campbell Hay, Douglas Young, Crombie Saunders, Sydney Goodsir Smith, W. S. Graham, Ruthven Todd, Sorley MacLean, Mac-Diarmid and I were all in some degree associated — Maclellan also gave support to a somewhat self-conscious Celtic revival movement. Scott reported: "The night before Francise, Lovey and I left Glasgow, Tonge, who has been working for Reid and Lefevre in London, brought along J. D. Ferguson and Margaret Morris of the Margaret Morris Movement—the MMM as it is familiarly called. This MMM has settled in Glasgow as its last refuge and abiding city, has linked up with the Saltire Society, and the Dunedin Society, kicking off with the Celtic Ballet Club and looking all round the horizon for pupils. Willa Muir, I learn, attended a meeting of all three movements in Glasgow and said she would write scenario . . . and expressed the hope that she'd get FGS to write music for it! J. D. Ferguson, living in unlawful conjugal relationship with Margaret Morris, has left Paris for good and settled down in Glasgow. He is also, as needs must, highly interested in Celtic this and that as something quite new in the way of culture, so I send you warning of a new epidemic — a veritable sandstorm from three airts . . . So look to your rigging, Christopher — the Kennedy-Fraser, Hi, Ho, Horo is nothing to what's coming; I reckon you'd better move off to the Faroes before it strikes you at Whalsay."

Later in the month he tells MacDiarmid that Mrs Scott and the boys are remaining at Taynuilt until at least the end of December, and that the boys are now going to and from Oban High School by train. At Munro Road his second daughter, Lilias (Lovey), and he were "in the meantime carrying on as best we can, leaving the house empty during the forenoons and tackling, at least she is, the fires and blackouts and teas when we again foregather after the lunch hour. In this fashion one day follows another (an occasional air-raid breaking the even tenor of existence); I see nobody but an occasional girl friend of Lovey's and the ignorant colleagues I have to mix with up the hill. The one good point about it is that I've lots of free time, and better still that I'm making very good use of it. The orchestral 'Seven Deadly Sins' have been knocked into something like shape . . . The whole work, as I now see it, is the quintessential of Scottish dance idioms, plain as a house-end in its objectivity and ridiculously easy to understand."

There was good news, too, about Saurat's son, who was not, after all, killed, but a prisoner of war. Scott confesses: "I am not able to express any opinion of my own on the subject of the war. I just curse everything and everybody, Hitler, Stalin, Mussolini, Petain, etc. etc. Indeed, you are almost the only man alive I've any use whatever for, and I rather envy your but-and-ben in Whalsay."

A letter written from Taynuilt on 29th December recalled "an episode that occurred over in Woodville Gardens during a visit from Mr and Mrs William Jeffrey.[11] Jeffrey and I were talking of some attempts of his in Scots when that very respectable university lecturer of a wife of his came out with: 'Well, Willie, if you *do* write anything in Scots, I hope you'll just put it in the fire!' To be immediately followed by my unspoken comment 'Ye bitch! If this Willie of yours ever writes *any* poetry in any language, it'll be more than you'll deserve!' " This letter also acknowledged a presentation copy of MacDiarmid's *Golden Treasury*. The limitations of Scott's taste becomes apparent in his "hesitation about Davidson" but "none about Macfie's 'In Memorium' ". as dated a piece of contrived poeticism as anything in the book. Scott regrets that Mac-Diarmid did not include the "Michael Bruce 'Cuckoo' I set to music last summer. It's a mighty good bit of writing worthy to lay alongside Wordsworth's." He had received a commission from Nelson to write "an original 'Sight Singing Book', for schools, and needless to say have done nothing about anything since I came up here a fortnight ago." This was to be yet another unfulfilled commission.

The war continued. "We've had alerts and raids — no mistake about it — and all the indignities of getting below tables and waiting like rats for what's coming. It can't be helped. Perhaps human beings will learn some day how to avoid war — how to abolish it rather, but there it is — human fools and all their folly, and unfortunately we too are just human."

At the beginning of October 1941, the Scott family left Taynuilt and were re-united in Glasgow. Scott reported to MacDiarmid his growing friendship with Soutar, though, as we have seen, he held a limited opinion of the effectiveness of the Perth poet's work. His "things to me seem very facile and competent, but at the same time void of significance, and I just told him so. Willie seems from a subsequent letter to have imbibed from you or somebody a good deal of nonsense of a dialectical kind about the poet being the product of the society he lives in, and failed to realise the real poet *makes* the society as well as being made by it. He thinks the contemporary poet just can't possibly produce lyrical poetry in this year of chaos — to which, of course, I replied — of course not, if he isn't enough of a poet."

Writing from Taynuilt 25th August 1942, while on holiday, Scott tells MacDiarmid that the family has had "a grand time with Willie Johnstone, and he's back in London working out designs for my synopsis of the Dunbar poems. No news yet from the Sadlers Wells folk."

He had apparently submitted to them the score of the "Seven Deidly Sins", but nothing came of his proposal that they should stage it.

Soon after, the Grieves left Shetland for south and came down to Glasgow, where Grieve took up war work. There is a gap in Scott's correspondence with MacDiarmid until May 1944. Most of the letters that follow are factual reportage about domestic or organisational matters, though Scott also announces that he is now trying to get George Campbell Hay to provide him with words for a Gaelic national anthem. He was no more successful with this request that he had been with MacDiarmid over the provision of words for a Scottish national anthem.

Scott records his pleasure at the recitals devoted to his songs given by Joan Alexander, John Tainsh, and William Noble in Glasgow, Edinburgh and Ayr — Scott managed to attend the Ayr concert, organised by the Saltire Society, and including all the songs contained in *Thirty-five Scottish Lyrics,* then newly published under their imprint. On 6th December 1951 Scott tells MacDiarmid that he is revolving in his mind: "the idea of publishing, on my own, another book of songs and that the volume will include five of your short poems taken from your *Pennywheep,* 'Sabine', 'Blind Man's Luck', 'In Mysie's Bed', 'Song' (beginning 'There's an unco tune') and 'At the Window', which comes from 'The Lucky Bag'. My idea is to keep them together in the volume as 'Five Miniatures'— they're all quite short: some of them were written long ago, but all have been revised so thoroughly that they have quite lost their first look.

George Campbell Hay is responsible for 'The Two Neighbours', 'The Smokey Mirr o' Rain', the title of which I have changed to 'A Misty Morning', as there's enough of the 'smokey smirr' in each of the stanzas. Quite recently I set music to a very good sonnet by Muir which appeared in 'The Listener', and the other songs are 'Oh Wat ye what my Minnie did?' (Burns), 'Of the False Fire of Purgatorie' from the Guid and Godly Ballatis', 'To Love Unluvit' (Alex Scott) and "My Daddy is a cankert carle' (old Scottish). That is the bunch of twelve I am thinking of for the new volume." It is thus clear that at least twelve of Scott's unpublished songs were considered by him to be worthy of presentation to the public.

On 29th January 1952 he was reporting that he had "resolved to go on with the business, even though it now runs to almost £150: £130 for the volume of songs and another £20 for the separate issue of Jimmy Hogg's 'Skylark'. I'm maybe not quite sane in taking on such a venture, but having money in a bank these days is just putting it to sleep, and I'd rather see it doing something worthwhile for *me,* if not for Scotland." He now tells MacDiarmid that he has decided to cut out one of his five short lyrics — the 'Unco Tune' — and has substituted his daughter Lovey's 'In Normandy', "rather a touching expression of a yearning for the home land. I had to limit myself to twelve songs equal to a 40 page book of 36 plates, cover and heaven knows what else."

Unfortunately, only the Hogg song was actually published, the prospect of increasing costs deterring Scott from continuing with what would have been volume 6 of *Scottish Lyrics.*

On 30th May he was discussing with MacDiarmid the songs to be sung at the mismanaged London recital (see pages 139 - 141). That letter finishes: "I take it that you are introducing the show and the songs. Your explanations needn't be long, except maybe in your own poems. I have no idea how Bill Maclellan intends to run the concert — I don't know if there's any arrangement about programmes . . . I've had a letter from London asking particulars about myself, but I am not going to *London* — I've just no money, what with the expense of publishing another volume of songs, and a pension that's steadily diminishing in value."

Scott's last letter to MacDiarmid, dated 27th October, announces the abandonment of the proposed final volume, and gives another indication of his worsening financial situation: ". . . The damned Corporation of Glasgow are this year making my rates 53 times 19/10½ in the £, vis £52, which is more than two months of my pension."

A few months before Scott's death, his wife, Burges, acknowledged a note from MacDiarmid:

"I know you have been grieved to hear . . . about F.G. It is now quite a long time since he showed signs of forgetfulness and lack of interest. At times, he would say to me — after playing a few bars on the piano — 'No, I can't do it now-a-days'. He never seemed to be able to conquer this apathy or to recover his interest in his or in other people's intellectual efforts. During this period, I called in a specialist who suspected a brain tumour. After examination, the result was negative. Since then, he has continued quite happily and I must say he is usually cheerful. This is a blessing. He could have been still at home and we could have been taking our usual short walks; but ever since Christmas the degenerative process has gone on and after Easter another phase of the trouble had developed — the habit of incontinence. This was a very difficult matter and I got another specialist who urged me to let him go to hospital and diagnosed the trouble as deterioration of the head arteries. What can be done!

F.G. is looking well and able to be up and about most of the day. Although his thinking is rather confused, he is at times quite clear.

I have always considered that his unwillingness to try to understand your own changed points of view — in various fields — was not helpful to himself, and I think it might have been beneficial during those less productive years of his had he taken an interest in the intellectual affairs of others. I am extremely sorry that the honour you paid him in your brochure, which he read, and I too enjoyed reading, also your congratulations — remained unacknowledged by any of us. He did appreciate everything, but latterly he became a very irregular correspondent.

One day lately I gave him the news of Saurat's death, and he was very much affected. On another occasion, recently, he mentioned your name, and I can see that he is about to say something which he has difficulty in expressing. I go to see him every afternoon, and some of the others go in the evenings.

I've always felt that you knew F.G. better than anyone else in Scotland did, and that you may be able to understand how empty an experience it is to be without him and his inspiration."

The appearance in 1966, eight years after Scott's death, of Mac-

Diarmid's book *The Company I've Kept,* alleging anti-semitism on Scott's part and claiming that he was of Jewish ancestry, caused distress both to Burges and to the Scott family. On 31st January 1967, George Scott wrote to MacDiarmid after reading the book: "Perhaps you can guess the references to my father's ancestry . . . has occasioned us all, and especially my mother, a certain amount of surprise and indeed displeasure. Naturally, I should like to know how you came by this information." Naturally, no explanation was ever forthcoming!

"The other matter which seemed to us to be unexpectedly and, may I say it, unnecessarily laboured," George continued, "was the description of the 'rift' between my father and yourself. I am conscious of the fact that circumstances and differences of opinion during the latter years of my father's life made these meetings with you sometimes strained and unproductive; I am not aware that his attitude towards you as a proven artist of outstanding worth diminished at any time.

Perhaps you know less of my father's condition than we thought; it would have been good for him to have seen you more often at the end. He was your friend, and the 'illusion of friendship' which you submitted as an explanation of his attitude towards you, bearing in mind your previous reference to him as a life-long friend and collaborator, seems to me to be a case of how to lose friends and be influenced by people."

Writing after his mother's death on 15th October, George Scott thanked the poet for his letter of condolence. "May I say, without bitterness, that my mother meant to write to you about your references to F.G. in 'The Company I've Kept', and that I have the rough draft of the letter she always meant to send. When I wrote to you at the beginning of the year I wanted to put on record (perhaps I was rather ungracious) what we all felt . . . Before she died, my mother had put the sale of 44 Munro Road into the hands of the lawyers, and by the time this reaches you I expect the transactions to be completed." Thus ended, rather sadly, the long association between Scotland's greatest twentieth century poet and her finest and most-versatile song-writer.

NOTES

1. *Jamieson's Dictionary of the Scottish Language* (1866).

2. Vasily Vasilievich Rozanov (1859 - 1919), Russian philosopher, journalist and critic. His literary criticism of Gogol and Dostoevsky is highly regarded outside the U.S.S.R., where he has been rejected as representing turn-of-the-century decadence.

3. Major C. H. Douglas (1879 - 1952), consulting engineer and economist, whose Social Credit theories at one time greatly interested MacDiarmid.

4. Book 4 *Scottish Lyrics,* for which Scott had apparently considered the possibility of a preface by Tovey.

5. This would not seem as absurd a suggestion as it might now, since between 1934 and 1938, Erik Chisholm mounted the first complete performances in English in Scotland of Mozart's *Idomoneo,* Gluck's *Iphigenia in Tauris,* Berlioz's *The Trojans* and *Benvenuto Cellini.* While they remained inadequate performances by modern professional standards Chisholm had the gift of being able to draw from amateur singers and musicians more than they ever thought they had to give.

6. *Creative Art in England from the Earliest Times to the Present* (with illustrations) by William Johnstone (Stanley Knott, London 1936).

7. The reference is to MacDiarmid's poem "Talking with Five Thousand People in Edinburgh", which first appeared in *Poetry Scotland, Second Collection,* though not so acknowledged in *The Complete Poems of Hugh MacDiarmid:*

   "For I am like Zamyatin. I must be a Bolshevik
   Before the Revolution but I'll cease to be one quick
   When Communism comes to rule the roost . . ."

8. Dr Robert R. Rusk was Principal Lecturer, Education Department, at Jordanhill College of Education from 1923 until 1946, when he left to become Lecturer in Education at the University of Glasgow.

9. A famous Glasgow business college, now disbanded, that specialised in typing and office procedures.

10. Sir Patrick Dollan (1885 - 1963), journalist and councillor representing Govan Ward on Glasgow Corporation, and Lord Provost of the City from 1938 until 1941.

11. William Jeffrey (1896 - 1946), a Scottish poet, associated with the Scottish literary renaissance.

12. Ronald Campbell Macfie (1867 - 1931), a doctor of medicine and lecturer at the University of Aberdeen, wrote many books on medical matters as well as several volumes of Georgian verse brought together in *Collected Poems.*

INDEX

O